PEARSON

my World

GEOGRAPHY

ProGuide

EAST AND SOUTHEAST ASIA

East and Southeast Asia

Boston, Massachusetts • Chandler, Arizona • Glenview, Illinois • Upper Saddle River, New Jersey

ISBN-13 978-0-13-369591-5
ISBN-10 0-13-369591-3

5 6 7 8 9 10 **V064** 14 13 12 11

Master Teachers and Contributing Authors

George Sabato
Past President, California Council
    for the Social Studies
Placerville Union School District
Placerville, California

Michael Yell
Past President, National Council
    for the Social Studies
Hudson Middle School
Hudson, Wisconsin

Program Authors

Gregory H. Chu
Professor and Chair of Department
    of Geography
University of Wisconsin-La Crosse
La Crosse, Wisconsin

Don Holtgrieve
Department of Planning, Public
    Policy, and Management
University of Oregon
Eugene, Oregon

Susan Hardwick
Department of Geography
University of Oregon
Eugene, Oregon

Program Consultant

Grant Wiggins
President of Authentic Education
Hopewell, New Jersey

Teacher Consultants

James F. Dowd IV
Pasadena, California

Susan M. Keane
Rochester Memorial School
Rochester, Massachusetts

Timothy T. Sprain
Lincoln Middle School
La Crosse, Wisconsin

Marilyn Weiser
North Dakota Geographic
    Alliance Coordinator
Minot State University
Minot, North Dakota

CONTENTS

East and Southeast Asia

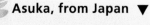

Asuka, from Japan ▼

Ridwan and his family, from Indonesia, in Southeast Asia ▶

Xiao, from
China ▼

East and Southeast Asia

- Prepare to learn about East and Southeast Asia and activate prior knowledge by creating KWL (Know, Want to know, Learned) tables, filling out only the K and W columns. Correct any misconceptions or misinformation in the tables.

- Have students preview maps, photos, and other visuals and predict what they will learn about East and Southeast Asia.

GUIDE ON THE SIDE

What time is it there? Have students look at the time zone display to determine by how many hours the times in Washington, D.C., and Beijing, China differ. (13 hours)

Analyze Maps Point out the political map and have students answer the following questions.

- What are the capitals of North Korea and South Korea? (P'yongyang and Seoul)

- What major bodies of water surround Southeast Asia? (Bay of Bengal, South China Sea, the Indian Ocean, and the Pacific Ocean)

- Why might some people say that China is not just part of East Asia? (Western China extends into Central and South Asia.)

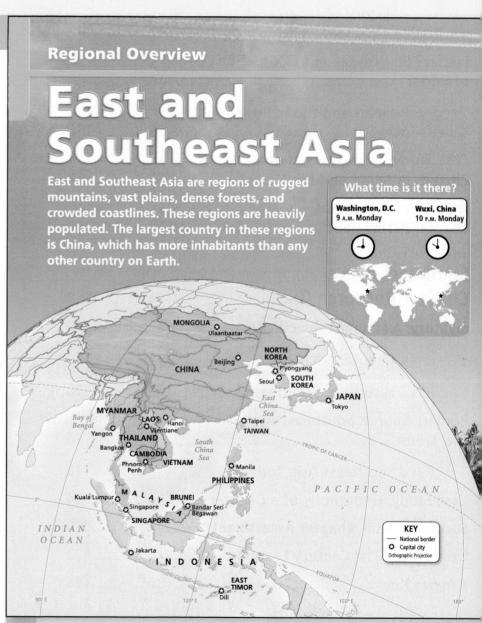

Regional Overview

East and Southeast Asia

East and Southeast Asia are regions of rugged mountains, vast plains, dense forests, and crowded coastlines. These regions are heavily populated. The largest country in these regions is China, which has more inhabitants than any other country on Earth.

What time is it there?

Washington, D.C.	Wuxi, China
9 A.M. Monday	10 P.M. Monday

KEY
— National border
✪ Capital city
Orthographic Projection

THE UNIT AHEAD

In this unit students will

- study the geography of East and Southeast Asia.
- get to know teenagers from China, Japan, and Indonesia.
- go On Assignment in China, Japan, and Indonesia.
- make connections between the physical geography, history, and politics of East and Southeast Asia.

The Unit Ahead

➡ Chapter 14 China and Its Neighbors

➡ Chapter 15 Japan and the Koreas

➡ Chapter 16 Southeast Asia

my worldgeography.com

Plan your trip online by doing a Data Discovery Activity and watching the myStory Videos of the region's teens.

my Story

Xiao
Age: 18
Home: Wuxi, China
Chapter 14

my Story

Asuka
Age: 18
Home: Yokohama, Japan
Chapter 15

my Story

Ridwan
Age: 19
Home: Bukittinggi, Indonesia
Chapter 16

Rice fields in Bali, Indonesia

my Story

Make Predictions Make predictions about the teen students you will get to know in this unit.

- Do you think Xiao is familiar with rural life in China? Explain. (Sample: Yes, Xiao lives in a village, which is probably located in a rural area.)

- Locate Yokohama on a map. Based on its location, do you think Asuka lives in a crowded area? Explain. (Sample: Yes, Asuka lives in an area that has several large cities, including Yokohama and Tokyo.)

- Ridwan is videotaping an important event. What event do you think he is videotaping? (Samples: a wedding, a birthday party)

NOTES

GEOGRAPHY

The Himalayas The Himalaya ranges hold some of the tallest mountain ranges in the world and include the world's tallest peak, Mt. Everest, at 29,035 feet (8,850 meters). These mountains began forming approximately 45–50 million years ago, but geologists consider them young mountains. In fact, they are still growing at the rate of 10 millimeters per year. These mountains are the result of a collision between two tectonic plates, the Indian and Eurasian plates. Due to the fact that India continues to press into Eurasia, the region is physically unstable and experiences frequent earthquakes and avalanches. These high mountains protected China from invasion but also created a barrier to trade and exchange during its long history.

Analyze Visuals Ask students to look at the labeled satellite photo, which shows key physical patterns in the region.

- What type of livelihood might be common in the Gobi?
  (Samples: herding, trading)

- How does the physical geography of Japan differ from China? (China has a large plateau, desert, and wide open flood plains. Japan has mostly a small area of coastal land and mountains in the center of its islands.)

Regional Overview
Physical Geography

Tian Shan
Taklimakan Desert
Kunlun Shan
Plateau of Tibet
Himalayas
Mt. Everest
29,035 ft (8,850 m)

Gobi
Huang (Yellow) River

North
China Plain
Chang (Yangtze) River

The Himalayas are one of the many mountain ranges in East Asia.

Malay Peninsula
Gulf of Thailand

South China Sea

INDIAN OCEAN

Java Sea

Active volcanoes lie throughout the islands of Southeast Asia.

QUICK FACTS

China's Rivers East Asia boasts the world's third-longest river. Only the Nile and the Amazon rivers are longer than the Chang River (also called the Yangtze River) at 3,915 miles (6,300 kilometers). China's Huang River (also called the Yellow River) at 3,395 miles (5,464 kilometers) is also among the world's longest rivers.

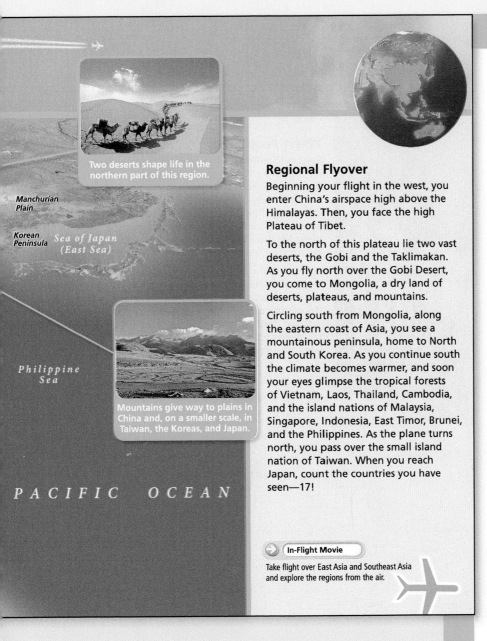

Two deserts shape life in the northern part of this region.

Manchurian Plain

Korean Peninsula

Sea of Japan (East Sea)

Philippine Sea

Mountains give way to plains in China and, on a smaller scale, in Taiwan, the Koreas, and Japan.

PACIFIC OCEAN

Regional Flyover

Beginning your flight in the west, you enter China's airspace high above the Himalayas. Then, you face the high Plateau of Tibet.

To the north of this plateau lie two vast deserts, the Gobi and the Taklimakan. As you fly north over the Gobi Desert, you come to Mongolia, a dry land of deserts, plateaus, and mountains.

Circling south from Mongolia, along the eastern coast of Asia, you see a mountainous peninsula, home to North and South Korea. As you continue south the climate becomes warmer, and soon your eyes glimpse the tropical forests of Vietnam, Laos, Thailand, Cambodia, and the island nations of Malaysia, Singapore, Indonesia, East Timor, Brunei, and the Philippines. As the plane turns north, you pass over the small island nation of Taiwan. When you reach Japan, count the countries you have seen—17!

> **In-Flight Movie**
> Take flight over East Asia and Southeast Asia and explore the regions from the air.

Regional Flyover

Analyze Visuals Read the Regional Flyover and ask the following questions about the labeled satellite photo.

- What parts of the region appear to have the least vegetation? (the Gobi and Taklimakan deserts north of the Plateau of Tibet)
- When during your flyover of the region would you expect to see a lot of vegetation? (later in the trip, heading south)
- Where do you think would be the best place to farm? (Sample: where it is greenest, along plains and river valleys)

> **In-Flight Movie**

Before playing the In-Flight movie, ask
- What have you seen or would you expect to see while looking out the window of a plane?
- What can you find out about a place by flying overhead?
- How is this information important to understanding the geography of a place?

GEOGRAPHY

Sky City Architects in Tokyo are trying to solve one of the world's worst urban crowding challenges by building a mega-skyscraper that would house over 35,000 residents. Since land in Japan is some of the most expensive in the world, engineers have been forced to consider vertical solutions. Some criticize the plan as unsafe due to the threat of earthquakes.

Some also might consider it inhuman to have such large numbers of people living in one building complex. Meanwhile, other architects think that a project such as Sky City is not only a way to relieve population congestion but also to create additional "green" space in cities where parks and gardens are severely lacking.

GUIDE ON THE SIDE

Where People Live

Analyze Visuals Indicate the population distribution map and the satellite photo. Have students use these visuals with the text to better understand the human geography of East and Southeast Asia.

- What parts of China are most densely populated? (the eastern half, the river valleys, the coast)

- Find Japan in the satellite photo by using information from the population map. What can you guess about Japan from the information in these maps? (Japan is very bright in the satellite photo and almost completely red in the population distribution map. The country is modern with many cities.)

- Why do you think one side of Taiwan appears dark and the other side appears bright in the satellite photo? (Sample: The western side is flatter and more heavily populated and the eastern side less so because of the rugged landscape.)

Regional Overview
Human Geography

Downtown Tokyo is lit up brightly every night.

Where People Live

East and Southeast Asia's physical features have influenced where people in the region live. Many nations in these regions do not have much land that is good for farming or settlement. Not very many people live in the rugged mountains and dry deserts. The dry climate in the north of these regions is particularly challenging. Even in the south, where water is more plentiful, there are many hills and very little land that is flat enough to farm.

As a result, the huge population of these regions is packed into the areas where life is easier—on the plains and along rivers and flat coastal areas. Japan, the Koreas, and many of the nations of Southeast Asia have forested mountains running through their centers, so in those countries people live mainly in valleys and in coastal cities. China and Mongolia both have large plains where people can farm or raise livestock.

This map shows where people live in East and Southeast Asia.

The lights in this satellite photo show electricity use in heavily populated areas of East and Southeast Asia.

PRIMARY SOURCE

Technology and Urbanization Bill Gates, founder of Microsoft, stated, "I thought digital technology would eventually reverse urbanization, and so far that hasn't happened. But people always overestimate how much will change in the next three years, and they underestimate how much will change over the next 10 years." Ask students to consider ways that access to the Internet might either increase or decrease the number of people moving to cities.

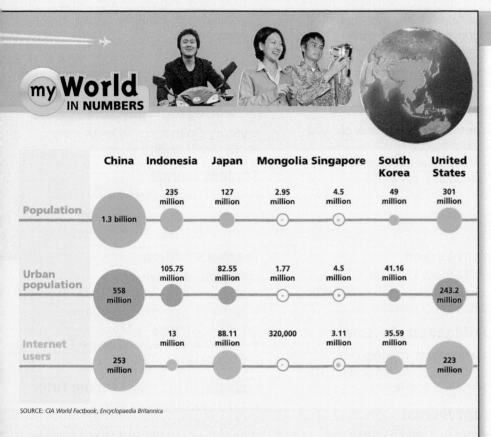

my World
IN NUMBERS

	China	Indonesia	Japan	Mongolia	Singapore	South Korea	United States
Population	1.3 billion	235 million	127 million	2.95 million	4.5 million	49 million	301 million
Urban population	558 million	105.75 million	82.55 million	1.77 million	4.5 million	41.16 million	243.2 million
Internet users	253 million	13 million	88.11 million	320,000	3.11 million	35.59 million	223 million

SOURCE: *CIA World Factbook, Encyclopaedia Britannica*

Put It Together

1. What physical features prevent western China from being heavily settled?

2. Where do many of the rivers in China and Southeast Asia begin?

3. Compare the number of Internet users to the number of urban dwellers. Which country has more Internet users than urban residents?

 Data Discovery

Find your own data to make a regional data table.

Size Comparison

East and Southeast Asia are more than twice as large as the United States but have 7 times the population.

PUT IT TOGETHER **1.** Western China's rugged landscape and lack of rainfall make it harder to farm. **2.** Many major rivers in China and Southeast Asia begin in the Himalayas. **3.** Japan

myWorld in Numbers

Analyze Charts Point out the table and use the questions below to help students analyze the data and draw conclusions.

- Which three countries have the most Internet users? (China, United States, Japan)

- Is there a relationship between the number of Internet users and the number of urban dwellers? If so, what is it? (The countries with the greatest percentages of urban dwellers have the most Internet users, except for Indonesia.)

Data Discovery

Students can practice chart and graph skills online with the Data Discovery feature. Students can use their trackers to save data for their On Assignment stories later in the unit.

Eastern Hemisphere **617**
World Geography **741**

Plan With Understanding by Design*

Chapter Objectives
Begin With the End in Mind

Students will demonstrate the following enduring understandings:
- The successes of a large country or empire might not benefit all citizens.
- A market economy leads to more economic development than a command economy due to competition, innovation, and free trade.
- Abrupt economic growth can have major impacts on a country's population distribution, culture, and environment.

Connect
Make Learning Meaningful

Student Edition
- **Essential Question** How can you measure success?
- **myStory** Xiao discusses the issue of pollution in his village.

my worldgeography.com
myStory Online: Get to know more about Xiao through a video.

Student Journal
Essential Question Preview

Experience
Teach Knowledge and Skills

Student Edition
- Read Sections 1, 2, and 3.
- Answer Reading Checks and Section Assessment questions.

my worldgeography.com
On Assignment: myStory Video, Active Atlas, Timeline, Culture Close-up, Data Discovery, and Self-Test

Student Journal
- Sections 1, 2, and 3 Word Wise
- Sections 1, 2, and 3 Outline Map and Take Notes

Teacher's Edition
🏃 **myWorld Activities:**
- Section 1: Should I Migrate?, p. T10
- Section 2: Command Economy vs. Market Economy, p. T16
- Section 3: Take a Stand on the Three Gorges Dam, p. T24

21st Century Learning Online Tutor
- Read Special Purpose Maps
- Make Decisions
- Identify Main Ideas and Details
- Compare and Contrast
- Compare Viewpoints

Understand
Assess Understanding

Assessment Booklet
- Chapter Tests   • Benchmark Tests

Teacher's Edition
🏃 **myWorld Chapter Activity:**
Students gather data on the effects of economic growth in China, chart their findings, and write a report to an economic leader.

Student Journal
Essential Question Writer's Workshop

my worldgeography.com
On Assignment: Students write and submit a blog or multimedia slideshow about China's successes and challenges in recent years.

Success Tracker™
Online at myworldgeography.com
Administer chapter tests and remediate understanding.

Student Edition
Chapter Assessment

Connect to the Essential Question

Essential Question

How can you measure success?

Use the Essential Question poster and follow these steps to help students understand the Essential Question.

Connect to Their Lives

1. Have students explain what success means to them. (If students have already studied this Essential Question, encourage them to note changes in the way they define success now.) As students respond, emphasize the diversity of ways success can be measured, as with grades, sports, drama, or relationships with peers or teachers. Ask, Should there be common measures for success such as grades?

2. Have students identify evidence for these measures of personal success. Post the following table for them to complete or have students turn to the *Essential Question Preview* page in their **Student Journals:**

Measures of Personal Success			
Family	Friends	School	Other (sports, arts, chores)

3. Discuss students' responses. Ask, Why might different people measure success differently?

Connect to the Content

4. Now have students brainstorm ways to measure a country's success. Students might say to look at violence or poverty levels.

5. Ask students to identify evidence for these measures of national success. Post the following table for them to complete: (Help them to understand what might be included in each category, e.g. education under Social Services.)

Measures of National Success			
Economy	Politics	Social Services	Environment

6. After previewing the chapter, have students make chapter-related predictions on the *Essential Question Preview* page in the **Student Journal.**

7. Remind students that they will answer a prompt related to the Essential Question on each section's *Take Notes* page in the **Student Journal.**

Explore worldgeography.com

ON ASSIGNMENT: China and Its Neighbors

For this chapter's assignment, students will
- take a digital trip to China, Mongolia, and Taiwan.
- take on the role of a journalist.
- gather notes, images, and data for their story throughout their journey.
- write an article or create a multimedia slideshow connecting the information and images gathered during their trip to this chapter's Essential Question: *How can you measure success?*

ITINERARY

During their trip, students will make the following stops:

myStory Video

Learn more from Xiao about life in China.

Active Atlas

Read more maps of China.

Timeline

Explore important dynasties in Chinese history.

Data Discovery

Gather data from charts about life in China.

Culture Close-up

Check out life in the far reaches of East Asia.

Self-Test

Assess their own knowledge of chapter content.

While on their trip, students will practice the following skills:

- **Interpret** graphic representations of data
- **Synthesize** evidence into an interesting blog or multimedia slideshow
- **Evaluate** factors that determine a country's success or failure

TIGed
TakingITGlobal for Educators

Extend the reach of every lesson by helping students connect to a global community of young people with common interests and concerns. Visit myworldgeography.com to
- explore Country Pages relating to China and Its Neighbors.
- delve deeper into this chapter's Essential Question, *How can you measure success?*
- find online alternatives to and solutions for the Unit Closer 21st Century Learning Activity.
- encourage learning through social networking in a safe, global environment.

 worldgeography.com

TEACHER CENTER

Preview and assign student materials, enrich your teaching, and track student progress with the following resources:
- Online Lesson Planning and Resource Library
- Presentations for Projection
- Online Teacher's Edition and Ancillaries
- Google Earth Links

Assess Enduring Understandings

 **myWorld Chapter Activity**   **Step-by-Step Instructions**   2 hrs

A Changing China: Who Benefits the Most?

Teach this activity at the end of the chapter to assess enduring understandings.

OBJECTIVES

Students will demonstrate the following enduring understandings:

- The successes of a large country or empire might not benefit all citizens.
- A market economy leads to more economic development than a command economy due to competition, innovation, and free trade.
- Abrupt growth can have major effects on a country's economy, population distribution, culture, and environment.

Students will provide the following evidence of understanding:

- Growth Analysis Chart
- Growth Report

LEARNING STYLES

- Logical
- Verbal

MATERIALS

- Activity Support: Student Instructions and Rubric, p. T6
- Activity Support: Issue Analysis Worksheet, p. T7
- Activity Cards: #121–126
  - 121. Wealth Gap
  - 122. Resource Gap
  - 123. Income Gap
  - 124. Education Gap
  - 125. Communication Gap
  - 126. Health Gap

Activity Steps

1. **Set Expectations:** Tell students that they will divide into small groups and that each group will be a research team. Each activity card addresses a major issue that affects China. Using the activity cards, information from Sections 1–3, and myworldgeography.com, teams will collect data on how China's growth is affecting various Chinese people in different ways. They will chart the data and then write a report to China's leaders. Review the activity instructions and rubric.

2. **Field Research Jigsaw:**
   - Divide the class into six research teams. Give each student a copy of *Issue Analysis Worksheet* and each team one Activity Card.
   - Tell students to imagine that each group is gathering data about the issue on their activity card. Tell them that the Chinese government wants information about the impact of this issue on its people.
   - Have students read and discuss the card and record data on the Activity Support. Then

rearrange students using a jigsaw strategy. Ask students to pool their data to examine how different issues affect different people. Students should take notes about the effects of the different issues.

3. **Chart the data:** Have students create a table with three columns and six rows. The first column should list the six Activity Card issues. The second column should list who benefits from each issue. The third column should list who is harmed by each issue.

   L2 Extra Support Complete **21st Century Online Tutor** Categorize.

4. **Report:** Have students write a report that answers the questions on the following page. Make sure that students compare their issue and its effect to other issues and their effects.

   ELL Advanced Provide a word bank of transitional phrases with definitions for help writing their reports. Sample phrases are *in addition, furthermore, as a result, according to,* and *therefore.*

Name _____ Class _____ Date _____

 myWorld Chapter Activity Support **Student Instructions and Rubric**

A Changing China: Who Benefits the Most?

Activity Instructions: Read the following summary.

1. Work with your teammates to gather information about the issue assigned to your team and the effects of this issue on Chinese people. Then complete the Issue Analysis Worksheet.

2. Your teacher will rearrange teams. Share your data to find out how different issues affect different people. Take notes.

3. Create a table with three columns and six rows. The first column should list the Activity Card issues. The second column should list who benefits from each issue. The third column should list who is harmed by each issue.

4. Write a report using knowledge from the activity cards, the chapters, and myworldgeography.com. Your report should describe to a Communist Party official how China's growth is affecting the general public in different ways. It should answer the following questions:
   a. What are the effects of China's growth?
   b. Who benefits from each issue? Who doesn't? Explain.
   c. What recommendations would you make to promote more equal benefits from China's growth?

myWorld Chapter Activity Rubric	3 Exceeds Understanding	2 Reaches Understanding	1 Approaches Understanding
Graph: Organization	Complex organization	Basic organization	Not organized and hard to read
Graph: Data	Groups data in categories more complex than "Benefit" and "Does not benefit"	Groups data in categories "Benefit" and "Does not benefit"	Does not group data into categories
Report: Sources	Uses information from all three sections, more than three cards, and two online features	Uses information from at least three cards and one other source	Uses information only from the cards
Report: Completeness	Answers all questions in detail	Answers most questions with some detail	Answers some questions with vague responses
Report: Audience	Uses a formal tone for writing to an official	Mostly uses a formal tone for writing to an official	Uses a casual tone

Name _____ Class _____ Date _____

myWorld Chapter Activity Support   **Issue Analysis Worksheet**

A Changing China: Who Benefits the Most?

Directions: Fill out this survey, gathering information from the Activity Card.

Name of Issue _____

Data Formats   ☐ chart   ☐ line graph   ☐ bar graph

☐ pie graph   ☐ map

Differences Between Chinese Citizens	
What two groups does the data compare?	
Benefits	
Which group is better off?	Provide at least one reason.
Disadvantages	
Whom do you think this issue harms? How do you think it harms them?	Provide at least one reason.

Notes about other issues

_____

_____

_____

_____

T7

China and Its Neighbors

- Introduce the Essential Question so that students will be able to understand the big ideas of this chapter (see earlier page, Connect to the Essential Question).

- Help students prepare to learn about China and Its Neighbors by looking at the chapter's maps, charts, and photos.

- Have students make and record chapter predictions with the *Essential Question Preview* in the **Student Journal.**

- Ask them to analyze maps on this page.

GUIDE ON THE SIDE

Explore the Essential Question . . .

Have students complete the Essential Question Writer's Workshop in their **Student Journal** to demonstrate in-depth understanding of the question in the context of this chapter.

Analyze Maps Point out the political map of China, Mongolia, and Taiwan.

- Which country is landlocked? (Mongolia) Which is an island? (Taiwan)

- What are the three major rivers flowing through China? (Huang River, Chang River, Xi River)

- What might explain the location of the city of Shanghai? (Sample: It is located at the mouth of a major river. This location would be good for shipping and transportation.)

China and Its Neighbors

Essential Question

How can you measure success?

KEY
- National border
- ⊕ Capital city
- ○ Other city

0 ___ 400 mi
0 ___ 400 km
Lambert Conformal Conic Projection

Ulaanbaatar ○

MONGOLIA

Beijing ⊕
Tianjin ○

Yellow Sea

CHINA

Wuxi ○ Shanghai

Wuhan ○

East China Sea

Chongqing ○

Taipei ○
TAIWAN

TROPIC OF CANCER

Hong Kong ○

South China Sea

Where in the World Are China and Its Neighbors?

★

★

Washington, D.C., to Wuxi: 7,440 miles

INTRODUCE my Story

Get students excited to learn about China and Its Neighbors by first experiencing the region through the eyes of Xiao.

- Read myStory and watch the myStory Video about his life.

- Have students complete *Xiao's Lake* in the **Student Journal** to prepare to learn about the challenge of pollution in China.

my Story

Xiao's Lake

In this section you'll read about Xiao, a young man helping to care for his family. He lives in eastern China. What does his story tell you about the challenges China faces?

Explore the Essential Question
- at my worldgeography.com
- using the myWorld Chapter Activity
- with the Student Journal

Story by Megan Shank for myWorld Online

Xiao lives with his father, mother, grandmother, and older brother in a tiny village near Wuxi (woo shee), an ancient city in the east of China. After learning of his father's diabetes diagnosis, 17-year-old Xiao found a full-time job to help support his family.

Xiao (whose name is pronounced show, as in *shower*) and his brother both work at a factory that produces machines that make ice cream. His mother works at a different factory and tends the family's orange and peach orchard. His father is a part-time driver.

Every morning at 7 A.M., Xiao rides his motorcycle to Wuxi. There are many factories in this area. They have easy access to railways and canals that transport goods to large cities, such as Shanghai. Xiao works 10 hours a day, five days a week. Many local youth leave to make their fortunes, but Xiao wants to stay close to his family.

Life has changed as China has become wealthier. Meat used to be too expensive to eat every day. Thirty years ago, few people could afford a television. Now, most families in Xiao's village own one.

Xiao rides home from work.

GUIDE ON THE SIDE

my Story

Xiao's Lake

- **Identify Details** Where does Xiao live in China? (Sample: He lives in a village near the city of Wuxi in the east of China.)

- **Summarize** How do Xiao and his parents make a living? (Sample: Xiao works in a factory. His father is a driver and his mother tends the family's orchard and also works in a factory.)

On Assignment

Have students go to myworldgeography.com to receive their assignments from a virtual editor. Students will explore China and its neighbors to better understand Xiao's story and the key idea of the chapter.

QUICK FACTS

Algae Algae are aquatic plants that can vary in size from a fraction of an inch to 200 feet in length. They do not have a true root, stem, or leaf. Many species of algae are ancient, but some have developed more recently. Algae have both positive and negative qualities. They provide much of the world's oxygen and are also a source of crude oil. In addition, many products are made from algae. However, algae can be poisonous. Some species create toxins. When fish or shellfish eat this type of algae, they become unfit for human consumption. Also, several algae are poisonous to fish and have caused major fish kills.

GUIDE ON THE SIDE

A street in Xiao's village

Xiao's mother applies pesticides to the orange trees in the family orchard.

Xiao's mother prepares dinner in a large wok.

Xiao's family shares these dishes at dinner.

- **Identify Evidence** What evidence shows that something is wrong with Lake Tai's environment? (terrible odor from the lake, algae bloom covering the lake, fish float on surface of lake)

- **Cause and Effect** What caused Lake Tai's environmental problems? (pollution and pesticides from factories and farms around the lake)

Unlike his parents' generation, which suffered famine and shortages of many goods, Xiao doesn't remember a time when food was scarce.

He does remember when the waters of Lake Tai were clean and clear. Lake Tai is China's third-largest body of fresh water. It is just a five-minute jaunt from Xiao's house. As a boy, he learned to swim there. He collected snails in the lake and had mud fights with friends.

Walking through the family's fruit orchard, it's hard to imagine this place ever smelled like anything other than sun-ripened oranges. Yet in the summer of 2007 a terrible odor crept from the lake across the orchard and into their home.

An algae bloom covered the lake with green slime. The algae bloom was caused, in part, by pollution and pesticides from the farms and factories around the lake. The algae used up the oxygen in the lake. Suffocated fish floated to the surface, belly up.

"You didn't even want to use the water to bathe, much less to drink," says Xiao.

Thirty million people rely on Lake Tai for drinking water. That summer, families in Xiao's village avoided the lake water. They drew water from local wells or bought bottles of water. Bottled water was rushed to Wuxi during the crisis.

Xiao's family shut the windows and put up with the stench. Flies and mosquitoes swarmed.

HISTORY

Lake Tai's History People first settled in the Lake Tai region around the 1st century B.C. By the 7th century A.D., they had started to build an irrigation system. This network consists of an intricate pattern of canals and channels that connect to the lake. Over the years, many improvements have been made to this network. For example, dikes have been built, and the canal system has become more complex. Throughout its history, Lake Tai's scenery has attracted many people. Emperors, ministers, and scholars have taken cruises on the lake. Also, many poets and scholars have been inspired by its beauty. Several islands on the lake are Daoist or Buddhist religious sites.

A factory by the lake is torn down.

Algae and trash float on this small pond near Xiao's home.

Small ponds where neighbors had once washed their fruit and rinsed their rice filled with algae and muck. People started to throw their garbage into these pools, as well.

"If the environment is better, people behave better," says Xiao. "When there's pollution, people throw their garbage where they shouldn't."

The city of Wuxi has started to solve the problem. They hired people to remove the algae. They have also shut down some factories around the lake to reduce the pollution.

Towns are also being bulldozed. Citizens in the village next to Xiao's village were forced to move when the government claimed the area for a park. Xiao has never lived anywhere else and worries the government will make his family move, too.

He has mixed feelings about his parent's use of pesticides and fertilizers in their orchard. He knows these chemicals run off into the lake and cause more harm. He also knows that the factory where he works may be adding to the pollution. Still, Xiao needs his job. He hopes to save money, marry, and start a family—preferably, he says, by the time he's 23— so there are no easy answers.

"How can you choose between your family and your home?"

- **Problem Solve** How has the city of Wuxi attempted to solve the environmental problems of Lake Tai? (The city of Wuxi has hired people to remove algae and shut down factories around the lake.)
- **Express Opinions** Do you think Xiao should tell his family to stop using pesticides? Explain. (Samples: Yes, the pesticides are harming the lake, which everyone in the area depends on. No, the pesticides are probably needed in order to have a productive orchard that can feed the family.)

Meet the Videographer

Name Carl Thelin
Favorite Moment Eating dinner with Xiao's family

 myStory Video

Join Xiao as he shows you more about his life and Lake Tai.

myStory Video

Have students watch the video at myworldgeography.com about Xiao's life and the village where he lives. Tell students to use their trackers to take notes on the issue of pollution in China.

Chapter Atlas

OBJECTIVES

Students will know

- the population distribution of China, Mongolia, and Taiwan.
- the climate of China, Mongolia, and Taiwan.

Students will be able to

- label outline maps of China, Mongolia, and Taiwan.
- analyze why people migrate in China.

SET EXPECTATIONS

In this section, students will

- read the Chapter Atlas.
- form an opinion about migration to a Chinese city.
- go On Assignment in China, Mongolia, and Taiwan and listen to phrases in Mandarin Chinese.

CORE CONCEPTS

You may wish to teach or reteach the following lessons from the Core Concepts Handbook:

- Population Distribution, pp. 76–77
- Migration, pp. 78–79
- Urbanization, pp. 80–83

KEY

Differentiated Instruction	English Language Instruction
L1 Special Needs **L2** Extra Support	**ELL** Beginner **ELL** Early Intermediate **ELL** Intermediate
L3 On-Level **L4** Challenge	**ELL** Early Advanced **ELL** Advanced

1 Connect
Make learning meaningful

Make Connections Ask students to list some minority ethnic groups in the United States in their journals. Then have them identify the minority group that they think is the largest. Then ask them if they think China has any minority groups. Have them explain their answer in their journals.

L2 Extra Support Review with students the meaning of the term "ethnic group." What makes ethnic groups different from one another?

Activate Prior Knowledge Have students call out adjectives that describe China and write these adjectives on the board. (large country, many people.) Ask students to predict whether or not Mongolia and Taiwan are similar to China.

L3 On-Level Draw students' attention to the political map on the chapter opener. Have them compare the location and size of China to that of Mongolia and Taiwan.

Prepare Follow the steps in the section **Preview.** Preteach the Key Terms. Then have students complete *Word Wise* in their journals using in-text clues and the glossary for help.

2 Experience
Teach knowledge and skills

Read Use **Background** notes and **Guide on the Side** questions to model active reading. Have students use *Take Notes* in their **Student Journal** to record important places to know in China on an outline map. Students should use the maps in the Chapter Atlas and the Active Atlas at myworldgeography.com for assistance.

L1 Special Needs Have students read Section 1 and write down words that they do not understand. Then define these words using basic vocabulary.

ELL Intermediate Post this model for writing cause and effect sentences. Bill went to _____ because he wanted to _____. Because of this trip, Bill _____.

L4 Challenge Have students read *Enrichment: Tibet's Conflicts With China* to learn more about Tibetan culture and the conflict between Tibetans and the Chinese government.

Practice: myWorld Activity Students will make decisions about migrating from a small town to a large city in China to explore some of the strengths and weaknesses of this type of migration. **Step-by-Step Instructions** and **More Activities** follow on the next page.

SECTION 1 RESOURCE GUIDE

FOR THE STUDENT

my worldgeography.com Student Center
- Language Lesson
- Active Atlas
- Culture Close-up

Student Edition (print and online)
- Chapter Atlas

Student Journal (print and online)
- Section 1 Word Wise
- Section 1 Outline Map

21st Century Learning Online Tutor
- Make Decisions

FOR THE TEACHER

my worldgeography.com Teacher Center
- Online Lesson Planner
- Presentations for Projection
- SuccessTracker

ProGuide: East and Southeast Asia
- Lesson Plan, pp. T8–T9
- 🏃 myWorld Activity Step-by-Step Instructions, p. T10
- Activity Support: Role Playing, p. T11
- myWorld Geography Enrichment, p. T12
- Section Quiz, p. T13

Accelerating the Progress of ELLs
- Peer Learning Strategies, p. 46

3 Understand
Assess understanding

Review Review *Word Wise* and *Outline Map* in the **Student Journal.**

Assess Knowledge and Skills Use the Section Assessment and Section Quiz to check students' progress.

Assess Understanding Review students' responses to the Section Assessment Essential Question prompt.

Remediate Use these strategies to review and remediate.

If students struggle to . . .	Try these strategies.
Understand pollution in China	Replay the **myStory Video** of Xiao's story.
Analyze cause and effect	Assign additional practice with the **21st Century Online Tutor.**
Identify Main Ideas and Details	Review main ideas using visuals from the lesson. Ask students if any of these issues apply to their own lives. Then ask them why they think these ideas are important.

ELL Support

ELL Objective Students will be able to identify words related to *migration.*

Cultural Connections To connect students to migration in China, let them use their native languages to describe why they think people they know migrate from one place to another.

ELL Early Advanced Content Tip Have students skim Section 1 for Key Terms and other important words. Provide definitions using basic vocabulary for terms or words that students are unable to understand. Then ask students to write out sentences that use these terms and words correctly.

ELL Activity Have students select three terms or academic words that deal with migration and draw a picture that represents each word. Then have students view each other's drawings and guess the words. For further reinforcement, make a word web and ask students to brainstorm related words such as *migrant, migrate, immigration,* etc. **(Visual/Verbal)**

myWorld Activity   **Step-by-Step Instructions**

   30 min

Should I Migrate?

OBJECTIVES

Students will

- analyze the pros and cons of migrating from a small town to a city in China.
- make a decision about whether to migrate from a town to a city in China.

Activity Steps

1. Tell students they will be asked to divide into small groups and make a decision about migrating from a town to a city in China. Each group will then share its decision and the reasons for it with the class.

2. Have students divide into small groups of five or six. Tell each group to imagine that they are a family unit in China. The members of each group should read over the roles described on *Activity Support: Role Playing*. Then each member should choose a role.

   L1 **Special Needs** To help students understand role playing, have them name a favorite TV show and two characters in that show. Then have them identify the actors playing these roles. Tell them that in this activity, they are like actors who play a role in a TV show.

   L3 **On Level** If students have trouble understanding the activity, ask them to think about

LEARNING STYLE

- Interpersonal
- Verbal

21st Century Learning

- Make Decisions

MATERIALS

- Scissors
- Activity Support: Role Playing, p. T11

the family in terms of problems and solutions. Ask them to list what problems this family might deal with and possible solutions.

3. Students in a group should take turns expressing their opinion about whether or not they want to stay in their small town or migrate to the city for better work. The city is about 200 miles away. Each student should support his or her opinion with reasons.

4. Each group as a whole should then discuss who, if any, will stay and who, if any, will migrate. After a decision is made, each group should answer all the questions listed at the bottom of the *Activity Support: Role Playing*.

5. Each group should then share its decision and the reasons for it with the class. If time allows, have the class discuss the various decisions.

More Activities From myWorld Teachers

Local Connections Ask students to name contributions that the Chinese have made to U.S. culture. List them on the board. Add any major ones that are missing. Then have students identify which contributions they have experienced. **(Verbal)**

Debate Post the following statement: "The one-child policy is good for China." Have pairs debate whether or not they agree with the statement. One

student in a pair should support the statement and the other disagree with it. **(Verbal/Logical)**

On the Go Have students research the lifestyle of nomadic herders in Mongolia. Then have them write a summary of their findings. Make sure that they include information about gers, festivals, and games. Also, have them draw a picture that depicts some aspect of Mongolian life. **(Verbal/Visual)**

my **worldgeography.com** (**Teacher Center**) → Find additional resources in the online Teacher Center.

Name _____ Class _____ Date _____

myWorld Activity Support   **Role Playing**

Should I Migrate?

Directions Imagine that your group is a family unit in China that lives in a small village. This family is poor and barely has enough food. Read the descriptions of the roles below. Then cut out each role, mix the pieces of paper in a container, and have each person select a role.

✂ -

Grandfather: 75 years old, has poor eyesight, has never been far from the village, does light work around the house but nothing heavy, is very attached to his family, has many lifelong friends in the village

Grandmother: 72 years old, has severe illness that needs medical attention, nearest medical clinic is 100 miles away and is expensive, is very attached to her family, has many lifelong friends in the village

Father: 45 years old, rice farmer, fishes in the nearby river, where recent pollution has killed many fish, is very attached to his family, lives in poor conditions, has many friends in the village, does not trust city people

Mother: 40 years old, does domestic chores and also helps her husband in the rice fields, is very attached to her family, moved to the village from another village when she got married, has two close friends in the village, wants her children to have a better life

Son: 20 years old, helps his father in the rice fields, is attached to his family, wants to learn more about better farming methods but can't afford an education, has only one good friend in the village, is not attracted to city life

Daughter: 18 years old, helps her father in the rice fields, is attached to her family, wants to see more of the world, wants an education, has several good friends in the village

Make a Decision Make a decision about how many people, if any, from your family unit will migrate to the city for better work. Then answer the following questions on a separate sheet of paper.

Which members of your family unit will go to the city? Support your answer with reasons.

What are the advantages of your decision?

What are the disadvantages of your decision?

Name _____ Class _____ Date _____

Enrichment: Tibet's Conflicts With China

Directions Read the selection below. Answer the questions that follow and complete the activity.

Tibetans are an important ethnic minority group in China. They live in a region called Tibet, which is located in southwest China. Tibet contains the highest plateau in the world, so it is often called the "Roof of the World."

Most Tibetans practice a form of Buddhism called Lamaism. The Dalai Lama is considered by his followers as the political ruler of Tibet and its supreme spiritual ruler. The Dalai Lama first rose to power in Tibet in 1642. However, by the early 1700s, China conquered the region. In 1911, Tibet revolted against China and regained its independence. China, though, still claimed that Tibet was part of their domain.

Then in 1949, the Chinese Communist Party (CCP) gained control of China and, a year later, took over Tibet. The CCP closed or destroyed many monasteries in Tibet and discouraged religious practice. Soon tensions between the Tibetans and the CCP intensified. In the late 1950s, riots broke out. The Dalai Lama and more than 100,000 Tibetans fled to India.

At first, the Communists harshly enforced restrictions on religion. Then in the 1980s, the CCP loosened its restrictions. For example, many Buddhist monasteries were allowed to reopen. However, the government still does not allow full religious freedom.

After the Dalai Lama left China, he has tried to gain more religious freedom for the people of Tibet. He has met with the Chinese government, but no resolution has been achieved.

1. What is the role of the Dalai Lama?

_____

_____

2. How has China's approach to Tibet changed over the years?

_____

_____

3. Activity Create a timeline that traces Tibet's relationship with China. Based on your research, decide how many centuries to include.

Name _____ Class _____ Date _____

Section Quiz

Directions Answer the following questions using what you learned
in Section 1.

1. _____ Which of the following stretches
from southern Mongolia toward the
Huang River in China?
a. the Gobi
b. the Himalayas
c. the North China Plain
d. the Tibetan Plateau

2. _____ Which of the following is the staple
crop of the North China Plain?
a. barley
b. rice
c. soybeans
d. wheat

3. _____ Which of the following places would
most likely have hot, humid summers and
mild winters?
a. Mongolia
b. northern China
c. Taiwan
d. Tibet

4. _____ China's policy of population control
is called the
a. best-family policy.
b. one-child policy.
c. small-family policy.
d. more-children policy.

5. _____ Which of the following is the largest
ethnic group in China?
a. Han
b. Tibetan
c. Uighurs
d. Hui

6. China is sparsely populated in the north and west and densely
populated in the south and east. Explain how geographic factors,
such as climate and landforms, influence this distribution.

_____

_____

_____

Chapter Atlas

- Model preparing to read by previewing the Key Ideas, Key Terms, headings, visuals, and captions. Have students make predictions about what they will learn. For ELL support, post the prompt, "I predict I will read about . . ."

- Preview and practice the reading skill, Label an Outline Map, by using examples from your community.

- Preteach this section's high-use Academic Vocabulary and Key Terms using the chart on the next page and in-text definitions. Have students practice Key Terms by completing the *Word Wise* page in their journals.

Physical Features

Identify Details Have students read to identify details about China's physical features.

- In what part of China are the Himalayas located? (the southwest border)

- What are the two largest rivers in China? (the Chang and the Huang)

Reading Skill

Label an Outline Map While they read, have students identify the Place to Know! on the outline map of the region in the **Student Journal.**

Section 1

Chapter Atlas

Key Ideas
- Most people live on the plains and in the coastal areas of this region.
- Climate, especially rainfall, influences the economic activities in this region.
- Cities have grown rapidly in China in recent years.

Key Terms
- loess
- staple crop
- nomadic herder
- arable land
- one-child policy

Visual Glossary

Reading Skill: Label an Outline Map Take notes using the outline map in your journal.

A fisherman uses a cormorant bird to catch fish on the Li River, China.

Physical Features

Travelers who enter China from the west must struggle over a barrier of high mountains. The Himalayas, along China's southwest border, are the highest mountain range in the world.

North of the Himalayas, travelers cross the Tibetan Plateau, the highest and largest plateau in the world. Many rivers begin here. They flow south and east to many countries, providing drinking water for one third of the world's population.

China's largest rivers—the Chang (or Yangtze) and the Huang (or Yellow)—begin on the Tibetan Plateau. These rivers

ACADEMIC VOCABULARY

High-Use Word	Definition and Sample Sentences
fertile	*adj.* rich in nutrients, capable of growing many plants *Because of the fertile soil, the farmers had a plentiful harvest.*
enforce	*v.* to make someone follow a rule or law *The dictator enforced very strict laws on his people.*

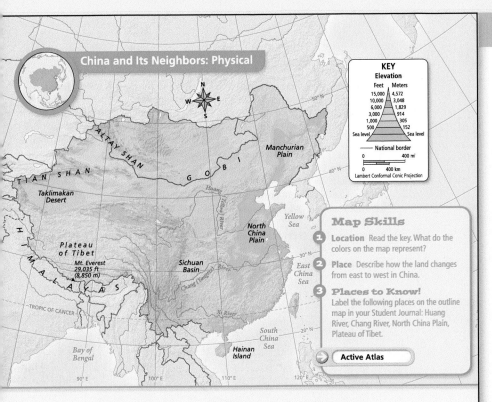

China and Its Neighbors: Physical

KEY
Elevation

Feet	Meters
15,000	4,572
10,000	3,048
6,000	1,829
3,000	914
1,000	305
500	152
Sea level	Sea level

— National border

0   400 mi
0   400 km
Lambert Conformal Conic Projection

Map Skills

1 **Location** Read the key. What do the colors on the map represent?

2 **Place** Describe how the land changes from east to west in China.

3 **Places to Know!** Label the following places on the outline map in your Student Journal: Huang River, Chang River, North China Plain, Plateau of Tibet.

Active Atlas

tumble from the highlands down to the plains on the east coast. The island of Taiwan, by contrast, has mountains on the east and <u>fertile</u> plains on the west side.

Mountains and highland plateaus cover much of Mongolia. A huge desert called the Gobi stretches from southern Mongolia toward the Huang River. Winds from the desert carry **loess** (LOH es) into China. Loess is a dustlike material that can form soil. It can pile up more than 100 feet deep. People carve caves into the loess hills and build their homes in them.

The Huang River cuts through these deposits, picking up the loess. Huang

means "yellow" in Chinese. If you hopped on board a boat along the river, you would see that the loess makes it look yellow and muddy. The Huang created the North China Plain by flooding many times. Each flood left behind fertile soil. For thousands of years, Chinese people have farmed the flat lands along the country's rivers.

Landforms, such as rivers, affect where people live. Climate is also important when people decide how to use the land.

Reading Check What physical feature do China and Mongolia share?

fertile, *adj.,* rich in nutrients, capable of growing many plants

MAP SKILLS **1.** elevation levels **2.** The land becomes more mountainous in the west. **3.** The outline map should be labeled correctly.

READING CHECK China and Mongolia share the Gobi Desert.

Cause and Effect While they read, have students look for causes and effects that involved China's physical features.

- What caused loess to form in central China? (Winds from the desert carry fine dust, called loess, into the area.)

- What effect did the flooding of the Huang River have in northern China? (Over thousands of years, the flooding of the Huang deposited rich soil, which formed the North China Plain.)

Analyze Visuals Have students analyze the physical map on this page.

- What is the elevation range of the Manchurian Plain? (about sea level to 1,000 feet or 305 meters)

- What region of China has the highest elevation? (Plateau of Tibet)

Active Atlas

Have students go to myworldgeography.com to see more maps about China, Mongolia, and Taiwan.

CORE CONCEPTS: TYPES OF CLIMATE

Review Core Concept 3.5 before discussing the climate in China. Review the characteristics of various types of climate found throughout the world. Then have students look over the climate map of China on this page. Ask, What types of climate are found in China? Do these climates reflect the climate patterns discussed on this page? Also, which of China's climates would best support rice farming? What climates found in China would have low population densities? Have students explain their answers.

Climate and Land Use

- **Compare and Contrast** How is the climate in north China different from the climate in south China? (The climate in the south is warmer.)

- **Cause and Effect** What effect do the mountains in western China have on the climate of Mongolia? (The mountains block moist winds, causing a dry climate in Mongolia and western China.)

- **Draw Conclusions** Do you think China, south of the Chang River, gets a lot of rain? Explain. (Yes, tea and rice, which both need a lot of water, grow well in this area.)

Analyze Visuals Analyze the climate map on this page.

- What type of climate is found in Beijing? (continental, warm summer)

- In what region of China is tundra found? (southwest China or Plateau of Tibet)

Climate and Land Use

Across this region, there are two important climate patterns. The first is that the climate is generally colder in the north and warmer in the south. The southern islands of Taiwan and Hainan have hot, humid summers and mild winters. Cities such as Ulaanbaatar (oo lahn BAH tawr) in the north of Mongolia and Beijing in northern China have hot summers. Winters there are freezing cold.

The second major climate pattern is that the climate in the west is drier than in the east. Winds blowing from the south carry moisture from the Pacific Ocean to Taiwan and eastern China. Tall mountains block these winds, so the climate of Mongolia and western China is dry. Two great deserts, the Gobi and the Taklimakan, stretch for hundreds of miles across this area.

These climate patterns influence how people use the land. South of the Chang River, crops that need abundant water, such as tea and rice, are grown. People here, such as Xiao's family, generally eat rice with their daily meals. Taiwan's wet western plains grow rice and other tropical crops, such as sugar and bananas.

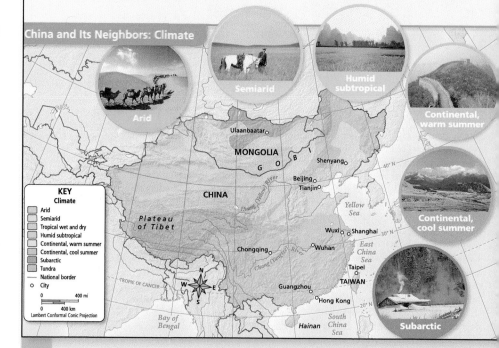

China and Its Neighbors: Climate

Arid · Semiarid · Humid subtropical · Continental, warm summer · Continental, cool summer · Subarctic

KEY
Climate
- Arid
- Semiarid
- Tropical wet and dry
- Humid subtropical
- Continental, warm summer
- Continental, cool summer
- Subarctic
- Tundra
— National border
○ City

0   400 mi
0   400 km
Lambert Conformal Conic Projection

MONGOLIA · CHINA · Plateau of Tibet · GOBI · Ulaanbaatar · Shenyang · Beijing · Tianjin · Yellow Sea · Wuxi · Shanghai · Chongqing · Wuhan · East China Sea · Taipei · TAIWAN · Guangzhou · Hong Kong · Hainan · South China Sea · Bay of Bengal · TROPIC OF CANCER · 40° N · 30° N · 20° N · Huang (Yellow River) · Chang (Yangtze) River

COMMON MISCONCEPTIONS

Chinese Eat Mostly Rice Although rice is an important food in China, the Chinese eat many other types of grains, especially wheat. In some regions, rice is not eaten much at all. Various cuisines have developed throughout China. Each cuisine makes use of local foods. For example, Cantonese cuisine was developed in the Guangdong province. Since this region borders the ocean, Cantonese cooking uses a lot of seafood. To the north, the province of Sichuan grows many chiles. This ingredient, therefore, is often used in Sichuan cooking, making it spicy. Hunan is known as "the land of rice and fish" because these foods are abundant there.

Between the Chang River and the Huang River both rice and wheat are grown. The fertile North China Plain north of the Huang River is too dry for rice. Here, wheat is the **staple crop,** that is, the major crop that is the basis of the diet. Common foods in northern China include steamed bread, dumplings, and noodles made of wheat flour.

Still farther north and west, the climate is usually too dry for growing crops. People in these regions have lived mainly as **nomadic herders,** that is, they herd flocks and do not settle in one place. They must move their herds to find sources of water and grassland. This nomadic lifestyle is especially common in Mongolia and Tibet. Like the cowboys of the American West, Mongolian herders become skilled horseback riders at a young age.

In recent years, industry has expanded in China, Taiwan, and Mongolia. More people have moved to the cities to work in offices and factories, rather than working as farmers or nomadic herders. Large industrial areas have grown around the cities of the region. Peoples' lives across the region are changing.

Reading Check What are the two major climate patterns in this region?

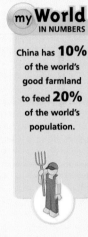

my World IN NUMBERS

China has **10%** of the world's good farmland to feed **20%** of the world's population.

GUIDE ON THE SIDE

- **Identify Evidence** Why is rice not the major crop north of the Huang River? (climate is too dry)
- **Express an Opinion** Why do you think Mongolian herders often become skilled horseback riders at a young age? (Sample: Knowing how to ride a horse is probably very helpful with herding. The younger a person can horseback ride, the sooner he or she can help with the herding.)
- **Predict** How do you think the lifestyle of a nomadic herder would change if he or she got a job in a city? (Sample: The person would live in one place instead of moving a lot. Also, the person would live in a more confined area in the city than in the country.)

Analyze Visuals Analyze the land-use map on this page.

- What type of land is found east of Guangzhou? (forest)
- What part of China is mostly barren? (western China)

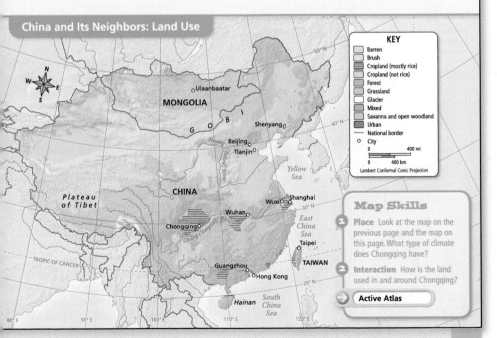

China and Its Neighbors: Land Use

KEY
- Barren
- Brush
- Cropland (mostly rice)
- Cropland (not rice)
- Forest
- Grassland
- Glacier
- Mixed
- Savanna and open woodland
- Urban
- National border
- City

0   400 mi
0   400 km
Lambert Conformal Conic Projection

MONGOLIA
Ulaanbaatar
GOBI
Shenyang
Beijing
Tianjin
Yellow Sea
CHINA
Plateau of Tibet
Wuhan
Chongqing
Wuxi
Shanghai
East China Sea
Taipei
TAIWAN
Guangzhou
Hong Kong
Hainan
South China Sea
TROPIC OF CANCER

Map Skills

① **Place** Look at the map on the previous page and the map on this page. What type of climate does Chongqing have?

② **Interaction** How is the land used in and around Chongqing?

Active Atlas

MAP SKILLS 1. humid subtropical
2. rice farming

READING CHECK A major climate pattern in the region is that the climate is generally colder in the north and warmer in the south. Another pattern is that the climate in the west is drier than the climate in the east.

Active Atlas

Point out the map of land-use.
- Have students go to myworldgeography.com to learn more about the land use in China, Mongolia, and Taiwan.

PRIMARY SOURCE

The Great Leap "The push of the crowded countryside and the pull of urban opportunity are simply too strong [in China]. One sweaty night, I drove with Wen out beyond Beijing's fifth ring road, past a huge new condo development with its own McDonald's, and into a totally different world—a once-rural village now surrounded by city, soon to be swallowed up itself, but for the moment serving as home to tens of thousands of migrant families."

—Bill McKibben, "The Great Leap," *Harper's*, Dec. 2005

Growing Cities, Crowded Coasts

- **Summarize** What is the one-child policy? (Married couples, especially in the cities, are only allowed to have one child.)

- **Cause and Effect** Why are China's resources limited? (Deserts and mountains cover much of the country. Only 15 percent of the land is arable land.)

- **Infer** Why do you think so many Chinese prefer to work in a city rather than in the country? (Sample: Most jobs in cities pay better.)

Analyze Visuals Ask students to compare and contrast the photographs of the Pudong district.

- What are the differences between the two photographs? (The large photo is filled with modern buildings. The small photo only has a few buildings, but more open space.)

- How do you think most people earned a living in the Pudong district before development? (Sample: Most people probably earned a living by farming.)

 myWorld Activity

Should I Migrate? Find Step-by-Step Instructions and an Activity Support on pp. T10–T11. **(Interpersonal/Verbal)**

ANSWERS

Growing Cities, Crowded Coasts

People are not evenly spread across the countries in this region. People have settled where it is easiest to make a living. Today, this is a region on the move with millions of people migrating to find work.

More people live in China than in any other country. Yet China's resources are limited. Deserts and mountains cover much of the country. Only about 15 percent of China's land is **arable land,** that is, land that can be used to grow crops. Most of the arable land is in the eastern part of the country. More than nine tenths of China's people live in the east, and this area can be very crowded.

The Chinese government realized decades ago that China's large population was a problem. If the population contin-ued to grow quickly, there would not be enough food in the country for everyone.

In the late 1970s, the government started a **one-child policy.** Under this law, many married couples are only allowed to have one child. Couples who have more children are punished. There are some exceptions to this rule. Couples in rural areas may sometimes have more than one child. In the cities the one-child policy has been strictly <u>enforced</u>.

Still, China's cities are large and are growing quickly. This is because millions of people are leaving rural areas and moving to the cities to look for work. Many of these workers find jobs in factories or on construction sites.

A migrant worker in Chengdu explains why she and her husband moved to the city to work:

> We lived in a village that's surrounded by big mountains. Where we were, you really can't make a cent. . . you raise a little livestock, some crops, but that's really not sufficient [enough].
> —Cai Zisheng, Chinese migrant

Most people in China still live in rural areas. Only about 45 percent of Chinese people live in cities—in the United States almost 80 percent of people live in cities. China's population is much larger than that of the United States, and so many cities in China are very large. China's capital, Beijing, is home to more than 14 million people. Shanghai is the largest city in the country with more than 16 million people.

Like China, some parts of Taiwan are very crowded. A ridge of mountains runs

enforce, *v.,* to make someone follow a rule or law

 myWorldActivity Migration Decisions

In 1990, parts of the Pudong area of Shanghai were covered by farmland (inset). Now, towering skyscapers and even an airport have been built over the fields.

GEOGRAPHY

Shantytowns As huge numbers of people migrated to cities in China, many shantytowns sprang up in urban areas. A shantytown consists of ramshackle dwellings. These towns often have no running water, no central heating, no paved roads, and no primary school. The population of shantytowns is mostly made up of people who have been laid off from work or who have a very low income. The Chinese government started a program to renovate many shantytowns, especially in the northeast region. This program builds homes with features such as running water and central heating and sells them at a very low price. In fact, a shanty dweller gets a new home free if it is not larger than his shanty. By 2007, the Liaoning construction bureau had improved shantytowns in 14 cities by building proper housing and better infrastructure. This transformation helped about 1.2 million people.

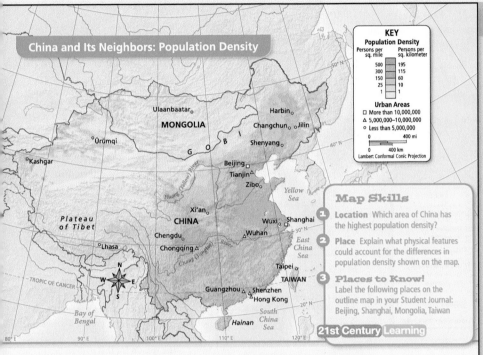

China and Its Neighbors: Population Density

KEY
Population Density

Persons per sq. mile	Persons per sq. kilometer
500	195
300	115
150	60
25	10
1	1

Urban Areas
☐ More than 10,000,000
△ 5,000,000–10,000,000
○ Less than 5,000,000

0   400 mi
0   400 km
Lambert Conformal Conic Projection

Map Skills

1 **Location** Which area of China has the highest population density?

2 **Place** Explain what physical features could account for the differences in population density shown on the map.

3 **Places to Know!** Label the following places on the outline map in your Student Journal: Beijing, Shanghai, Mongolia, Taiwan

21st Century Learning

along the east coast of the island, so most cities and farms are on the flatter west coast of the island. Almost three quarters of Taiwan's population lives in these coastal cities.

In contrast, Mongolia is a landlocked nation, or a nation without a coastline. About half of all Mongolians are nomadic, moving their homes to follow herds of livestock across the country's grassy plains. The nomads live in tents called gers (gehrz). Most of the rest of the population lives in cities. Almost a third of the population lives in the capital city of Ulaanbaatar.

In Mongolia, cities grow or shrink depending on the weather. When a hard winter strikes, livestock may die from a lack of food. Nomadic herders must go to the cities to find work, and the cities grow. During mild winters, some city workers give up their jobs to return to herding. In this region, as in many others, many people move to find of work.

Reading Check Why do many people in both China and Taiwan live along the coast?

Mongolian nomads often live in gers, which can be easily moved. ▼

▶ Culture Close-up

MAP SKILLS 1. eastern China, especially along the coast **2.** the mountains and deserts of western China **3.** The outline map should be correctly labeled.

READING CHECK Cities are located along the coast to take advantage of easy shipping. These cities provide many job opportunities.

GUIDE ON THE SIDE

- **Identify Details** In what city does about a third of the population of Mongolia live? (Ulaanbaatar)

- **Infer** Why do you think Mongolian herders live in tents? (Sample: Tents are easy to move.)

Analyze Visuals Analyze the population map of China on this page.

- About how many people per square mile live in the region around Shanghai? (500 or more people per square mile)

21st Century Learning

Read Special-Purpose Maps
Have students develop this skill by using this interactive online tutorial and activities. Students will learn how to read special-purpose maps and use the knowledge to solve problems.

▶ **Culture Close-up**

Discuss the photograph.
- How can you tell the gers are easy to move? (They have cloth sides that are tied down by ropes)
- Go to myworldgeography.com to learn more about Mongolia's nomads.

CULTURE

The Zhuang The Zhuang are the largest ethnic minority in southern China. In the early 2000s, these people numbered about 16 million. About 2,500 years ago, the Zhuang started to be pushed south by the Han, who eventually dominated China. The Zhuang adopted some of the cultural traits of the Han but also kept some distinct characteristics. For example, after marriage, brides stay with their birth family until the birth of the first child. The Zhuang are known for their handcrafted items, especially carpets, tablecloths, and curtains. They are also known for making a type of brocade, which is sold around the world.

Ethnic Diversity in China

- **Summarize** What are some of the larger minority groups in China? (the Tibetans, the Uighurs)

- **Cause and Effect** China's many ethnic groups are not spread evenly across the country. What caused this type of distribution? (As the Han people took control of China, the people they conquered mostly stayed in their traditional homelands.)

Analyze Visuals Analyze the ethnic diversity map on this page.

- In what part of China do most of the Uighurs live? (northwest China)

- What is the dominant ethnic group north of Beijing? (Mongolian)

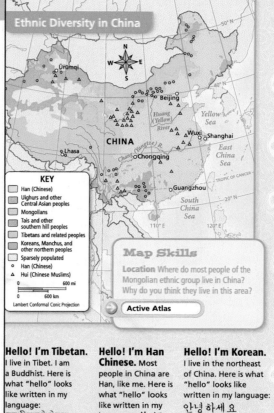

Ethnic Diversity in China

KEY
- Han (Chinese)
- Uighurs and other Central Asian peoples
- Mongolians
- Tais and other southern hill peoples
- Tibetans and related peoples
- Koreans, Manchus, and other northern peoples
- Sparsely populated
- ○ Han (Chinese)
- △ Hui (Chinese Muslims)

0   600 mi
0   600 km
Lambert Conformal Conic Projection

Map Skills

Location Where do most people of the Mongolian ethnic group live in China? Why do you think they live in this area?

Active Atlas

Hello! I'm Tibetan. I live in Tibet. I am a Buddhist. Here is what "hello" looks like written in my language:
བཀྲ་ཤིས་བདེ་ལེགས།

Hello! I'm Han Chinese. Most people in China are Han, like me. Here is what "hello" looks like written in my language: 你好

Hello! I'm Korean. I live in the northeast of China. Here is what "hello" looks like written in my language:
안녕 하세요

Language Lesson

Ethnic Diversity in China

About 92 percent of Chinese people today belong to the Han ethnic group. More than 50 ethnic groups make up the rest of the population.

Some of the larger minority groups are the Uighurs (WEE goorz) of northwestern China and the Tibetans.

These groups have their own languages, traditional clothing, and holidays. Some of these groups are closely identified with a religion. For example, many Uighurs are Muslim. Many Tibetans practice a unique form of Buddhism.

China's many ethnic groups are not evenly spread across the country. People of the Han ethnic group live mostly in the east. Many people who belong to minority groups live near the borders of the country.

The reason for this pattern lies in China's history. The Han people built their earliest kingdoms in the east along the Huang River. Later, these kingdoms joined together and created a powerful Chinese empire.

The Chinese emperors conquered new lands. They came to control regions whose people were not Han. These people kept many of their own customs and stayed near their traditional homelands.

People from all ethnic groups have played an important role in China's history. Some emperors were not from the Han ethnic group. Mongolian lead-

Active Atlas

Point out the ethnic diversity map.
- Have students go to myworldgeography.com to learn more about ethnic groups of China.

MAP SKILLS Most Mongolians live in northern China. They most likely live there because northern China borders Mongolia.

READING CHECK The Han people built their earliest kingdoms in the east along the Huang River. So areas on the outskirts of China, along its borders, were not dominated by the Han. As a result, minority groups flourished in these areas.

QUICK FACTS

Lunar Calendar The Chinese New Year does not fall on January 1 but rather can take place anytime in late January or February. The reason for the difference lies with the Chinese calendar. This calendar is based on the cycles of the moon. Because of this, it is called a lunar calendar. Each month starts with a new moon. In the Northern Hemisphere, the year begins at the second new moon after the start of winter. This can happen from January 21 to February 19, depending on the year. The Muslims also use a lunar calendar to track Islamic holy days and the holy month of Ramadan. Ramadan is observed by Muslims as a month of fasting. Fasting takes place each day from dawn until dusk. Ramadan falls during the ninth month of the lunar calendar.

ers ruled China for almost a hundred years. The last emperor and his ancestors belonged to a people called the Manchu.

China's current government has tried to protect the country's rich cultural heritage. For example, the one-child policy only applies to Han Chinese people. Families of other ethnic groups are allowed to have more than one child.

However, the Chinese government has made other rules that control cultural and religious life in China. People cannot freely form groups to practice religion. The government limits the number of churches and religious organizations.

All Chinese people, including the Han, must follow these restrictions. However, these rules make it harder for groups with special religious traditions to preserve their cultures.

Tibetans and Uighurs have protested against the government. Some have called for more autonomy from China. The Chinese government has attacked and imprisoned people who protest against its policies. The government is trying to improve the economy of borderland areas, but conflict continues because of its rules controlling cultural life.

Reading Check Why are many minority groups found along China's borders?

Uighur schoolgirls in China's western province of Xinjiang ▼

Section 1 Assessment

Key Terms

1. Use the following terms to describe land use in this region: loess, staple crop, nomadic herder, arable land.

Key Ideas

2. Why is there little farming in Mongolia?

3. Why did the Chinese government introduce the one-child policy?

4. Where were the early Han kingdoms in China?

Think Critically

5. **Analyze Information** Look at the population density map. Which areas have the highest population density? Why do so many people live in these areas?

6. **Summarize** Why are cities growing in China?

? Essential Question

How can you measure success?

7. How can the Chinese government measure whether or not the one-child policy has been successful? Go to your Student Journal to record your answer.

SECTION 1 ASSESSMENT **1.** Answers will vary. **2.** The climate is too dry for agriculture. **3.** to control China's population and thereby enable the country to use its resources to feed its entire population **4.** The Han built their earliest kingdoms along the Huang River. **5.** Areas in the east of China have the highest population density. Many people locate there for work in the numerous cities in the area. **6.** Millions of people are leaving rural areas and moving to cities to look for work. **7.** The goal is to control population growth. If the population is not increasing, then the policy would seem to be working.

ANSWERS

GUIDE ON THE SIDE

- **Identify Evidence** Does the one-child policy apply to all ethnic groups in China? Explain. (No, the one-child policy only applies to Han Chinese people.)

- **Infer** Why do you think Tibetans do not like the Chinese government's control of religious life? (Sample: Buddhism is very important to them and they don't want it controlled.)

Analyze Visuals Ask students to analyze the children in the photograph.

- Do you think these children belong to families with high incomes? Explain. (No, the children are wearing simple clothing that is probably inexpensive.)

- What emotions are these children conveying? (happiness, humor, joy)

→ **Language Lesson**

Have students go to myworldgeography.com to find out about the languages of China.

History of China and Its Neighbors

OBJECTIVES

Students will know
- the extent of China's advanced empire.
- how Communists created a command economy in China and Mongolia.
- how China and Mongolia changed to a market economy.

Students will be able to
- identify main ideas and details in the region's history.
- compare viewpoints.

SET EXPECTATIONS

In this section, students will
- read History of China and Its Neighbors.
- participate in models for command and market economies.
- go On Assignment in China, Mongolia, and Taiwan to track important dates in the region's history.

CORE CONCEPTS

You may wish to teach or reteach the following lessons from the Core Concepts Handbook:
- Economic Systems, pp. 62–63
- Economic Development, pp. 64–65
- Measuring Time, pp. 118–119

KEY

Differentiated Instruction	English Language Instruction
L1 Special Needs **L2** Extra Support	**ELL** Beginner **ELL** Early Intermediate **ELL** Intermediate
L3 On-Level **L4** Challenge	**ELL** Early Advanced **ELL** Advanced

1 Connect
Make learning meaningful

Make Connections Ask the class to name some of the major companies found in the United States. Write the names of these companies on the board. Then ask them to name what these companies produce. Do they think these companies are told what to produce by the government? Explain.

L2 Extra Support Have students write down some of the major businesses that can be found in their area.

Activate Prior Knowledge Remind students that in the previous section, they learned about the many ethnic groups found in China and its neighbors. Ask them to predict if any of these ethnic groups had conflicts during China's history. Why or why not?

L3 On-Level Draw students' attention to the visuals in the previous section that show the ethnic diversity in China.

Prepare Follow the steps in the section **Preview.** Preteach the Key Terms. Then have students complete *Word Wise* in their journals using in-text clues and the glossary for help.

2 Experience
Teach knowledge and skills

Read Use **Background** notes and **Guide on the Side** questions to model active reading. Have students use *Take Notes* in their **Student Journal** to identify main ideas and details. Have students complete **21st Century Online Tutor:** *Identify Main Ideas and Details*, and apply this skill to reading the section.

L4 Challenge Have students imagine that they are the revolutionaries trying to overthrow the Qing Dynasty. Have them write a speech that explains the reasons that the Qing Dynasty should be toppled.

ELL Intermediate Have students reread The Qing Dynasty Struggles. Define the word *viewpoint* as a way of looking at something. Then ask students to identify two groups with different viewpoints in the section, and have them explain how they are different.

L4 Challenge Have students read *Enrichment: Silk Making* to learn more about the history of silk making in China and how it is made.

Practice: myWorld Activity Students will participate in an activity that demonstrates a command economy and a market economy. Then they will evaluate both economies and compare and contrast them. **Step-by-Step Instructions** and **More Activities** follow on the next page.

SECTION 2 RESOURCE GUIDE

FOR THE STUDENT

my worldgeography.com Student Center

- Timeline

Student Edition (print and online)

- History of China and Its Neighbors

Student Journal (print and online)

- Section 2 Word Wise
- Section 2 Take Notes

21st Century Learning Online Tutor

- Identify Main Ideas and Details
- Compare Viewpoints

FOR THE TEACHER

my worldgeography.com Teacher Center

- Online Lesson Planner
- Presentations for Projection
- SuccessTracker

ProGuide: East and Southeast Asia

- Lesson Plan, pp. T14–T15
- myWorld Activity Step-by-Step Instructions, p. T16
- Activity Support: Resource Summaries, p. T17
- myWorld Geography Enrichment, p. T18
- Section Quiz, p. T19

Accelerating the Progress of ELLs

- Reading Support Strategies, p. 42

---

3 Understand
Assess understanding

Review Review *Word Wise* and *Take Notes* in the **Student Journals.**

Assess Knowledge and Skills Use the Section Assessment and the Section Quiz to check students' progress.

Assess Understanding Review students' responses to the Section Assessment Essential Question prompt.

Remediate Use these strategies to review and remediate.

If students struggle to . . .	Try these strategies.
Describe a command economy	Reread the **China and Mongolia Under Communism** subsection and review the main elements of a command economy.
Identify main ideas and details	Assign additional practice with the **21st Century Online Tutor.**
Compare Viewpoints	Have the class compare and contrast command and market economies. Use a concept web to list similarities and differences.

ELL Support

ELL Objective Students will be able to identify main ideas in English text.

Cultural Connections Explain that the main idea is the most important idea. Let students share how to say "most important" their native language.

ELL Early Intermediate/Intermediate Content Tip Tell students that there are sometimes clues in the text for finding the main idea. Words like "mostly," "greatest," "in general," "many," or "often" might signal that the author is trying to say this idea is important. Read text from the section and ask students to say which clue words they hear.

ELL Activity Make and distribute index cards with phrases corresponding to command economy and market economy. For example, "control" would go with command economy and "choice" would go with market economy. Post a chart with two columns, "Command Economy" and "Market Economy." Have pairs discuss their phrases, post them, and explain why. **(Kinesthetic/Verbal)**

myWorld Activity   **Step-by-Step Instructions**

 20 min

Command Economy vs. Market Economy

OBJECTIVES

Students will

- evaluate a command economy and a market economy.
- compare and contrast a command economy and market economy.

LEARNING STYLE

- Interpersonal
- Kinesthetic

21st Century Learning

- Compare Viewpoints

MATERIALS

- Activity Support: Resource Summaries, p. T17

Activity Steps

1. Tell students that they will be asked to participate in an activity that demonstrates a command economy. During this activity, students will think about the challenge of making a plan for the whole economy.

2. Divide the class into four groups. Assign a region in China to each group. The regions are north, east, south, and west. You will represent the Chinese government. Have the members of each regional group cut out the resource summary from the *Activity Support: Resource Summaries* that applies to their region.

   L2 Extra Support Hold a class discussion about which resources produce certain products.

   ELL Early Intermediate Ask students to define the word *command*. Ask them why they think it is used to describe a command economy.

3. Read the government's goal from the *Resource*

Summaries and decide which product the government wants to increase the production of. Then tell each region to produce a large amount of this product that is high in quality. Each region, based on its resource summary, should then determine if it can meet this quota. Each regional group should then tell the class whether or not it can meet the quota and why.

4. Then have each regional group use their summaries to decide what product they could best produce large amounts of at high quality. Have each region tell the class which product and why.

5. Ask the class to discuss the drawbacks of having the government set goals for all provinces. What does the government group need to know to make a good plan for everyone? Why might it be difficult for the government of a country as large as China to have the right information to make these decisions?

More Activities From myWorld Teachers

Local Connection Have students research a Chinese invention that they have used in everyday life. Then have them write a brief history of the invention and draw a picture showing a modern day use of the invention. **(Verbal/Visual)**

Person Place Thing Give each student a notecard with the name of a person, place, or thing that is important in Chinese history. Then have each student write three statements that apply to

the person, place, or thing on their notecard without naming it. After this, have each student read aloud their statements and other students guess what these statements refer to. **(Logical/Verbal)**

 Timeline Have pairs create a timeline of the important events in Chinese history. The timelines should include the date and brief description of each event. **(Verbal/Logical)**

my worldgeography.com (**Teacher Center**)   Find additional resources in the online Teacher Center.

Name _____ Class _____ Date _____

myWorld Activity Support   **Resource Summaries**

Command Economy vs. Market Economy

Directions Read the government's goal and the region resource summaries. Cut out the summary that applies to your region. Choose one of the following products for a massive production increase: tanks, rice products, wooden furniture, or canned fish. Answer the questions below.

✂ -

Government's Goal: The Chinese government wants to increase the total national production of one good. The government will trade this good for other goods. It wants all regional groups to produce large amounts of their chosen product at a high quality.

Northern China
- Some forests; limited types of wood
- Some fisheries; limited variety of fish
- Large iron deposits; good-quality iron ore
- Few rice farms; low-grade rice

Eastern China
- Large forests; many types of wood
- Many fisheries; wide variety of fish
- Few iron deposits; low-quality iron ore
- Large rice farms; high-grade rice

Southern China
- Large forests; many types of wood
- Many fisheries; wide variety of fish
- Few iron deposits; low quality iron ore
- Large rice farms; high-grade rice

Western China
- No forests; limited types of wood
- No fisheries; limited variety of fish
- Large iron deposits; high quality iron
- No rice farms; no rice

Wrap-Up Explain whether a command economy and a market economy would benefit your region based on what you know about its resources. Also explain whether your region was more or less successful when you had a choice or no choice about what to produce and why.

_____

_____

_____

_____

_____

Name _____ Class _____ Date _____

Enrichment: Silk Making

Directions Read the selection below. Answer the questions that follow and complete the activity.

Silk is a strong, shiny fiber with a natural beauty. Indeed, it is often called the "queen of fibers." Silk is used to make a lightweight cloth that is warmer than linen or cotton.

Legend has it that silk was invented in China around 2700 B.C. by Xi Ling-Shi, the wife of Emperor Huangdi. She noticed white worms eating the emperor's mulberry leaves. The worms spun shining cocoons. After she accidently dropped a cocoon in hot water, Xi Ling-Shi saw that it separated into a tangled thread. In this way, Xi Ling-Shi supposedly discovered silk. Scholars are not sure how much of this story is true. However, silk did originate in China. In fact, the Chinese kept the knowledge of silk making a secret for hundreds of years.

Today silk is made in a very controlled environment. On silk farms, moths called the *Bombyx mori* lay hundreds of eggs. Eventually, the eggs hatch young silkworms, which have large appetites. They are fed mulberry leaves day and night. Once fully grown, the silkworm stops eating and spins its cocoon. The silkworm does this by emitting a fluid that hardens immediately into silk threads. Most cocoons are then placed in a hot oven, which kills the worm.

Then the cocoons are soaked in hot water, causing them to unravel into silk filaments. The raw silk is strengthened by twisting the strands together. After this, a glue-like substance is boiled off the fabric, revealing the natural beauty of the silk. Then silk yarns are often dyed bright colors.

1. How does the silkworm form its cocoon?

_____

_____

2. Do you think that Xi Ling-Shi discovered silk? Explain.

_____

_____

3. Activity Make a brief illustrated how-to guide for making silk.

Name _____ Class _____ Date _____

Section Quiz

Directions Answer the following questions using what you learned
in Section 2.

1. _____ Around 1800 B.C., China began to be
ruled by a series of
   a. dictators.
   b. emperors.
   c. kings.
   d. sultans.

2. _____ In the 1200s, many tribes of Mongols
joined together under the leadership of
   a. Confucius.
   b. Genghis Khan.
   c. Jiang Jieshi.
   d. Mao Zedong.

3. _____ Which of the following did Britain
trade with China in exchange for tea?
   a. iron
   b. opium
   c. rice
   d. tobacco

4. _____ After the Communists took over
China in 1949, the Nationalists mostly fled
to
   a. Hong Kong.
   b. Japan.
   c. Mongolia.
   d. Taiwan.

5. _____ The Great Leap Forward called for
huge increases in the production of
   a. coal.
   b. lumber.
   c. steel.
   d. wheat.

6. How did China both change and stay the same after Mao died?
Give examples.

_____

_____

_____

_____

_____

History of China and Its Neighbors

- Model preparing to read by previewing the Key Ideas, Key Terms, headings, visuals, and captions. Have students make predictions about what they will learn. For ELL support, post the prompt, "I predict I will read about . . ."

- Preview and practice the reading skill, identify main ideas and details, by using examples from your community.

- Preteach this section's high-use Academic Vocabulary and Key Terms using the chart on the next page and in-text definitions. Have students practice Key Terms by completing the *Word Wise* page in their journals.

GUIDE ON THE SIDE

The Empires of China and Mongolia

- **Identify Main Ideas** When did China's civilization begin? (when farming villages formed on the fertile North China Plain thousands of years ago)

- **Identify Details** In what year did the Communists come to power in China? (1949)

Reading Skill

Main Ideas and Details While they read, have students practice this skill by completing the *Take Notes* graphic organizer in the **Student Journal.**

 Timeline

Have students go to myworldgeography.com to learn more about the chronology of Chinese history.

Section 2

History of China and Its Neighbors

Key Ideas
- For much of its history, China was an advanced, powerful empire.
- Communists created command economies in both China and Mongolia.
- In recent years, Mongolia and China have changed to market economies to increase economic growth.

Key Terms • dynasty • Confucianism • Daoism • command economy • famine

 **Visual Glossary**

Reading Skill: Main Ideas and Details Take notes using the graphic organizer in your journal.

A statue of a warrior from the tomb of Emperor Qin Shi Huangdi ▼

For much of China's long history, it was a successful empire with great achievements in art and technology. The Mongolians also built a huge empire. But for thousands of years, China was the most powerful country in the region. Yet by the 1900s, China had become weak. The Communists promised to make China powerful again when they came to power in 1949.

The Empires of China and Mongolia

The great empires of China and Mongolia were very different. The Chinese empire was based on agriculture. The Mongols' power came from their skill as warriors on horseback.

The Powerful Chinese Empire
China's civilization began when farming villages formed on the North China Plain thousands of years ago. Geographic features

Timeline

Major Chinese Dynasties				Qin ▼	
Shang		Zhou			Han
1500 B.C.	1000 B.C.		500 B.C.	A.D. 1	

■ Period of war or division

ACADEMIC VOCABULARY

High-Use Word	Definition and Sample Sentence
uniform	*adj.* the same; consistent *The new law has a uniform penalty for stealing.*
resource	*n.* something, such as coal, timber, or land, that a country can use *Ancient China had many valuable resources, including silk.*

isolated China from other early civilizations. High mountains limited communication to the west. By sea, all but a few neighbors were too far to reach. Around 1800 B.C., a series of emperors began to rule China. Usually, emperors were members of a **dynasty,** or a ruling family that held power for many years.

Powerful emperors unified and protected China. The Qin (chin) emperor Shi Huangdi (shur hwahng DEE) created a <u>uniform</u> written language for the whole empire. This made communication easier and helped unite the country. It is the basis of China's written language today.

Shi Huangdi also began to connect scattered walls to build the Great Wall, which still stands. The wall was meant to protect farmers from nomadic invaders. Later rulers added to it, extending it more than 4,000 miles.

Chinese Achievements Under the Dynasties The Chinese had many accomplishments during their history. They built roads and canals to make trade and travel easier. The Grand Canal is the longest man-made waterway in the world. It stretches for over a thousand miles from Beijing to Hangzhou. It passes Wuxi where Qian Xiao works.

Chinese inventions include paper, silk, and the magnetic compass. In the Song dynasty, the Chinese developed gunpowder. At first they used it for fireworks. Later, they began to use it in weapons.

A Mongolian Empire Many groups of nomads have lived on the plains north of China. One group, called the Mongols, united under the leadership of Genghis Khan in the 1200s. They were the ancestors of today's Mongolians. They swept over the Great Wall and conquered China. They also rapidly took control of much of Asia. The Mongol empire was the largest empire the world had ever seen, but it was short-lived. In 1368, the Chinese overthrew the Mongols, and the Ming dynasty came to power.

Reading Check Why did the Chinese build the Great Wall of China?

uniform, *adj.,* the same, consistent

Today, tourists climb the Great Wall of China. ▼

Sui		Mongol Rule	Republican Era	Communist Era
Tang	Song	Ming	Qing	

A.D. 500   A.D. 750   A.D. 1000   A.D. 1250   A.D. 1500   A.D. 1750   A.D. 2000

CULTURE

Mogao Caves A complex of about 500 Buddhist temple caves were created in northwest China, from the 300s to the 1300s. Merchants and nobles often stopped in the Mogao caves, situated in the Silk Road, to refresh their bodies and souls. The temple caves contained elaborate murals and valuable manuscripts. Eventually the caves were abandoned, but they were later discovered in 1900. Soon after this, an amazing collection of 60,000 paper manuscripts, which include Buddhist and Daoist scripture, were found in a hidden room in a cave.

Important Ideas and Beliefs

- **Express an Opinion** Do you think applying Confucianism to government is a good idea? (Sample: Yes, Confucianism stresses respect for authority.)

- **Problem Solve** Did Confucius believe that his belief system could help society? If so, how? (Yes, his belief system called for people to follow strict roles in society. If people did this, he thought, order would be established in society.)

Analyze Visuals Ask students to compare and contrast the images at the bottom of the page.

- Based on how the statue of the Buddha looks, do you think it shows someone who has achieved the Buddhist form of enlightenment? (Sample: Yes, the statue looks calm and free from pain and suffering.)

- Why do you think the statue of Confucious shows him holding a scroll? (Sample: The teachings of Confucius were used to set up values and laws in Chinese society. The scroll suggests written values and laws.)

Important Ideas and Beliefs

As dynasties rose and fell, three belief systems strongly influenced this region's culture. **Confucianism** (kuhn FYOO shuh niz um), is based on the ideas of the thinker Confucius. **Daoism** (DOW iz um) is a philosophy of seeking the natural way of the universe. The third philosophy, Buddhism, grew from the teachings of Siddhartha Gautama. He taught that people can become free from suffering if they give up selfish desires.

Confucianism Confucius (551–479 B.C.) believed society could be peaceful and harmonious if people acted strictly according to their roles. In the family, the young should respect the old. In government, the ruler should care for his subjects. In return, subjects had a duty to respect and obey the ruler.

Three hundred years after Confucius's death, the influence of his teaching increased. It was then that Emperor Wudi of the Han dynasty began to use Confucianism in government. Dynasties after the Han also supported the ideas of Confucius. Confucianism was taught in schools throughout China. This system of values greatly influenced Chinese culture.

Daoism The ideas of Daoism developed at around the time Confucius was teaching. The word *dao* (dow) means "the

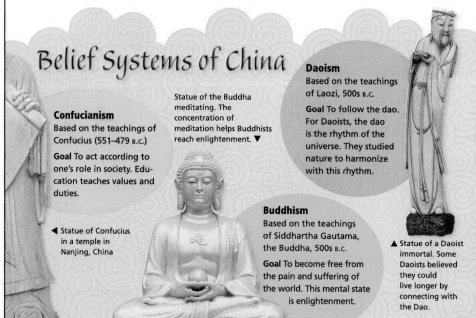

Belief Systems of China

Confucianism
Based on the teachings of Confucius (551–479 B.C.)

Goal To act according to one's role in society. Education teaches values and duties.

◄ Statue of Confucius in a temple in Nanjing, China

Statue of the Buddha meditating. The concentration of meditation helps Buddhists reach enlightenment. ▼

Daoism
Based on the teachings of Laozi, 500s B.C.

Goal To follow the dao. For Daoists, the dao is the rhythm of the universe. They studied nature to harmonize with this rhythm.

Buddhism
Based on the teachings of Siddhartha Gautama, the Buddha, 500s B.C.

Goal To become free from the pain and suffering of the world. This mental state is enlightenment.

▲ Statue of a Daoist immortal. Some Daoists believed they could live longer by connecting with the Dao.

GOVERNMENT

The Nationalist Party The Nationalist Party started as a league of revolutionaries who overthrew China's imperial system. By 1926, it had become a political party led by Chiang Kai-shek. Chiang's rule through the party was dictatorial. The Nationalist Party claimed that it wanted to form a democracy, but this goal was never taken seriously. Riddled with corruption, the party bred discontent and resentment among many Chinese. After World War II, the Communists pushed the Nationalists out of mainland China. Chiang and his followers fled to Taiwan and set up a Nationalist state. For many years, the Nationalist Party was the only real political force in Taiwan. At first, this party was determined to reconquer mainland China. However, over the years, the Nationalists have given up this goal. The Communists, though, view Taiwan as a rogue province of China that should be brought under the control of the Chinese government.

path" or "the way." Daoists believe people should try to find this path. Often, they see evidence of the Dao in natural things, such as water.

> There is nothing in the world more soft and weak than water, and yet for attacking things that are firm and strong, nothing is better than water ...
> —Laozi

Water, through patient effort over time, is even stronger than rock. By acting like water, people were following the Dao.

Buddhism Monks and other travelers from India brought Buddhism to China during the Han dynasty. Over time, Buddhism attracted a wide following. Buddhists built monasteries and temples across the country. Buddhism also became popular in Mongolia. Buddhism was much more influential than Daoism and Confucianism on Mongolia's culture.

Reading Check **What did Confucius think people should do to bring order to society?**

The End of the Dynasties
China's last dynasty, the Qing (ching), fell early in the 1900s. New, communist governments took control in both China and Mongolia.

The Qing Dynasty Struggles In 1839, the Qing dynasty fought with Britain over the opium trade. Opium is an addictive drug that Britain had been trading for Chinese tea. The Qing saw the bad effects of the drug and tried to stop the trade. The British sent warships to bombard some Chinese cities. China's weak military could barely put up a fight.

The British won. They forced the Chinese to accept the opium trade and foreign domination.

This was just the beginning of the Qing dynasty's troubles. It lost Taiwan to Japan after a brief war in 1895. Taiwan stayed under Japanese control through World War II. The Chinese people were shocked that their country could be defeated by the small island nation of Japan.

Revolution, Civil War, and Invasion Many Chinese people blamed the Qing for the country's weakness. In 1911 and 1912, revolutionaries took power from the Qing dynasty.

The revolutionary leaders hoped to make China a strong, modern nation. Yet, they could not bring peace. China suffered nearly 30 years of almost constant fighting followed by a Japanese invasion during World War II.

Nationalists under Jiang Jieshi (jahng jeh shur), also know as Chiang Kai-shek, fought Communists led by Mao Zedong (mow dzuh doong) for control of the country. Finally, in 1949, the Communists won the long civil war. They set up a stable government on mainland China.

The Nationalists fled to Taiwan. There, they set up a rival government, which continues to this day.

Mongolia's Revolution The Qing dynasty controlled much of Mongolia. Mongolia's Communist leaders won independence from China in 1921 after the Qing dynasty fell. Mongolia became a new nation.

Reading Check **Why did the Chinese overthrow the Qing dynasty?**

Dr. Sun Yixian served as the first president of China's republic after revolutionaries overthrew the Qing dynasty.

- **Compare Viewpoints** How does Daoism differ from Confucianism? (Daoism strives to be in harmony with the Dao, which is often found in nature. Confucianism applies a strict structure to society.)

The End of the Dynasties

- **Identify Details** Why did the Chinese government try to stop the opium trade with Britain? (because of the bad effect of opium on the people of China)

- **Cause and Effect** What caused the Nationalists to leave China? (The Communists took control of the country.)

READING CHECK behave strictly according to their roles in society

READING CHECK Many Chinese people blamed the Qing leaders for the country's weakness.

CORE CONCEPTS: ECONOMIC SYSTEMS

Review Core Concepts 5.3 before discussing how a command economy was used in China. Review the various economic systems. Also, discuss why most nations have mixed economies. Then have students identify the type of economy that the Communists first implemented in China. After this, ask what made this system a command economy. Does this economy seem liked a mixed economy? Explain. Have student's identify what were strong and weak points of China's command economy.

China and Mongolia Under Communism

- **Problem Solve** How did Communists attempt to distribute a country's wealth more equally? (They abolished the market economy and replaced it with a command economy.)

- **Identify Main Ideas** Was Communism a democracy? Explain. (No, only one political party was allowed.)

Analyze Visuals Have students analyze the images that show a command economy and a market economy.

- Why do you think the image of Mao Zedong was chosen to represent a command economy? (Sample: Command economies are controlled by leaders from the top.)

- Why do you think the image of a business was used for a market economy? (Sample: In a market economy, businesses decide what to produce.)

myWorld Activity

Command Economy vs. Market Economy Find Step-by-Step Instructions and an Activity Support on pp. T16–T17. **(Interpersonal/Kinesthetic)**

Command Economy vs Market Economy

In a *command economy*, the government makes most of the decisions about what goods to produce and how to produce them.

In a *market economy*, individuals interact in the marketplace to make economic decisions. If consumers buy a large quantity of something, companies make more of it.

Three Basic Economic Questions
What goods and services should be provided?
How should goods and services be produced?
Who consumes the goods and services?

Advantage Government tries to distribute resources fairly. **Disadvantages** Lack of choice for the consumer; possibility that government will not plan the economy well, leading to shortages or waste.

Advantage Greater freedom of choice **Disadvantages** Markets might change quickly and drastically; some people gain more than others.

myWorldActivity
Command Economy vs. Market Economy

resource, *n.,* something, such as coal, timber, or land, that a country can use

China and Mongolia Under Communism

Communist leaders in China and Mongolia brought great change to their countries. They had little economic success, though, and had to make major changes to their economic systems.

The Command Economy Communism is based on the idea that everyone should share a country's wealth equally. The Communists argued that a society could not reach this goal with a market economy. Instead, the Communists created a **command economy,** an economic system based on government planning and control.

In a command economy, the government owns the land, businesses, and resources of the country. The government makes an economic plan for the country. It decides which goods and services will be produced. People have jobs based on this plan, and the government has great control over the lives of the people. The Communists did not create a democracy. People could not vote. A small number of Communist Party leaders held power.

In both Mongolia and China, the Communists took land, livestock, and businesses away from their owners. These <u>resources</u> were supposed to be managed fairly according to the government's economic plan.

These governments also started programs to help people. Doctors, for example, traveled to small villages to provide basic healthcare.

READING CHECK The country started to move from a command economy to a market economy.

SECTION 2 ASSESSMENT 1. Confucians believe that people should behave strictly according to their roles in society. Daoists believe that people should find harmony with the Dao, which is often found in nature. **2.** a system of planned economy with government control **3.** China was technologically advanced, had a strong

HISTORY

Mao Zedong Mao Zedong was born in 1893 into a peasant family. In 1918, he became influenced by Communist ideas. Three years later, he formed the Chinese Communist Party (CCP) with 11 other people. The leader of China, Chiang Kai-shek, attacked and almost wiped out the Communists in Jiangxi province. Then in 1934, Mao led about 100,000 of his followers from Jiangxi to Shaanxi. This brutal trip is referred to as the Long March. Only a few thousand people survived the journey. However, the Long March helped to unify the Communists under Mao's leadership. After World War II, Mao and the Communists pushed Chiang and his followers out of mainland China. Many of Mao's economic policies, like the Great Leap Forward, were not successful. However, Mao remained in charge of China until his death in 1976.

Command Economy Problems The command economy often did not work well. When the Mongolian government tried to take livestock away from nomads to create the command economy, many herders decided to kill their animals rather than give them to the government. In part because of this, a **famine**, or severe food shortage, followed.

Poor planning by the Communists in China also led to famine. In 1958, Mao introduced the Great Leap Forward. This policy called for the country to rapidly increase production of steel, as part of an effort to make China's economy more modern.

Making steel took farmers away from their fields. The shift in focus away from agriculture combined with poor weather created food shortages. Historians believe that as many as 30 million Chinese people may have died of hunger between 1958 and 1962. This tragedy took place because the economic plan ignored the needs of the people.

New Leaders Leave the Command Economy Behind When Mao Zedong died in 1976, a Communist leader named Deng Xiaoping (dung show PING) rose to power. He began reforms that opened China up to international trade.

He also started to move China toward a market economy. New businesses opened. They competed with one another to make the best, cheapest goods. China's economy began to grow rapidly.

At the same time, Deng and other Communist leaders had no intention of allowing political power to slip out of their hands. The Chinese Communist Party's hold on the government stayed as strong as ever.

By contrast, political and economic reforms came at almost the same time in Mongolia. Both the political and economic systems changed in the 1990s. Mongolia became a democracy with a market economy.

Reading Check How did China change after Deng Xiaoping took power?

- **Identify Evidence** What evidence shows that China suffered from famine? (About 30 million people probably died of hunger from 1958 to 1962.)

- **Cause and Effect** Name one reason why famine hit Mongolia after the Communists took control of the country. (Many Mongolian herders killed their livestock rather than give them to the government.)

Section 2 Assessment

Key Terms

1. Describe the beliefs of Confucianism and Daosim.

2. What is a command economy?

Key Ideas

3. **Draw Conclusions** Why was China the most powerful country in the region for much of its history?

4. **Cause and Effect** What policies caused famine in China and Mongolia in the 1900s?

Think Critically

5. **Sequence** What was the sequence of events from China's war with Britain to the formation of a new government led by Mao Zedong?

Essential Question

How can you measure success?

6. Do you think the Qing dynasty was unsuccessful? Go to your Student Journal to record your answer.

military, and built the Great Wall to keep out invaders. **4.** The Great Leap Forward in China and taking over livestock in Mongolia caused famine in these countries. **5.** In 1911–1912, revolutionaries forced the Qing leaders from power. Nearly 40 years of fighting followed. Nationalists fought Communists for control of the country. In 1949, Communists won the long civil war and set up a government. **6.** Sample: Yes, the Chinese were defeated by the British and the Japanese under the Qing.

Confucianism and Imperial Law

OBJECTIVES

Students will

- use primary sources to learn about Confucianism and its influence on the legal system of imperial China.
- **21st Century Learning** develop cultural awareness by understanding how cultural values influence laws.
- **ELL** understand the relationship between the words *law* and *punishment*.

SET EXPECTATIONS

In this lesson, students will

- read and analyze the two documents from *The Analects* and the legal case of Fan Gui.
- write a law and its related punishment based on the ideas of Confucius.

1 Connect

In order to help students understand the fairness and unfairness of punishment for breaking the law, have them think about times in their life when they broke rules set down by their parents or guardians. Ask students if they were punished for breaking these rules. If so, did they think these punishments were fair? Explain.

L2 Extra Support Help students think of various behaviors that parents or guardians often set up rules about, such as doing homework, watching TV, or eating junk food.

2 Learn

Preview Have students preview the two pages and identify the image of Confucius and Chinese officials. Looking at the image of the officials, ask students to predict if they think these officials would establish strict laws or lenient laws. Have them explain their answers. Read the Key Ideas, glossary terms, and definitions. Clarify any questions about the meaning of these words by providing examples. Read the introduction.

Read Slowly read aloud the excerpt from *The Analects* without stopping. Read the document again, this time stopping to read the questions at the left and prompt students to rethink and analyze the meaning of the words. Have students answer the questions using the location of the letters to provide clues. Do the same for "The Case of Fan Gui." Lead a discussion starting with their responses to the questions. Ask, How do these documents help us to understand the influence of Confucianism on ancient Chinese law? Do you think current Chinese law is influenced by Confucianism? Explain.

ELL Intermediate Explain that a law is a rule made by government. Tell students that laws say what you can and cannot do. Then say that punishment is what happens when you do what the law says you cannot do. Post a diagram to demonstrate.

myWorld Activity: Law and Punishment Tell the students to imagine that they live in imperial China. The emperor has asked them to write a legal code based on Confucius's ideas. Review with students *The Analects*, the case of Fan Gui, and also what they read about Confucianism in the text. Pairs of students should write one paragraph describing a new law and another paragraph describing the punishment for breaking it. **(Verbal/Logical)**

30 min

3 Understand

Review Go back to the Key Idea. Discuss with students the similarities and differences between the two documents.

Assess Have each student complete **Analyze the Documents.** Review their answers to determine if students have met the lesson objectives.

Remediate Students may have difficulty thinking of laws. Ask students to brainstorm a list of crimes and classify them as very serious, serious, and minor. Then suggest they write a law relating to one of the crimes.

Name _____ Class _____ Date _____

Law and Punishment

Directions Brainstorm possible laws and punishments based on Confucius's ideas. Then pick one law and one punishment and write a paragraph about each.

Steps for Writing a Law and a Punishment

1. Choose a partner. Imagine that you both live in imperial China. The emperor has told you to write a legal code based on the ideas of Confucius.

2. Review *The Analects* excerpt, the case of Fan Gui, and what Section 2 says about the ideas of Confucius. Based on these sources, what type of laws do you think Confucius would want? List possible laws and punishments below.

Law	**Punishment**
1. _____ _____	1. _____ _____
2. _____ _____	2. _____ _____
3. _____ _____	3. _____ _____
4. _____ _____	4. _____ _____

3. Write a paragraph describing one of these laws for the emperor's new legal code. Describe the law clearly to avoid misunderstandings. In your paragraph, answer the following:

- To what situation does this law apply?

- Who has to follow this law?

4. Write a paragraph describing the punishment for breaking this law. Consider what type of punishment would be fair and why. Include levels of punishment for breaking the law more than once. Share your work with the class.

T21

CORE CONCEPTS: FAMILIES AND SOCIETIES

Review Core Concept 7.2 before discussing family and society in China. Review the key ideas of nuclear family and extended family. Also, make sure students understand that all societies share certain common institutions, such as government. Then ask students if they think the values of Confucius applied to the nuclear family, the extended family, or both. To what societal institutions did the values of Confucius apply in China? Have students explain their answers.

Develop Cultural Awareness Have students use the primary source excerpts to improve their understanding of how the values of a culture can influence that culture's legal system.

ANSWERS

(A) Sample: Parents might be anxious that their children are not working or are in trouble with the law.

(B) People require more than food. Proper treatment of a parent includes respect and caring. Providing only for parents' physical needs is treating them like animals, not human beings.

(C) By filial piety, Confucius means having a sense of respect and obligation toward one's parents.

Primary Source

Confucianism and Imperial Law

Key Idea
- The ideas of Confucius have influenced many aspects of Chinese society, including the legal system of the Qing dynasty.

▲ A copy of *The Analects,* compiled by 200 B.C.

Confucius did not write any books. His students wrote down his ideas. A book called *The Analects* is a collection of his teachings. This book includes his ideas for maintaining an orderly society. Those ideas have influenced Chinese life and government for hundreds of years. For example, Confucius emphasized the value of filial piety, that is, love and respect for one's parents and ancestors. The court case of Fan Gui, from the Qing dynasty, China's last imperial dynasty, shows how the idea of filial piety was part of the law.

Stop at each circled letter on the right to think about the text. Then answer the question on the left with the same letter.

(A) **Infer** How might adult children cause their parents "anxiety"?

(B) **Summarize** Why is providing only for parents' physical needs treating them like farm animals?

(C) **Synthesize** What does Confucius mean by *filial piety*?

anxiety, *n.,* upset or worry
filial, *adj.,* proper for a son or daughter
piety, *n.,* devotion, dutiful respect

Filial Piety

Confucius

66 [A student] asked about the treatment of parents. The Master said, behave in such a way that your father and mother have no **anxiety**
(A) about you. . . .
'Filial' sons' are people who see to
(B) it that their parents get enough to eat. But even dogs and horses are cared for to that extent. If there is no feeling of respect, wherein lies the difference?
Filial **piety** does not consist merely in young people undertaking the
(C) hard work. It is something much more than that. 99
—Confucius, *The Analects*

ANALYZE THE DOCUMENTS 1. Fan Yuan is described as an "unfilial rascal," which sounds as if he was disrespectful or didn't help his mother—behaviors that would probably have upset her. He was also deported from his home region, which would be upsetting too.

2. Fan Gui's sentence of death shows that harming one's parent—even by accident—was considered a serious offense. His pardon shows how much Chinese society valued respect and care of parents. Even though he was a convicted criminal and his brother was

21st Century Learning — DEVELOP CULTURAL AWARENESS

To assist your students in developing cultural awareness, point out that the ideas of Confucius still have an influence on the legal system in China today. Although China's current legal system is fundamentally different from the legal system during imperial times, the influence of filial piety can still be seen. Article 49 of the constitution states that adult children have an obligation to support their elderly parents. Have students identify values described in these documents and compare them to values in the United States. Ask students to share opinions about whether they should be held responsible for the care of their elder family members.

Stop at each circled letter on the right to think about the text. Then answer the question on the left with the same letter.

D Summarize Why was Fan Gui sentenced to death?

E Paraphrase What is one reason that a criminal could be released according to Chinese law?

F Analyze How did Fan Yuan's behavior influence the Board's decision about Fan Gui?

petition, v., to make a formal, written request

provisionally, adv., until a final arrangement is made

deport, v., to send away by force

Filial Piety in the Court

❝ Mrs. Fan . . . petitioned to have her eldest son, Fan Gui, released from his criminal sentence to care for her. Fan Gui accidentally wounded his mother when quarreling with his younger brother. Fan Gui was tried and **D** provisionally sentenced to immediate death. . . .

[W]e again received a petition [from] Mrs. Fan [stating] that her third son had died, and Fan Yuan, her second son, had been **E** deported. Moreover, he is truly an unfilial rascal. Hence, she requests that her eldest son, Fan Gui, be allowed to remain at home.

This Board . . . submitted a palace memorial to the emperor proposing approval of the petition. . . . **F** Fan Gui [was able] to remain at home. ❞
—The Case of Fan Gui, Qing Dynasty, 1821

▲ A magistrate in a Chinese court during the Qing dynasty

ANSWERS

D Fan Gui was sentenced to death for accidentally injuring his mother while quarreling with his brother.

E A criminal could escape punishment if he was an only son who had to care for his parents.

F Fan Yuan's unfilial behavior and wildness showed that he would not take care of his mother, so Fan Gui was the only son available for the job.

A scene from Confucius's hometown of Qufu in Shandong province, China ▼

Analyze the Documents

1. **Draw Inferences** In what way might Fan Yuan have caused his mother anxiety?
2. **Writing Task** Write a paragraph explaining how Fan Gui's sentence and pardon both show the importance of filial piety.

not, he was released since he was the son who would take proper care of his mother.

China and Its Neighbors Today

OBJECTIVES

Students will know

- changes to the governments and economies of China and its neighbors.
- characteristics of Chinese society.
- changes to China's environment.

Students will be able to

- compare and contrast life in rural and urban China.
- evaluate recent changes in China.

SET EXPECTATIONS

In this section, students will

- read China and its Neighbors Today.
- act out their point of view on the Three Gorges Dam.
- go On Assignment in China, Mongolia, and Taiwan and explore Mongolian culture.

CORE CONCEPTS

You may wish to teach or reteach the following lessons from the Core Concepts Handbook:

- People's Impact on the Environment, pp. 52–55
- Economic Systems, pp. 62–63
- Migration, pp. 78–79

KEY

Differentiated Instruction

- **L1** Special Needs
- **L2** Extra Support
- **L3** On-Level
- **L4** Challenge

English Language Instruction

- **ELL** Beginner
- **ELL** Early Intermediate
- **ELL** Intermediate
- **ELL** Early Advanced
- **ELL** Advanced

---

1 Connect
Make learning meaningful

Make Connections Ask students to think about the **myStory Video** of Xiao and the environmental problems that his village faces. Then have students think about environmental problems in the region where they live. Ask, How are the environmental problems faced by Xiao and the people in his village similar to or different from the environmental problems that you face?

L1 Special Needs Allow students who struggle to focus to rewatch the video on a personal computer.

Activate Prior Knowledge Remind students that in the previous section, they learned about China's shift from a command economy to a market economy. Ask them to predict how this shift might affect daily life in China.

L2 Extra Support Draw students' attention to the visuals in the previous section that compare command and market economies.

Prepare Follow the steps in the section **Preview.** Preteach the Key Terms. Then have students complete *Word Wise* in their journals using in-text clues and the glossary for help.

2 Experience
Teach knowledge and skills

Read Use **Background** notes and **Guide on the Side** questions to model active reading. Have students use *Take Notes* in their **Student Journal** to track the similarities and differences of the governments in China, Taiwan, and Mongolia. Have students complete **21st Century Online Tutor:** *Compare Viewpoints*, and apply this skill to reading the section.

L3 On-Level Have students draw a poster that shows their view of the Communist Party in China.

ELL Intermediate Have students make dictionaries out of notebooks with a few pages for each letter of the alphabet. Students should note unknown words they come across as they read. Assist students in writing definitions and sample sentences.

L4 Challenge Have students read *Enrichment: The Chinese River Dolphin* to learn more about the effects of industrial growth on China's ecosystems.

 Practice: myWorld Activity Students will take a stand on controversial statements about the benefits and drawbacks of the Three Gorges Dam to explore some of the effects of economic growth in China. **Step-by-Step Instructions** and **More Activities** follow on the next page.

SECTION 3 RESOURCE GUIDE

FOR THE STUDENT

my worldgeography.com Student Center
- Culture Close-up
- Data Discovery

Student Edition (print and online)
- China and Its Neighbors Today

Student Journal (print and online)
- Section 3 Word Wise
- Section 3 Take Notes

21st Century Learning Online Tutor
- Compare and Contrast
- Make Decisions

FOR THE TEACHER

my worldgeography.com Teacher Center
- Online Lesson Planner
- Presentations for Projection
- SuccessTracker

ProGuide: East and Southeast Asia
- Lesson Plan, pp. T22–T23
- ⚹ myWorld Activity Step-by-Step Instructions, p. T24
- Activity Support: Opinion Statements, p. T25
- myWorld Geography Enrichment, p. T26
- Section Quiz, p. T27

Accelerating the Progress of ELLs
- Organizing Information Strategies, p. 48

3 Understand
Assess understanding

Review Review *Word Wise* and *Take Notes* in the **Student Journals.**

Assess Knowledge and Skills Use the Section Assessment and the Section Quiz to check students' progress.

Assess Understanding Review students' responses to the Section Assessment Essential Question prompt.

Remediate Use these strategies to review and remediate.

If students struggle to . . .	Try these strategies.
Describe the effects of economic growth in China.	Reread the **A More Unequal Society** subsection. Review the main effects of economic growth in China.
Evaluate different viewpoints	Assign additional practice with the **21st Century Online Tutor.**
Compare and contrast	Review the chart in the subsection **Politics: One Party or Many?** Ask, How is China similar to or different from Taiwan and Mongolia?

ELL Support

ELL Objective Students will be able to use English to express comparisons.

Cultural Connections To help students learn the differences between governments, have them describe similarities and differences between the government in their family's home country and the government here. Remind them to use words such as same, different, more and less.

ELL Early Advanced/Advanced Content Tip Have students find Latin-cognates in the section such as migration, divide, policy, and industry, then map the words including a translation, related words, and the Latin root defined.

ELL Activity Make and distribute index cards with terms corresponding to democracy or communism (one term per card). Post a diagram with two sides: democracy and communism. Have students discuss their term in pairs, decide where to post it, and explain why. **(Kinesthetic/Linguistic)**

Take a Stand on the Three Gorges Dam

OBJECTIVES

Students will

- evaluate benefits and drawbacks of building the Three Gorges Dam.
- describe the effects of the dam on the environment.

LEARNING STYLE

- Kinesthetic

21st Century Learning

- Make Decisions

MATERIALS

- Chart paper
- Markers
- Activity Support: Opinion Statements, p. T25

Activity Steps

1. Tell students they will be asked to consider whether they agree or disagree with statements about the Three Gorges Dam project. After they "take a stand," they will convene in small groups to decide whether or not they are in favor of building the dam.

2. Have students move their desks to the sides of the room to clear a long wide space. Assign one end of the room to represent Strongly Agree and the other end Strongly Disagree. Tell students that the middle is Neutral.

   L1 Special Needs To help students understand the concept of a continuum have them name a movie they loved, a movie they disliked, and a movie they felt so-so about.

3. Read the statements on *Activity Support: Opinion Statements* one at a time. After saying each

statement aloud, give students time to decide and move to their preferred place on the continuum. If time allows, have students volunteer to defend their positions.

   L2 Extra Support Have students read the statements first, cut them out, and place them in piles for Agree, Disagree, and Neutral.

4. Allow students five minutes of group discussion to decide if they would build the dam or not. They should write Yes or No on a sheet of chart paper along with three reasons to support their decision.

5. Post students' decision charts. If time allows, have one person from each group present their decision and answer questions from other groups.

 More Activities From myWorld Teachers

Local Connections Have students research local Chinese festivals, such as Chinese New Year, or the Dragon Boat Festival, and explain at least two. **(Verbal/Visual)**

Made In To reinforce that China manufactures many light goods, ask students to check items for "Made In" labels, and make a class list of the

countries where the goods were manufactured. Explore the patterns of where our goods are made. **(Kinesthetic/Logical)**

 Debate Post the following statement, and have pairs discuss its meaning as it relates to social change in China: "The past is a foreign country, and the present too." —Leslie T. Chang, "Gilded Age, Gilded Cage," *National Geographic*, May 2008. **(Verbal)**

my worldgeography.com (Teacher Center) → Find additional resources in the online Teacher Center.

Name _____ Class _____ Date _____

myWorld Activity Support   **Opinion Statements**

Take a Stand on the Three Gorges Dam

Directions Read the statements below and think about whether you agree or disagree. Consider the benefits and drawbacks of the dam. Cut out statements and place in piles for Agree, Disagree, and Neutral.

✂ -

The cost of the dam is worth it due to the energy it will create.

- -

Easier transportation and better flood control are more important than protecting historical monuments.

- -

Displaced people will find better jobs in new cities at newly built factories that will depend on the dam.

- -

Protecting China's historical and cultural monuments is more important than strengthening the economy.

- -

Defend Your Position Choose one of the above statements that you feel strongly about. Write down your reasons for agreeing or disagreeing.

_____

_____

_____

_____

_____

Name _____ Class _____ Date _____

Enrichment: The Chinese River Dolphin

Directions Read the selection below. Answer the questions that follow and complete the activity.

The baiji (BY gee), or Chinese river dolphin, was native to China's Chang, or Yangtze, River. The Chinese regarded the baiji as the "Goddess of the Yangtze." It had lived in China for 20 million years, making it one of the oldest species in the world. The dolphin was known to be blue-gray above and lighter below, growing to over 7 feet (about 2.4 meters).

As industry developed along the Chang River, the baiji soon became the world's most endangered cetacean, or mammal that lives in water. It became harder for the baiji to find food when their ecosystem was changed by pollution. People also think that the river dolphins died due to illegal fishing or collisions with cargo ships coming up river to pick up products from factories.

Despite a report of an encounter with the baiji in 2007, the last sighting that could be proved was in 2002. The species is now widely believed to be extinct. Many ecologists, scientists who study how ecosystems work, worry that more animal species will become extinct due to rapid economic development in China. Many of China's unique species of birds are suffering from air pollution and might meet the same fate as the Yangtze's goddess, China's river dolphin.

1. What are some reasons why the baiji is now extinct?

_____

_____

2. What are some reasons why people in China would be for or against taking action to protect endangered species?

_____

_____

3. Activity Map the area where the baiji used to live. Create an overlay with the location of major industrial cities in the same area.

Name _____ Class _____ Date _____

Section Quiz

Directions Answer the following questions using what you learned
in Section 3.

1. _____ Which of the following is an accurate
statement about Taiwan?
   a. Taiwan has several political parties.
   b. Taiwan is controlled by the Communists.
   c. Taiwan is a colony of Great Britain.
   d. Taiwan plans to take over mainland
     China.

2. _____ The Chinese Communist Party is
   a. controlling access to information
     about China.
   b. one of the three major political parties
     in the Chinese government.
   c. in favor of increasing freedom of
     speech.
   d. not interested in trading with other
     countries.

3. _____ What resource does hydroelectricity
come from?
   a. coal
   b. oil
   c. wood
   d. water

4. _____ What does the term "floating
population" mean?
   a. people who live on islands
   b. illegal migrant laborers
   c. workers who permanently move to the
     city
   d. laborers who travel to factories by
     riverboat

5. _____ Which of the following is Mongolia's
major trading partner?
   a. China
   b. India
   c. Japan
   d. Russia

6. Complete the chart below to show the impact of China's changing
economy.

What has been the impact of economic changes in China on . . .
the standard of living?
where people live?
the environment?

China and Its Neighbors Today

- Model preparing to read by previewing the Key Ideas, Key Terms, headings, visuals, and captions. Have students make predictions about what they will learn. For ELL support, post the prompt, "I predict I will read about . . ."

- Preview and practice the reading skill, compare and contrast, by using examples from your community.

- Preteach this section's high-use Academic Vocabulary and Key Terms using the chart on the next page and in-text definitions. Have students practice Key Terms by completing the *Word Wise* page in their journals.

GUIDE ON THE SIDE

Politics: One Party or Many?

- **Compare and Contrast** How are the governments of Mongolia and Taiwan different from the government of China? (In Mongolia and Taiwan, many parties can compete in political elections. In China, the people do not have the freedom to create parties or vote in open elections.)

- **Summarize** How did Mongolia gain a democracy? (demands of protesters)

Analyze Visuals Have students analyze the photographs on this page.

- Based on the large photograph, do you think the protest in Mongolia was successful? Explain. (Sample: Yes, the protesters seem happy.)

- Do you think the figure in the small photograph is a protester? Explain. (Sample: Yes, he is facing off against a row of tanks.)

Reading Skill

Compare and Contrast While they read, have students practice this skill by completing the *Take Notes* graphic organizer in the **Student Journal.**

Section 3

China and Its Neighbors Today

Key Ideas
- The governments of Mongolia and Taiwan have become more democratic, but China's has not.
- Exports have been important to the economies of all three countries.
- China's economy has grown rapidly, but it faces many challenges.

Key Terms
- single-party state
- wage
- life expectancy
- illiterate
- hydroelectricity

Visual Glossary

 Reading Skill: Compare and Contrast Take notes using the outline map in your journal.

Protests in Mongolia led to political reform. ▼

The Chinese government used the army to stop protests in Tiananmen Square. ▼

In recent years, China, Taiwan, and Mongolia have all experienced great changes. For Taiwan and Mongolia, the changes have been both political and economic. China, by contrast, has seen impressive economic growth with less change in the country's government.

Politics: One Party or Many?

Since the 1980s, Taiwan and Mongolia have changed their governments. In both countries, many parties can compete in elections. People in China, by contrast, do not have the freedom to create new parties. The people of Taiwan and Mongolia also enjoy more freedom in their religious and private lives than the people of China.

Reforms in Mongolia In 1989, protesters in Mongolia demanded change in the political system. The country's leaders responded and made many reforms. New parties could join free elections. Mongolian leaders also wrote a new constitution. This constitution states that the people directly elect the president and the parliament makes the laws.

ACADEMIC VOCABULARY

High-Use Word	Definition and Sample Sentences
access	*n.* ability to be used *The car's key gave Joe access to the car.*
benefit	*v.* to help, be of service to *The new medicine benefited the patients.*

The Communist Party is still important in Mongolia. Candidates from this party have won many elections. Now, though, this party competes with other parties for control of the government.

The new constitution also protects certain freedoms, such as religious freedom. In the past, the communists did not allow people to worship freely. Now, many people are again practicing Buddhism and other religions.

Democracy Grows in Taiwan After China's civil war, Jiang Jieshi left China and set up a government in Taiwan. He created a **single-party state,** that is, a country in which one political party controls the government. Jiang's Nationalist Party controlled the government. In the 1980s, some Taiwanese people began to push the government to become more open. Finally in 1989, the Nationalists allowed other parties to take part in elections. Like the communists in Mongolia, the Nationalists Party is still important in Taiwan. Now, though, the Taiwanese can choose from more than one party when they vote.

Limited Freedom in China China's leaders have not made major political changes. It continues to be a single-party state. The Chinese Communist Party (CCP) controls the government.

The CCP no longer controls the economy. It does control peoples' lives in other ways. For example, China does not have freedom of the press. That is, journalists are not free to report the news

as they see it. The CCP also blocks many Web sites. Chinese people do not have access to all information on the Internet.

Chinese people also do not have freedom of speech. The government may imprison people who say or do things to oppose the government.

In 1989, tens of thousands of people gathered in Tiananmen Square (tyen ahn mun skwehr) in Beijing. They called for more freedom and changes to the government. They refused to leave the square. China's leaders sent in tanks and troops to break up the demonstration. Thousands of people were killed or wounded.

The government refused to make any of the changes that the protesters had demanded. The freedoms of the Chinese people remain very limited.

Reading Check Is Taiwan a single-party state today?

access, *n.,* ability to be used

Political and Economic Systems: China and Its Neighbors

	China	Taiwan	Mongolia
Political Parties	Single-party system	Several parties	Several parties
Elections	Few elections, very limited	Open elections	Open elections
Freedoms	Freedoms limited by government	Religious freedom, freedom of the press	Religious freedom, freedom of the press
Economic System	Market system	Market system	Market system

Chart Skills

How is China different from Taiwan and Mongolia? How are all three countries similar?

> **Data Discovery**

CHART SKILLS China has a single-party system, few elections, and allows limited freedom. Taiwan and Mongolia have several parties, open elections, and allow freedom of religion and freedom of the press. All three nations have a market system.

READING CHECK No, Taiwan is a multiparty state.

ANSWERS

GUIDE ON THE SIDE

- **Draw Conclusions** What do you think is the Chinese government's attitude toward practicing religion in China? (Sample: tries to limit or prohibit religion)

- **Predict** Do you think the Chinese government will eventually allow more freedom for its people? Explain. (Sample: Yes; When China changed to a market economy, it became more open to the outside world. Eventually, these outside influences will cause many Chinese people to demand more freedom.)

Analyze Visuals Ask students to analyze the chart on this page.

- Based on the chart, do you think Taiwan is a democracy? Explain. (Yes, it has several parties, open elections, and allows freedom of religion and the press.)

- Which country has few elections? (China)

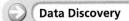

> **Data Discovery**

Have students go to myworldgeography.com to see more data about China, Mongolia, and Taiwan.

QUICK FACTS

Fast Food Hits China Fast food restaurants have become very popular in China. In 1987, the first fast food restaurant opened in China. By 2000, these restaurants were serving about 2 million Chinese consumers every day. Fried chicken is especially popular with the Chinese people.

Economic Growth: Importance of Exports

- **Identify Main Ideas** Why has Taiwan been called an "Asian Tiger"? (For decades, its economy has had strong economic growth.)
- **Cause and Effect** What caused the wages of the Taiwanese people to increase? (The Taiwanese were able to make goods cheaply, because of low wages. As a result, they began to export more goods, and their economy grew rapidly. Because of this, the wages of the Taiwanese people eventually began to increase.)

Analyze Visuals Ask students to analyze the photograph on this page.

- Does the photograph show that Taiwan is technologically advanced? Explain. (Yes, it shows that Taiwan can build a skyscraper.)
- Will this skyscraper attract businesses to Taiwan? Explain. (Sample: Yes, it is an impressive landmark.)

The skyscaper Taipei 101 towers over Taiwan's capital. ▼

Economic Growth: The Importance of Exports

Trade is important for the economies of all three countries in this region. Taiwan and China have had rapid economic growth. Mongolia struggles to strengthen its economy.

Taiwan: An Asian Tiger Taiwan has been called an "Asian Tiger" because for decades its economy had strong growth. In the mid-1900s, Taiwan began to manufacture more goods. At the time, many people still worked on farms. The country was relatively poor.

People were paid a low **wage,** that is, their pay was low. Factories paid their workers less than factories paid in wealthier countries. As a result, factories in Taiwan could make their products more cheaply. Other countries were happy to buy Taiwan's cheaper goods. Soon, the country was exporting goods. Its economy began to grow quickly.

As money from exports came into the country, Taiwanese people became wealthier and wages increased. The price of making goods in Taiwan went up.

The Taiwanese economy continued to grow even as wages went up. One reason is because the government improved the education system. Better education helped Taiwan to produce new, technologically advanced products, such as chemicals, medicines, and electronics. Taiwan now exports these complex, expensive products. By making this change, the economy continued to grow.

Mongolia's Mineral Resources Early in the 1990s, Mongolia changed to a market economy. This change was difficult. In the past, the Soviet Union gave Mongolia economic support. Mongolia struggled without this help.

Wages are not high in Mongolia, but transportation is difficult. This increased the cost of making goods in Mongolia. The country is landlocked. This means it has no coastline. Moving goods long distances across land is more expensive than shipping them the same distance by sea.

Railroads connect Mongolia to Russia and China. Now, China is one of Mongolia's major trading partners. Mongolia's main exports are its mineral resources. In addition, raising livestock is still important to Mongolia's economy.

With the market economy, Mongolia's economy has grown. More Mongolians now have cellphones and access to the Internet. Still, many people remain poor. The country has not had the strong growth of Taiwan and China.

China's Economic Miracle China's economic reforms began much earlier than Mongolia's. In the late 1970s, the Chinese government told farmers in some areas that they did not have to follow the government's economic plan. The farmers could decide what they wanted to grow. They could sell their harvest and keep the profits. Some farmers figured out how to use their land more efficiently than the government plan. They produced more than before.

COMMON MISCONCEPTIONS

China's Central Government and the Economy Many people think that China's central government still has a strong influence over China's economy. However, this is not true. For example, Chinese banks have been given much more autonomy. As a result, businesses can now get bank loans that are not part of the state plan. This approach has spurred economic growth. But, there has been a downside to this new autonomy. Recently, China has dealt with financial scandals caused by corrupt banking. Because of this, the government has started to crack down on this problem. In fact, an investigation of major banks claimed that it prevented $61 million from being lost to fraud.

Because these farmers were successful, the government expanded the policy. Farmers across the country could make their own decisions. The government also let more people start private businesses. Slowly, the government gave up the command economy.

As with Taiwan, trade became important to China's economic growth. Wages in China continue to be relatively low. Companies make their products cheaply and sell them abroad.

The Chinese government also encouraged foreign companies to come to China. These companies had money to build new factories. Most of these factories are along China's long coastline. Here, it is easy for companies to ship their goods around the world. The companies need many workers. People have moved to coastal cities to find jobs in these factories. Shenzhen is one coastal city where many factories have been built. In 1980, it was a town of 30,000 people. By 2006 it had become a city of more than 8 million people!

Now, China's economy is one of the largest in the world. Toys, clothing, and many other goods sold in the United States are made in China.

Reading Check Why is trade more difficult for Mongolia?

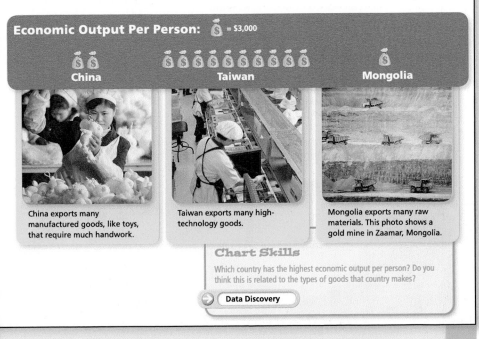

Economic Output Per Person: = $3,000

China

Taiwan

Mongolia

China exports many manufactured goods, like toys, that require much handwork.

Taiwan exports many high-technology goods.

Mongolia exports many raw materials. This photo shows a gold mine in Zaamar, Mongolia.

Chart Skills

Which country has the highest economic output per person? Do you think this is related to the types of goods that country makes?

Data Discovery

CHART SKILLS Sample: Taiwan has the highest economic output. Yes, Taiwan makes many high-tech goods, which can be mass-produced using assembly lines.

READING CHECK It is landlocked. Transportation is more expensive.

ANSWERS

GUIDE ON THE SIDE

- **Draw Conclusions** Why do many foreign companies in China build their factories along the coast? (It makes shipping goods around the world easier.)

- **Identify Evidence** Give some statistical evidence that shows the growth of China's cities. (In 1980, Shenzhen was a town of 30,000 people. By 2000, it had grown to become a city of more than 8,000,000 people.)

Analyze Visuals Have student compare and contrast the photographs on this page.

- Which country probably exports the most computers? (Taiwan)

- Which country relies on mineral exports? (Mongolia)

Data Discovery

Have students go to myworldgeography.com to see more data about China, Mongolia, and Taiwan.

ECONOMY

"Have Nots" Protest China's economic development has caused the income gap to widen. For example, in 2004, urban residents earned on average a little more than three times as much as rural residents. Also, a few people have gotten very wealthy, while many people remain in poverty. As a result, resentment from the poor and unemployed has increased, and protests have soared. In 2003, there were 60,000 public protests, which was a 15 percent increase from the previous year.

A More Unequal Society

- **Compare and Contrast** How do eastern and western China differ economically? (Eastern China has more industrial output than western China. As a result, eastern China has more wealth than the west.)

- **Summarize** When China switched to a market economy, how did health care services to rural areas change? (Under the command economy, the Chinese government provided more health care to rural areas.)

Analyze Visuals Ask students to analyze the photograph on this page.

- Do you think the school shown in the photograph is technologically advanced? (Sample: No, they don't seem to have computers or televisions.)

- Do you think most of these students have to travel a long way to get to school? Explain. (Sample: Yes, because the schools are probably built in larger towns, not small villages.)

A More Unequal Society

The economic growth in China has made many people wealthier. Now, more families can afford products such as televisions, refrigerators, and even cars. Still, some people have <u>benefited</u> from this new wealth more than others have.

benefit, *v.,* to help, be of service to

Greater Wealth in the East Trade has helped bring growth to coastal cities. Many factories are located along the south and east coasts. This area produces 60% of the nation's industrial output.

Areas in the west and center of China face many of the same challenges as Mongolia. Companies far from the coast find it expensive to transport their goods. In recent years, the Chinese government has tried to increase investment in the west and center of China. Still, growth there lags behind eastern China.

Many Rural Areas Struggle Many rural communities have also faced difficulties. Under the command economy, the national government provided some services to rural areas. They sent doctors to rural areas to give everyone basic medical care. The **life expectancy,** that is, the number of years that people live on average, rose rapidly.

Now, individuals or local governments often must pay for these services. Less wealthy areas struggle to pay the costs of basic services. For example, some villages do not have enough money to have their own school. Parents, then, have to pay to send their children to a school in a different town. Some parents cannot afford these fees. Children from rural areas are less likely than those from urban areas to go to college and get higher-paying jobs.

Many villages in rural China cannot afford to have their own school. Five small villages share this primary school. Mr. Dai teaches all classes at the school.

CULTURE

Education In China, there are six years of primary school. This is followed by three years of lower secondary school and then three more years of upper secondary school. This is followed by four years at a university. Most students get some lower secondary education. About one third of these students go on to upper secondary school. The number of university students is increasing rapidly.

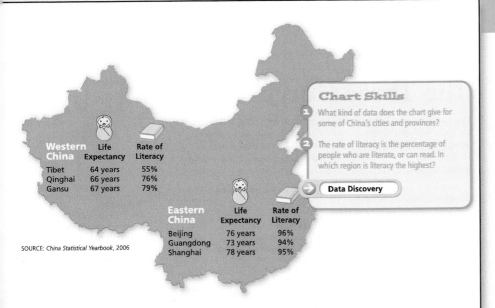

Chart Skills

1. What kind of data does the chart give for some of China's cities and provinces?

2. The rate of literacy is the percentage of people who are literate, or can read. In which region is literacy the highest?

Data Discovery

Western China

	Life Expectancy	Rate of Literacy
Tibet	64 years	55%
Qinghai	66 years	76%
Gansu	67 years	79%

Eastern China

	Life Expectancy	Rate of Literacy
Beijing	76 years	96%
Guangdong	73 years	94%
Shanghai	78 years	95%

SOURCE: *China Statistical Yearbook*, 2006

The Floating Population Because there are fewer opportunities for education and employment in rural areas, millions of people have been moving to cities.

These migrants are known as the "floating population." It is estimated at over 140 million people, or one tenth of China's total population. That is nearly half the population of the United States.

This floating population is moving illegally. The Chinese government has a rule allowing people to live only where they are registered, usually their birthplace. The government limits new registration in cities. Migrants who work in a city without registration often cannot receive healthcare or other government services. This is another challenge for people from rural areas as they try to improve life for their families.

Opportunities for Women Traditionally, couples live with the husband's family. The son takes care of his parents as they grow older. Therefore, many parents want to have at least one son.

The one-child policy changes this situation. If a couple has a daughter, they cannot have a son. They will help their daughter to be as successful as possible. Now, many daughters support their elderly parents.

Still, parents who have more than one child may send their son to school and keep their daughter at home to work. More women than men are **illiterate,** that is, more women than men do not know how to read. Women still do not have equal education and job opportunities.

Reading Check Why are migrant workers described as a floating population?

- **Cause and Effect** Why have such a large number of people been migrating to cities in China? (to improve living conditions for their families)

- **Draw Conclusions** How has the one-child policy given women more opportunities? (If a couple's one child is a daughter, the parents will invest their time and energy in helping the daughter to be successful in school and find a good job. Traditionally, sons were mostly given these opportunities.)

Analyze Visuals Ask students to analyze the statistical map.

- What region has the lowest life expectancy? (Tibet)

- Do you think education is better in western China or eastern China? (eastern China)

Data Discovery

Have students go to myworldgeography.com to see more data about China, Mongolia, and Taiwan.

READING CHECK They do not have a permanent residence.

CHART SKILLS **1.** life expectancy and rate of literacy **2.** eastern China

CORE CONCEPTS: ENVIRONMENT AND RESOURCES

Review Core Concept 4.1 before discussing the Three Gorges Dam. Review renewable and nonrenewable resources. Also, have students look over the table of Major Natural Resources. Then ask why soil is a renewable resource. Do the same for water, plants, and animals. After this, ask why fossil fuels and minerals are nonrenewable.

Then have students read the feature about Three Gorges Dam and study the images. Does Three Gorges Dam provide a renewable or nonrenewable resource? Explain. Have students discuss whether they think building the dam was worth the cost and consequences, such as relocation.

GUIDE ON THE SIDE

Three Gorges Dam

- **Connect** How does the Three Gorges Dam help to fill China's need for more energy? (by producing large amounts of hydroelectricity)

- **Analyze Visuals** Based on the relocation photograph, do you think many of the people who relocated were poor? Explain. (Yes, the person in the photo does not seem to have the money to hire people to move his belongings.)

- **Analyze Visuals** What part of the dam produces hydroelectricity? (the turbines inside the dam)

- **Express an Opinion** Do you think building the Three Gorges Dam was a good idea? (Sample: Yes, the extra energy the dam provides is well worth the time and cost of building it. No, the damage to the environment caused by the dam does not make it worthwhile.)

myWorld Activity

Take a Stand on the Three Gorges Dam Find Step-by-Step Instructions and an Activity Support on pp. T24–T25. **(Kinesthetic)**

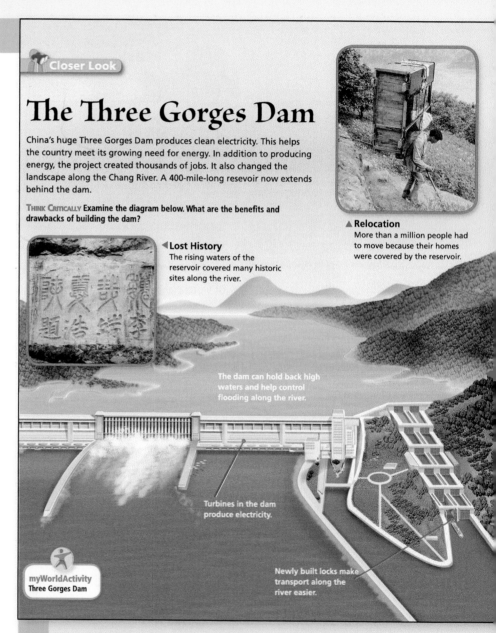

Closer Look

The Three Gorges Dam

China's huge Three Gorges Dam produces clean electricity. This helps the country meet its growing need for energy. In addition to producing energy, the project created thousands of jobs. It also changed the landscape along the Chang River. A 400-mile-long resevoir now extends behind the dam.

THINK CRITICALLY Examine the diagram below. What are the benefits and drawbacks of building the dam?

▲ **Relocation**
More than a million people had to move because their homes were covered by the reservoir.

◄ **Lost History**
The rising waters of the reservoir covered many historic sites along the river.

The dam can hold back high waters and help control flooding along the river.

Turbines in the dam produce electricity.

Newly built locks make transport along the river easier.

myWorldActivity
Three Gorges Dam

READING CHECK air pollution, water pollution, shortage of water

THINKING CRITICALLY Drawbacks include destroying historic sites and causing many people to relocate. A benefit is producing large amounts of hydroelectricity.

SECTION 3 ASSESSMENT 1. a country with just one political party **2.** not knowing how to read **3.** Mongolia's political reform has promoted democracy. However, China's reform has changed its economy but not its political system. As a result,

PRIMARY SOURCES

Pollution "Water pollution is a serious public health hazard in China, perhaps even more so than polluted air, some experts say. Nearly half of China's 1.3 billion people drink water contaminated with chemicals and biological wastes, and chronic water shortages plague much of the population."

— Charles W. Schmidt, "Economy and Environment: China Seeks a Balance," *Environmental Health Perspectives*, Sept. 2002

Environmental Challenges

As the Chinese economy has grown, pollution has become a major problem. China also uses many resources to feed, clothe, and house its large population.

Facing Environmental Problems Chinese cities have some of the worst air pollution in the world. Millions of cars, buses, and coal-burning electricity plants contribute to the smog around Chinese cities.

Water pollution is also a serious problem. Factories and farms dump dangerous chemicals into rivers and lakes near cities. Lake Tai near Xiao's home is one of many lakes affected by this issue.

Drier areas in the north and west are struggling with shortages of water. Factories, farms, and citizens compete to use this limited resource. At times, the Huang River dries up before reaching the sea. The land around Beijing is so dry that sandstorms blow into the city.

China has laws to limit pollution, but local governments do not want to punish polluters too harshly. People would lose their jobs if factories closed down.

Searching for Energy In the past, China could produce all the energy it needed. Now, more energy is needed to run its many new businesses. China has started importing oil. Also, it has been building more coal-burning power plants.

Burning oil and coal makes China's air pollution even worse, so China is looking for cleaner forms of energy. In western China, wind power produces electricity. The Chinese government also built the Three Gorges Dam along the Chang River to produces **hydroelectricity** (hy droh ee lek TRIH suh tee), or electricity made by water power. Building this dam was disruptive and expensive. China's leaders have to balance these costs with the need for new sources of energy.

Reading Check What kinds of environmental challenges does China face?

my **Story**   📷 Pho

Xiao, like many Chinese people, boils his water to make it safe to drink.

Environmental Challenges

- **Cause and Effect** What is a cause of water pollution in China? (Factories and farms dump dangerous chemicals into rivers and lakes.)
- **Identify Details** What resource does China import to help meet its energy needs? (oil)

my **Story**

Learn more from Xiao about life in China.

Section 3 Assessment

Key Terms

1. What is a single-party state?
2. What is illiteracy?

Key Ideas

3. **Compare and Contrast** How has reform been different in China and Mongolia?
4. What is one problem that China faces, and how might China solve it?

Thinking Critically

5. **Analyze Cause and Effect** What effect does geography have on Mongolia's economic growth?

? Essential Question

How can you measure success?

6. What is one way that China has been successful? Give evidence from the text and from figures to support your point. Go to your Student Journal to record your answer.

China's people still have little freedom. **4.** Sample: China uses large amounts of coal to produce energy, and, as a result, creates a lot of pollution. To reduce pollution, China could develop more solar and wind power. **5.** Because Mongolia has many mineral resources, its economy has relied on producing and exporting these minerals. **6.** China has developed one of the largest economies in the world. This economy is increasingly focused on manufacturing, technology, and services. As a result, China has received more wealth. More families can afford consumer goods such as televisions, refrigerators, and cars.

ANSWERS

Information Control in China

OBJECTIVES

Students will

- understand how the Chinese Communist Party's control of information has changed over the years.
- **21st Century Learning** analyze reactions to media restrictions in China following the 2008 protests in Tibet.
- **ELL** analyze word choice in a primary source.

SET EXPECTATIONS

In this case study, students will

- read Information Control in China.
- analyze two primary sources about freedom of the press in China.

1 Connect

Write the statement "I have complete freedom of speech" on the board. Ask student volunteers to share how they feel about the statement. They may respond that their freedom of speech is curtailed by rules in the classroom or the rules of their parents or caregivers. Tell them that citizens in China are not guaranteed freedom of speech, and outspoken critics are sometimes sent to prison for saying or writing opinions that don't agree with those of the ruling party.

L1 Special Needs If students are having trouble responding to the prompt, allow them to share answers with a partner before the whole class discussion.

2 Learn

Preview Have students preview the pictures and headings in the reading. Ask them if they think the following statement is true or false: "China has a free-market economy and a democratic government." Tell them they will return to this statement after reading.

Read While students read Information Control In China, stop frequently to check for comprehension. Ask questions found in **Guide on the Side** to build understanding of key ideas and objectives.

myWorld Activity: China and Freedom of Press Give students *Activity Support: Viewpoints* and ask them to read and analyze the two quotes presented there. Then ask them to choose partners and have a dialogue about freedom of the press in China. Ask them to discuss one of the following questions: What are the disadvantages of having only one source for news? Do you think that having many news sources threatens the government's power? They should work together to create three bullet points supporting their answers to either question. **(Verbal)**

20 min

ELL Intermediate Ask students to count how often the words *information* and *true* or *truth* are used in Quotation 1. Why do they think these words are used often?

L2 Extra Support If students are unfamiliar with reading media content, have them go to Analyze Media Content in the **21st Century Online Tutor.**

3 Understand

Review Discuss the student partners' response to the questions, probing for understanding of Key Ideas.

Assess Ask students to recall whether they thought that the statement they responded to during the Preview part of the lesson—"China has a free-market economy and a democratic government"—was true or false. *(It was false.)* Ask them to revise the statement so that it is true.

Remediate If students are struggling to understand the Key Ideas, have them create a table with the following headings: *Economic Reforms* and *Political Restrictions*. Then skim the text and fill in the table with examples of each.

Name _____ Class _____ Date _____

 myWorld Activity Support   Viewpoints

China and Freedom of Press

Directions Read the quotations below and respond to the questions that follow them.

In March 2008, protests by Tibetans led to rioting in parts of Tibet and other western provinces in China. The quotations below are reactions to how people within China got information about the rioting.

Quotation 1
"After the violent rioting in Tibet, the western media were stopped from getting into the area to cover it. So all the information released was from the Chinese government. It might be true but [it is] not a normal or fair information flow channel. The so-called truth is all based on the government releases. Until now, what's really going on during those rioting days is still uncertain. I mean, what the government says might be the truth, but it would be better if there were multiple sources."
—Chinese journalist

Quotation 2
"There was a lot of confusion on the Internet [because of] many people with many different ideas and opinions and voices. And then...message boards were closed and we were only able to read what the government wanted us to read. Maybe in an ideal world everyone would be able to say what they wanted to, but realistically when there's confusion on the Internet, it can harm social stability." —Chinese student, From How Do Chinese Citizens Feel About Censorship? Laura Sydell, NPR, Weekend Edition Saturday, July 12, 2008

1. According to the journalist, what was the only source of information on the riots in Tibet?

   _____

2. What do you think is the journalist's opinion about the information given out by the Chinese government?

   _____

3. According to the college student, who or what shut down the message boards when confusion erupted?

   _____

4. What does the college student think is the purpose of censoring the message boards?

   _____

5. How are the journalist's opinion and the student's opinion similar?

   _____

CORE CONCEPTS: POLITICAL SYSTEMS

Review Core Concept 8.2 before discussing the Communist Party in China. Make sure that students understand what a nation-state is. Also, review the key ideas of democracy, monarchy, and authoritarian government. Ask students if they think China had an authoritarian government before the death of Mao Zedong. Then ask them if the government of China changed after the death of Mao. If so, how did it change? Did the basic system of government change or remain the same? Have students explain their answers.

- **Identify Details** In what year did the Communist Party take control of China? (1949)

- **Infer** What do you think caused China to enter a period of isolation after the Communist takeover? (Sample: The Communists tightly controlled politics, information, and culture.)

Analyze Visuals Have students analyze the photograph on this page.

- Based on the photo, do you think the military was important in the Communist takeover of China? Explain. (Yes, soldiers dominate Beijing in the photograph.)

- Whose picture do you think is on the star on top of the truck? (Mao Zedong)

Case Study

Information Control in China

Key Ideas
- When Mao Zedong led China, the Communist Party controlled information as a way to change Chinese society.
- Today, the Communist Party still controls information on political issues.

Key Terms • liberate • propaganda • Cultural Revolution

The Communist Party won a civil war and took control of China in 1949. The leaders of the Party claimed that they **liberated** China, or made it free, but the Communist Party limited the political freedoms of the Chinese people. The Party tightly controlled information, and China entered a period of isolation. Since economic reforms in the 1980s, China has become less isolated. The Communist Party allows more freedom of expression but still controls political information.

Chairman Mao ▼

Victorious Communist troops march into Beijing in 1949 ▼

QUICK FACTS

China's Newspapers The CCP tightly controls the information that is presented in China's newspapers. Even so, China has dozens of daily newspapers. One of the largest is the *People's Daily*, which has a circulation of about 3 million. In fact, in 2005, it had the ninth-largest newspaper circulation in the world. In addition, the People's Daily Company publishes ten other newspapers and six magazines.

The Communist Transformation of China

The leaders of the Communist Party hoped to transform, or completely change, China. They took control of the economy. In addition, they wanted to sweep away many traditional beliefs and practices in China. For example, women had fewer rights than men. The Communists created laws to improve equality between men and women. They encouraged parents to send not only their sons but also their daughters to school. They gave women jobs in government-owned businesses, and more women began to work outside the home.

Despite new opportunities for some, the Communists did not create a free and open society. They wanted to change society quickly. The Party punished people who criticized its policies and began to control the information that people received. The Party took over newspapers and companies that published books. In addition, the Party began to supervise schools and colleges. Teachers had to use textbooks approved by the Party. Meanwhile, China became more isolated. News and information from foreign countries was strictly controlled.

Much of the information that Chinese people received was **propaganda,** that is, information that supported the policies of the government. Posters and newspaper articles showed the positive side of the changes taking place in China and hid the serious problems in the country.

Reading Check **Why did the Party take over newspapers in the country?**

The Cultural Revolution

China's leader, Mao Zedong, felt that cultural change was happening too slowly. He thought people who supported his ideas about communism should fight against people who held traditional values. In the 1960s, Mao called for a **Cultural Revolution.** This was a period of sometimes violent upheaval in China.

The "soldiers" in this revolution were students called Red Guards. Mao thought that respect for teachers and education was not a communist value. He closed schools across the country and encouraged students to join the Guards. Mao told them to rid the country of the traditional, Confucian ideas.

The Red Guards broke into peoples' homes looking for old books and art. They criticized and even attacked people who had these things. In addition, the Guards damaged temples and monuments to destroy traditional culture.

During this time, artists and performers had to show support for Mao and the ideas of the Cultural Revolution. People could only go to a few approved movies and plays.

The Cultural Revolution began to disrupt life across China. Workers joined the Revolution. Production at factories slowed. In addition, different groups of Red Guards began to fight with each other. Finally, Mao had to bring in the army to end the fighting between these groups and restore order to the country.

Reading Check **Who were the Red Guards?**

Chairman Mao's Little Red Book

Mao's "Little Red Book" was handed out to the Red Guards. The book contained quotes from Mao. These quotes were meant to build support for the Communist Party among soldiers.

The Communist Transformation of China

- **Identify Main Ideas** How did the Communist Party want to change China? (The Communist Party wanted to change the economy by taking control of it. The Party wanted to sweep away many traditional beliefs and practices, as well.)

- **Summarize** How did the Communist Party benefit women in China? (The Communist Party created laws to improve equality between men and women. Also, they encouraged parents to send their daughters to school. In addition, they gave women jobs in government-owned businesses.)

The Cultural Revolution

- **Infer** Why do you think Mao Zedong was against Confucian ideas? (Sample: because Confucian ideas supported traditional values, which conflicted with Communist values)

READING CHECK to control the information that the newspapers presented

READING CHECK students who became fanatic soldiers who supported the Cultural Revolution

CULTURE

China's Cinema Movies were first introduced to China in 1896. The first Chinese film, *Conquering Jun Mountain,* was made in 1905. The country started to make serious cinematic art during the 1930s. Many of these films had strong anti-imperialist messages. During World War II, Chinese filmmaking in Japanese-occupied Manchuria had pro-Japanese sentiments. Some of the films made in unoccupied China were anti-Japanese. After the war, a few great films were made, including *Spring River Flow Eastward* (1947). But under Mao Zedong's influence, filmmaking soon became very restricted. From 1966 to 1972, only a few films were shot in China, and these had to follow strict Communist guidelines. In the 1980s, more creative freedom was allowed. Soon a new wave of Chinese filmmakers, called the Fifth Generation, created great movies, including *Red Firecracker, Green Firecracker.* China's film industry continues to be active.

Analyze Tables Have students analyze the table on this page.

- Which of the four categories do you think changed the least? Explain. (Sample: News only seemed to change slightly. Now a limited amount of foreign news is allowed.)

- Which of the four categories do you think has the most freedom under Chinese rule today? (Sample: Books have the most freedom, since many types of books on many subjects are now allowed to be published.)

Analyze Visuals Have students analyze the visuals on this page.

- Describe the expressions on the figures in the top poster. (determined, harsh, angry)

- How are the top poster and the picture underneath it similar? (They both show a group of Chinese people. Also, they both show a person or people in uniform. Printed materials are also in both images.)

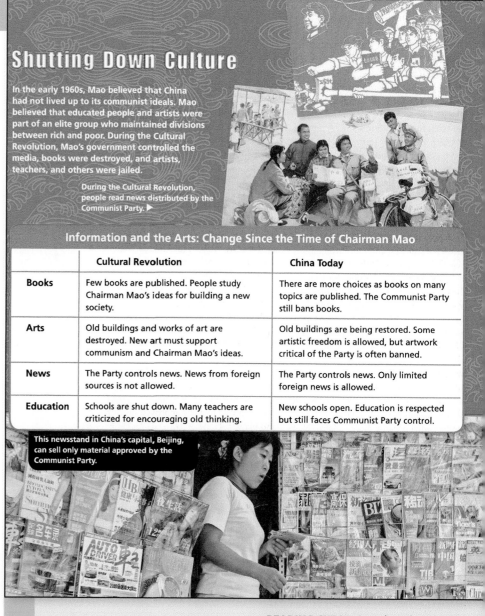

Shutting Down Culture

In the early 1960s, Mao believed that China had not lived up to its communist ideals. Mao believed that educated people and artists were part of an elite group who maintained divisions between rich and poor. During the Cultural Revolution, Mao's government controlled the media, books were destroyed, and artists, teachers, and others were jailed.

During the Cultural Revolution, people read news distributed by the Communist Party. ▶

Information and the Arts: Change Since the Time of Chairman Mao

	Cultural Revolution	China Today
Books	Few books are published. People study Chairman Mao's ideas for building a new society.	There are more choices as books on many topics are published. The Communist Party still bans books.
Arts	Old buildings and works of art are destroyed. New art must support communism and Chairman Mao's ideas.	Old buildings are being restored. Some artistic freedom is allowed, but artwork critical of the Party is often banned.
News	The Party controls news. News from foreign sources is not allowed.	The Party controls news. Only limited foreign news is allowed.
Education	Schools are shut down. Many teachers are criticized for encouraging old thinking.	New schools open. Education is respected but still faces Communist Party control.

This newsstand in China's capital, Beijing, can sell only material approved by the Communist Party.

READING CHECK Samples: The Chinese government tells those who run Web sites to censor their content, and blocks some foreign Web sites.

PRIMARY SOURCE

The CCP Losing the Information War "They [the CCP] know they're losing control [of information] mainly because of the Internet. And that worries them because they don't have a large answer for that very large question. They have an answer to individual things, some disaster comes along, [it] does get reported. They can handle that but if it's the overall question of how the press operates in an increasingly open atmosphere, that's something they don't have a counter for."

—Peter Herford, "Losing the Information War," reported by Jennifer Eaker, CBS News, July 6, 2006

The Party After the Cultural Revolution

Mao died in 1976. Deng Xiaoping and some other Party leaders did not agree with the goals of Mao's Cultural Revolution. These leaders ended the disruption of the Cultural Revolution, but they wanted to maintain Party control.

Deng opened universities that Mao had closed. In addition, the government has restored historic palaces and temples damaged by the Red Guards. Deng also ended China's isolation. Today, Chinese students study abroad, and many people travel to China each year. Chinese people also have more choices for news and entertainment. Magazines on a wide range of topics are now published. Television stations show comedies, drama, and even reality shows—not just the few plays allowed by the Communist Party during the Cultural Revolution.

Still, the Chinese government tries to control how people think and how much they know. The Communist government decides which books can be published. The government also continues to control news and entertainment. Every week, the Party gives newspapers a list of topics that must be covered and other topics that must be avoided. The Party still makes large posters to support its policies, such as the one-child policy.

Journalists who report news against the wishes of the Party may be fined, fired, or imprisoned. One event the media are forbidden to mention is the 1989 killings in Tiananmen Square. Journalists do not discuss it, and textbooks say nothing about it. An Internet search launched in China might yield hits about the square as a tourist site but nothing about the events of 1989.

The Internet is tightly controlled in other ways as well. Many Web sites are blocked. Those who run Web sites are expected to censor their content and are punished if they do not.

Even with these restrictions, Chinese people now pursue hobbies and interests that were not allowed in the past, especially during the Cultural Revolution. However, access to information, especially about many political issues, is limited.

Reading Check **How do the Chinese government and Communist Party control information on the Internet?**

The Party After the Cultural Revolution

- **Summarize** What cultural changes happened in China after Mao's death? (Universities reopened; historic palaces and temples were restored; Chinese students were allowed to study abroad; and the Chinese people were given more choices for news and entertainment.)

- **Express an Opinion** Why do you think the Communist Party forbids the Chinese media to cover the 1989 killings in Tiananmen Square? (Sample: The Party probably feels that this incident reflects badly on China's government and might stir unrest among the people.)

Assessment

1. What was Mao's goal for the Cultural Revolution?

2. What was the government's attitude toward education during the Cultural Revolution?

3. How does the government force journalists to report events from the government's point of view?

4. How does the government stop Internet users from looking up the events in Tiananmen Square in 1989?

5. Why do you think that the Chinese government still tries to control its people's access to information about politics?

ASSESSMENT 1. He wanted to free China from traditional ideas. **2.** Respect for teachers and education was not a Communist value. Schools were closed and teachers were jailed. **3.** The government fines, fires, or imprisons journalists who do not obey. **4.** Chinese Web sites cannot carry information about the events, and foreign sources are blocked. **5.** Sample: The CCP doesn't want to lose power. It restricts criticism that might lead to unrest.

1. Rural areas have fewer employment opportunities, so rural people migrate to cities to find work.

2. Some minority groups do not have to follow the one-child policy. However, the government has limited religious freedom, which has created tension among some minority groups.

3. In rural areas, parents often spend money to send their sons to school,

7. In the 1200s, many tribes of Mongolians joined together under the leadership of Genghis Khan. Under Khan, Mongolian raiders conquered China.

THINK CRITICALLY

8. Cars, buses, and coal-burning electricity plants contribute to air pollution. Factory waste, pesticides, and fertilizers contribute to water pollution. Enforce pollution control policies that make factories gradually reduce pollution without laying off many workers.

9. Most of the farmland and large cities in China are located in the east. As a result, more than two thirds of China's population is in the east, thus creating a high population density. In contrast, Mongolia has many grassy slopes, which support nomadic herders. As a result, these people are more spread out and less dense.

10. If wages are low, then a country can produce goods for a low price. This makes exporting goods easier because many countries want to buy low-priced goods.

11. What goods and services should be produced? China used to mainly produce agricultural products. Now it produces more manufactured products. How should goods and services be produced? China used to produce goods and services without using advanced technology. Now advanced technology is often used. Who uses those goods and services? China used to produce products mostly for the Chinese people. Now China exports many products.

while keeping their daughters at home to help around the house. More women than men in China are illiterate.

4. Followers of Confucius believe that society could be peaceful and harmonious if people acted strictly according to their roles. Daoists believe that people should try to find "the path" or "the way," which is found in natural things.

5. the Himalayas, the Tibetan Plateau, the Gobi, the Chang and the Huang rivers, the North China Plain

6. In a command economy, the government owns all the land, businesses, and resources of the country, and so determines what goods and services that country will produce. In contrast, with a market economy, individuals and private businesses make most of the economic decisions.

China and Its Neighbors

Chapter Assessment

Key Terms and Ideas

1. **Discuss** Why are people migrating from villages to cities in China?

2. **Summarize** How has the government of China helped and hurt China's minority groups?

3. **Compare and Contrast** How are men and women treated differently in China?

4. **Explain** What are the important beliefs of Confucianism and Daoism?

5. **Recall** What are some of the main physical features of China?

6. **Compare and Contrast** How do a command economy and a market economy differ?

7. **Describe** How and when did the Mongols conquer China?

Think Critically

8. **Problem Solving** What are some causes of air and water pollution in China? How could you lower pollution in China without forcing many people out of work?

9. **Identify Evidence** What might explain why China's population density is higher than Mongolia's?

10. **Draw Conclusions** Why is it easier for a country to export its goods if wages are low?

11. **Core Concepts: Economics** What three basic questions do economists ask when studying economies? How have the answers to these questions changed for China?

Places to Know

For each place, write the letter from the map that shows its location.

12. **Beijing**
13. **Chang River**
14. **Huang River**
15. **Mongolia**
16. **Shanghai**
17. **Taiwan**
18. **Estimate** Using the scale, estimate the distance between Beijing and Shanghai.

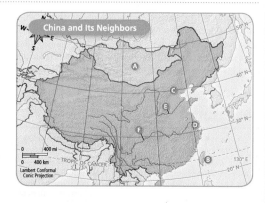

China and Its Neighbors

PLACES TO KNOW

12. C

13. F

14. E

15. A

16. D

17. B

18. about 500 miles, or 800 kilometers

myWorld Chapter Activity

A Changing China: Who Benefits the Most? Find Step-by-Step Instructions, Student Instructions and Rubric, and an Activity Support on pp. T5–T7.
(Logical/Verbal)

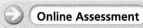

21st Century Learning

Evaluating Web Sites Students' tables should show a successful search and thoughtful evaluation of the Web sites. If students need help with this skill, direct them to the **21st Century Online Tutorial:** *Evaluate Web Sites.*

→ **Online Assessment**

Tailor review and assessment to each student's needs with an array of online assessments.
- On Assignment Article or Slideshow
- Self-Test
- Success Tracker

? Essential Question

How can you measure success?

A Changing China: Who Benefits the Most? Gather data about the changes taking place in China. Answer the question *How do these changes affect different people in different ways?* Organize your findings and write a report to an economic leader.

21st Century Learning

Evaluating Web Sites

Search for three different Web sites that give information on the Three Gorges Dam. Examine each site and answer the following questions. Create a table to record your answers.
- Who is the source of the information?
- How up-to-date is the information?
- Does the information seem accurate?
- Is the information easy to understand?

Document-Based Questions

Success ☆ Tracker™
Online at myworldgeography.com

Use your knowledge of the region and Documents A and B to answer Questions 1–3.

Document A

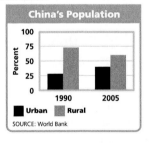

China's Population

Percent: 100, 75, 50, 25, 0

1990   2005

■ Urban   ■ Rural

SOURCE: World Bank

Document B

" There are no social benefits—all I get is my salary. Hands stop, mouth stops. If I get sick, I just have to keep my eyes open and sit here."

—a migrant worker in urban China

1. Which of the following might explain the change seen in Document A?
   A better health care in rural areas
   B better schools in rural areas
   C better-paying jobs in urban areas
   D natural disasters in urban areas

2. Which of the following best describes the worker quoted in Document B?
   A a member of the "floating population"
   B a person who was born in a big city and has health benefits
   C a government official in a city
   D a farmer in western China

3. **Writing Task** Do you think the situation described in Document B is common? Explain your answer.

WRITING TASK TIP

QUOTING DOCUMENTS Demonstrate how to integrate a quote into a paragraph or sentence before students complete question 3. Post an example such as, When the worker says, "hands stop, mouth stops," we understand that she has to work constantly in order to eat and survive. Draw students' attention to the use of commas and quotation marks to set the spoken words apart from the rest of the sentence.

DOCUMENT-BASED QUESTIONS

1. C

2. A

3. Students should use data from Document A to explain why the feeling expressed in Document B might be more and more common. If there are more people moving to urban areas, there are more people without benefits. Students may point out that factory workers have to go to work even if they are sick for fear of being quickly replaced by one of the millions of migrant workers.

Plan With Understanding by Design*

Chapter Objectives
Begin With the End in Mind

Students will demonstrate the following enduring understandings:
- Societies and individuals adapt in unique ways to the influences of their physical and cultural geography.

- Pollution and other environmental problems often occur when societies do not consider the scarcity of available resources.
- Scarcity of resources leads to economic interdependence between countries.

Connect
Make Learning Meaningful

Student Edition
- **Essential Question** How much does geography shape a country?
- **myStory** Learn about life in Yokohama as you read the myStory.

my worldgeography.com
myStory Video Get to know Asuka through a video of her life and home.

Student Journal
Essential Question Preview

Experience
Teach Knowledge and Skills

Student Edition
- Read Sections 1, 2, and 3.
- Answer Reading Checks and Section Assessment questions.

my worldgeography.com
On Assignment myStory Video, Active Atlas, Data Discovery, Culture Close-up, and Self-Test

Student Journal
- Sections 1, 2, and 3 Word Wise
- Sections 1, 2, and 3 Take Notes

Teacher's Edition
myWorld Activities
- Section 1: Trade Off, p. T38
- Section 2: Best of the Best, p. T44
- Section 3: Political Manga, p. T52

21st Century Learning Online Tutor
- Read Special Purpose Maps
- Problem Solve
- Make Decisions
- Identify Main Ideas and Details
- Set a Purpose for Reading
- Compare Viewpoints

Understand
Assess Understanding

Assessment Booklet
- Chapter Tests • Benchmark Tests

Teacher's Edition
myWorld Chapter Activity Plan a multimedia presentation that shows how Japan and the Koreas have adapted to and changed their environment.

Student Journal
Essential Question Writer's Workshop

my worldgeography.com
On Assignment Students write and submit an online article or multimedia slideshow about how geography shapes Japan and the Koreas.

Success Tracker™
Online at myworldgeography.com
Administer chapter tests and remediate understanding.

Student Edition
Chapter Assessment

* *"Understanding by Design" is registered as a trademark with the Patent and Trademark Office by the Association for Supervision of Curriculum Development (ASCD). ASCD has not authorized, approved or sponsored this work and is in no way affiliated with Pearson or its products.*

Connect to the Essential Question

Essential Question

How much does geography shape a country?

Use the Essential Question poster and follow these steps to help students understand the Essential Question.

Connect to Their Lives

1. Have students discuss how they think geography has shaped their lives. (If students have already studied this Essential Question, encourage them to note changes to their opinion.) As students respond, emphasize the diversity of ways that geography can shape their lives. Students might focus on parks, nearby lakes, local weather, crops grown in their region, the size of their school, and recreational activities. Ask, Have you ever lived in a place that had different geographic influences? Explain.

2. Have students identify how geographic elements mentioned in the chart below have affected their lives. Post the following chart for them to complete or have students turn to the *Essential Question Preview* page in their **Student Journal.**

Personal Influence of Geographic Elements				
Parks, Lakes, Rivers	Local Weather	Local Crops	Size of school	Recreational Activities

3. Discuss students' responses. Ask students how these elements affect each other. For example, how can cold weather affect the type of recreational activities in a region?

Connect to the Content

4. Now have students brainstorm ways that geographic elements can influence a country. For instance, amount of rainfall can affect what crops are grown.

5. In the chart, have students list influences of geographic elements on a country.

Influences of Geographic Elements on a Country				
Physical Features	Climate	Natural Resources	Population	Culture

6. After previewing the chapter, have students make chapter-related predictions on the *Essential Question Preview* page in the **Student Journal.**

7. Remind students that they will answer a prompt related to the Essential Question on each section's *Take Notes* page in the **Student Journal.**

Explore 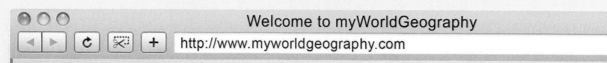 my worldgeography.com

Welcome to myWorldGeography

http://www.myworldgeography.com

ON ASSIGNMENT: Japan and the Koreas

For this chapter's assignment, students will
- take a digital trip to Japan and the Koreas.
- take on the role of a journalist.
- gather notes, images, and data for their story throughout their journey.
- write an article or create a multimedia slideshow connecting the information and images gathered during their trip and this chapter's Essential Question, *How much does geography shape a country?*

ITINERARY

During their trip, students will make the following stops:

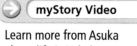 **myStory Video**

Learn more from Asuka about life in Yokohama.

 **Active Atlas**

Read physical, climate, and land use maps for Japan and the Koreas.

 **Data Discovery**

Gather data from the charts on Japan and the Koreas.

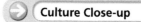 **Culture Close-up**

Examine urban planning in Japan.

 **Self-Test**

Assess their own knowledge of chapter content.

While on their trip, students will practice the following skills:

- **Interpret** graphic representations of data.
- **Synthesize** evidence into an interesting article or multimedia slideshow.
- **Evaluate** factors that determine the influence of geography on a country.

TIGed
TakingITGlobal for Educators

Extend the reach of every lesson by helping students connect to a global community of young people with common interests and concerns. Visit myworldgeography.com to
- explore Country Pages relating to Japan and the Koreas.
- delve deeper into this chapter's Essential Question, *How much does geography shape a country?*
- find online alternatives to and solutions for the Unit Closer 21st Century Learning Activity.

my worldgeography.com

TEACHER CENTER

Preview and assign student materials, enrich your teaching, and track student progress with the following resources:
- Online Lesson Planning and Resource Library
- Presentations for Projection
- Online Teacher's Edition and Ancillaries
- Google Earth Links

Assess Enduring Understandings

 myWorld Chapter Activity **Step-by-Step Instructions**   2 hr

Mission Earth

Teach this activity at the end of the chapter to assess enduring understandings.

OBJECTIVES

Students will demonstrate the following enduring understandings:
- Societies and individuals adapt in unique ways to the influences of their physical and cultural geography.
- Pollution and other environmental problems often occur when societies do not take into account the scarcity of available resources.

Students will provide the following evidence of understanding:
- Environmental Changes and Adaptations Chart
- Presentation to the United Nations Environment Programme

LEARNING STYLES
- Visual
- Verbal

MATERIALS
- Activity Support: Student Instructions and Rubric, p. T34
- Activity Support: Environmental Analysis, p. T35
- Activity Cards: #127–132
  - 127. Japan: Building More Land
  - 128. Japan: Moving Underground
  - 129. South Korea: Air Pollution
  - 130. South Korea: Solar Power
  - 131. North Korea: Building Dams
  - 132. North Korea: Ondol

Activity Steps

1. **Set Expectations** Tell the class that they will divide into six groups and that each group will be a research team. By using assigned Activity Cards, information from Sections 1 through 3, myworldgeography.com, and what they learn from other teams, each team will collect data on how Japan and the Koreas have changed and adapted to their environments. Each student will then chart the information and plan a multimedia report to the United Nations Environment Programme.

2. **Field Research Jigsaw**
   - Divide the class into six research teams. Give each team an Activity Card. Give each student a copy of *Activity Support: Environmental Analysis.*
   - Have each team research and discuss the environmental changes or the environmental adaptations presented on the team's activity card. Students should focus on the benefits and drawbacks of the changes or adaptations presented. Tell students to record their information on the *Environmental Analysis.*
   - Rearrange students using a jigsaw. Ask students to pool their information and use their *Environmental*

   Analysis to take notes on other countries.

   ELL Intermediate Review activity cards before the activity for potentially challenging vocabulary. Present a list of these words with translations and/or definitions to use while reading the information.

3. **Review and Discuss Research** Have students study their *Environmental Analysis* to compare how countries change and adapt to their environment.

4. **Multimedia Presentation** Then have each student plan a multimedia presentation that answers the questions on the following page. The plan should include descriptions of images and graphs that would be used in the presentation. The images and graphs should be listed in the order they will appear in the presentation. Also, students should write a narration to accompany their images and graphs. The plan should end with a summary that includes suggestions about how Japan and the Koreas could improve their environment.

   L4 Challenge Have students make presentations to the class by using presentation software.

  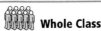

Name _____ Class _____ Date _____

myWorld Chapter Activity Support **Student Instructions and Rubric**

Mission Earth

Activity Instructions Read the following summary of your myWorld Chapter Activity. Then follow your teacher's directions.

1. Work with your teammates to gather information about how your assigned country has changed or adapted to its environment. Then complete the section of *Activity Support: Environmental Analysis* that focuses on your activity card.

2. Your teacher will then rearrange your teams. Share your activity card's information with your new group. Use the *Environmental Analysis* to take notes about other nations.

3. Review your *Environmental Analysis* and compare how the various countries have adapted and changed their environment. Examine benefits and drawbacks.

4. Plan a multimedia presentation to show the United Nations Environment Programme how Japan and the Koreas have changed and adapted to their environments. Your report should answer the following questions:
   a. What are some ways that Japan and the Koreas change and adapt to their environments?
   b. What are some benefits and drawbacks of these changes and adaptations?
   c. What suggestions would you make to the United Nations Environment Programme about how Japan and the Koreas can improve their environments?

myWorld Chapter Activity Rubric	3 Exceeds Understanding	2 Reaches Understanding	1 Approaches Understanding
Chart: Organization	Complex organization	Basic organization	Not organized and hard to read
Chart: Data	The information is accurate and detailed.	Basic information is presented accurately.	The information presented is basic and some of it is inaccurate.
Presentation Sources	Uses information from the cards, from all three sections, and two online features	Uses information from the cards and one other source	Uses information only from the cards
Presentation Visuals	Compelling visuals and two or more graphs or charts	Clear, helpful visuals and one graph or chart	Simple visuals or visuals are unclear, and no graphs or charts

Name _____ Class _____ Date _____

myWorld Chapter Activity Support · **Environmental Analysis**

Mission Earth

Directions Fill out this analysis, gathering information from the activity cards and other students during the jigsaw. Use extra paper if needed.

JAPAN

Description of Change	Benefits of Change	Drawbacks of Change
Description of Adaptation	**Benefits of Adaptation**	**Drawbacks of Adaptation**

SOUTH KOREA

Description of Change	Benefits of Change	Drawbacks of Change
Description of Adaptation	**Benefits of Adaptation**	**Drawbacks of Adaptation**

NORTH KOREA

Description of Change	Benefits of Change	Drawbacks of Change
Description of Adaptation	**Benefits of Adaptation**	**Drawbacks of Adaptation**

T35

Japan and the Koreas

- Introduce the Essential Question so that students will be able to understand the big ideas of this chapter (see earlier page, Connect to the Essential Question).

- Help students prepare to learn about Japan and the Koreas by looking at the chapter's maps, charts, and photos.

- Have students make and record chapter predictions with the *Essential Question Preview* in the **Student Journal.**

- Ask them to analyze maps on this page.

GUIDE ON THE SIDE

Explore the Essential Question ...

Have students complete the Essential Question Writer's Workshop in their **Student Journal** to demonstrate in-depth understanding of the question in the context of this chapter.

Analyze Maps Point out the political map.

- What is the capital of Japan? (Tokyo)

- What is the approximate distance between Seoul and Tokyo? (about 1,000 miles)

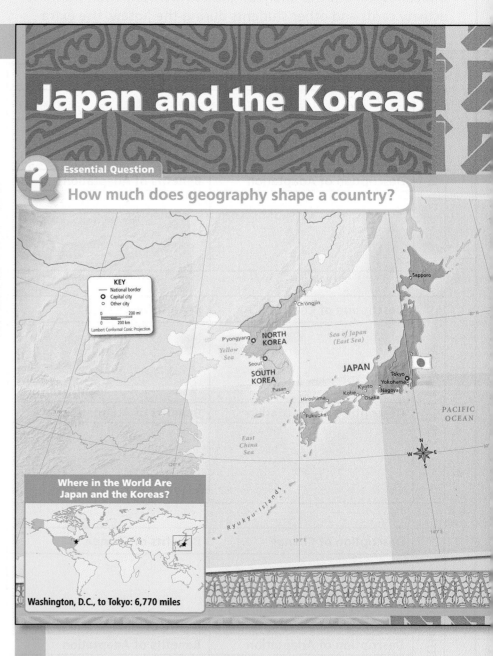

Japan and the Koreas

Essential Question

How much does geography shape a country?

KEY
— National border
✪ Capital city
○ Other city

0   200 mi
0   200 km
Lambert Conformal Conic Projection

Sapporo
Ch'ŏngjin
NORTH KOREA
P'yongyang
Yellow Sea
Seoul
SOUTH KOREA
Pusan
Sea of Japan (East Sea)
JAPAN
Tokyo
Yokohama
Kyoto
Kobe
Nagoya
Hiroshima
Osaka
Fukuoka
East China Sea
Ryukyu Islands
PACIFIC OCEAN

Where in the World Are Japan and the Koreas?

Washington, D.C., to Tokyo: 6,770 miles

INTRODUCE my Story

Get students excited to learn about Japan and the Koreas by first experiencing the region through the eyes of Asuka, a high-school student who lives in Yokohama, Japan.

- Read myStory and watch the myStory Video about her life.

- Have students complete *Asuka: A Girl on the Go* in the **Student Journal** to prepare to learn about the daily life of Asuka and the difficulties and benefits of living in Yokohama.

my Story
Asuka: A Girl on the Go

In this section you'll read about Asuka. She is a senior in high school and lives with her family in Yokohama, Japan. Life has not been easy for Asuka, but that has not stopped her from wanting to make the world a better place to live. What does Asuka's story tell you about the challenges young people face living in Japan?

Explore the Essential Question
- at **my** worldgeography.com
- using the **myWorld Chapter Activity**
- with the **Student Journal**

Story by Michael Condon for MyWorld Geography Online

In the bamboo- and -concrete-covered hills of Yokohama, a cluster of identical apartment blocks stands out. The drab, box-shaped buildings have numbers stenciled onto the top of their walls to identify them. On the third floor of one of the apartment buildings, in a small apartment no bigger than an average American living room, lives Asuka. The third-year high school student shares the apartment with her father, her grandmother, her 15-year-old brother, the family's pet turtle, and Max, a pet rabbit.

More than 35 million people live in the Greater Tokyo-Yokohama metropolitan area. This is almost twice as many people as live in Greater New York. With so many people needing housing, space is scarce. Most people live in small apartments. About 2,500 people live in this four-block square area of Yokohama. It is very crowded, and the cost of living in Yokohama is high.

---

my Story

Asuka: A Girl on the Go

- **Connect** What are some of the differences between where you live and where Asuka lives? (Sample: I live in a much larger place with more rooms than the apartment where Asuka lives.)

- **Express Opinions** Would you like to live in Yokohama? Explain. (Samples: No, it's too crowded. Yes, there seems to be a lot to do.)

On Assignment

Have students go to myworldgeography.com to take on the role of a journalist.

HISTORY

Yokohama The city of Yokohama was originally a small fishing village. Then in 1859, the nearby town of Kanagawa became the main port for foreigners in Japan. There, foreigners could live and trade goods. Because of this, the general area, including Yokohama, began to flourish. After the Meiji Restoration, trade with foreigners increased, which spurred the development of the Yokohama region. In 1889, the towns of Yokohama and Kanagawa combined to form the city of Yokohama. Soon this city became the second largest in Japan. In 1923, the Great Kanto Earthquake destroyed much of Yokohama. The city was also extensively damaged by U.S. air raids during World War II. Yokohama, though, has persevered to become a thriving metropolitan center. It has a large industrial area, an active cultural life, and many historic buildings.

GUIDE ON THE SIDE

- **Identify Details** How many hours does Asuka work a week? (20 hours)

- **Predict** What type of work do you think Asuka would like to do when she is an adult? (Samples: politician, history teacher, banker)

- **Infer** Do you think Japanese schools stress learning foreign languages? Explain. ` (Sample: Yes, Asuka is taking courses in English and Korean.)

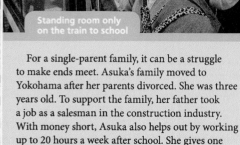

Standing room only on the train to school

Asuka's grandmother serving dinner in a small kitchen

A crowded bedroom and study area

For a single-parent family, it can be a struggle to make ends meet. Asuka's family moved to Yokohama after her parents divorced. She was three years old. To support the family, her father took a job as a salesman in the construction industry. With money short, Asuka also helps out by working up to 20 hours a week after school. She gives one third of her wages to the family and uses the rest to pay her other expenses.

Though her family does not have a lot of money, the 18-year-old high school senior considers herself fortunate. Every day she wakes up at 6:30 A.M., grabs the "bento" lunch box her grandmother has prepared, and heads off to school. She attends a high school in the middle of Yokohama, where she studies international affairs. Her curriculum is demanding. It includes courses in world history, politics, economics, Japanese, English, and Korean.

Asuka has developed a keen interest in politics, economics, and history. She plans to major in these subjects when she goes to college. Asuka thinks it is important to study politics and history because they explain how various countries have developed and the way their governments work. With that knowledge, she believes, "We can improve the living conditions of people and make things better."

CULTURE

Higher Education in Japan Japan has about 1,200 institutions of higher learning. These include junior colleges, colleges, and universities. The degree programs in junior colleges last two or three years. Colleges and universities have four-year programs. Japan also has many technical colleges that combine high school and college. These technical programs last five years. Since 1980, the number of female undergraduate students has increased. Even so, females still make up less than half of the entire student body. In addition, the number of foreign students attending colleges and universities in Japan has increased dramatically. Most of these students come from China and South Korea.

A Glocally field trip

Class is just about to begin.

Asuka is a high-energy person. In addition to her studies and her job, she takes part in extracurricular activities. These activities range from volunteer work to playing drums in a rock band. Asuka is also the leader of the school's "Glocally" Club. (The club's name is a combination of the words "global" and "locally.") As part of the club's activities, the students go on field trips to observe war ruins. They also learn how wars affect people and look for ways to achieve peace in the modern world.

The teacher in charge of the club has introduced the students to some serious issues that are far from the minds of the average high school student in most developed countries. Asuka is glad he challenges them to think about real-world issues.

Over the last couple of years, Asuka has also taken part in the Yokohama Student Forum. Last year she became a student leader and put together a forum on child labor—an issue that touches the lives of families across Asia.

Asuka appreciates all the opportunities she has had. "I have [led] a privileged life," she says, "while others are suffering elsewhere." After graduating from college, Asuka says she wants to do something to help others less privileged.

Judging by what she has achieved so far, the promising young student will be sure to put her talents to good use in the future.

 myStory Video

Join Asuka as she shows you about her life in Yokohama.

Meet the Journalist

Name Heath Cozens
Favorite Moment My favorite memory was Asuka doing karaoke.

- **Summarize** Name Asuka's extracurricular activities. (volunteer work, playing drums in a rock band, leader of the "Glocally" Club)

- **Draw Conclusions** Why do you think Asuka wants to learn about real-world issues? (Sample: Learning about these issues probably helps Asuka to better understand how and why people are suffering throughout the world.)

myStory Video

Have students watch the video at myworldgeography.com about Asuka's life and the city where she lives. Tell students to use their trackers to take notes on the issue of overcrowding in Japan.

NOTES

Chapter Atlas

OBJECTIVES

Students will know

- the physical features, climate, resources, and land use of Japan and the Koreas.
- how the people of Japan and the Koreas have adapted to their environment.

Students will be able to

- label outline maps of Japan and the Koreas.
- solve problems concerning lack of resources in Japan and the Koreas.

SET EXPECTATIONS

In this section, students will

- read the Chapter Atlas.
- play a trading game about the scarcity of resources.
- go On Assignment in Japan and explore the streets of Tokyo.

CORE CONCEPTS

You may wish to teach or reteach the following lessons from the Core Concepts Handbook:

- Forces On Earth's Surface, pp. 24–25
- Environment and Resources, pp. 48–49
- Land Use, pp. 50–51

KEY

Differentiated Instruction
- **L1** Special Needs
- **L2** Extra Support
- **L3** On-Level
- **L4** Challenge

English Language Instruction
- **ELL** Beginner
- **ELL** Early Intermediate
- **ELL** Intermediate
- **ELL** Early Advanced
- **ELL** Advanced

1 Connect
Make learning meaningful

Make Connections Ask students to think about the problem of limited space in their homes, school, or community. What kind of conflicts can limited space cause? How have they and people they know dealt with these problems? Then have students look at a map of Japan and the Koreas. Ask if they think Japan and the Koreas has a limited-space problem. Have them explain their answers in their journals.

L2 Extra Support To provide a visual for "limited space," have two volunteers try to fit their books into one desk or one bag and discuss the results.

Activate Prior Knowledge Remind students that in the previous chapter, they learned about China's economic development and how it has led to environmental problems. Ask them to predict ways in which Japan's and the Koreas' economic development might have caused environmental problems.

L3 On-Level Review some of the environmental problems in China. When reading about Japan and the Koreas, compare the types of environmental problems in the two regions.

Prepare Follow the steps in the section **Preview.** Preteach the Key Terms. Then have students complete *Word Wise* in their journals using in-text clues and the glossary for help.

2 Experience
Teach knowledge and skills

Read Use **Background** notes and **Guide on the Side** questions to model active reading. Have students use *Take Notes* in their **Student Journal** to record important places to know in Japan and the Koreas on an outline map. Students should use the maps in the Chapter Atlas and the Active Atlas at myworldgeography.com for assistance.

ELL Beginner Read aloud the Places to Know! in *Take Notes.* Define geographic features using basic vocabulary and visuals. For example, define *mountain* as "high land" and show a picture labeled in English.

L4 Challenge Have students read and complete *Enrichment: Japan's Temperatures* to learn more about the variations in Japan's temperature.

 **Practice: myWorld Activity** Students trade resource tokens to help them analyze and solve the problem of scarcity of resources. **Step-by-Step Instructions** and **More Activities** follow on p. T38.

SECTION 1 RESOURCE GUIDE

FOR THE STUDENT

my worldgeography.com Student Center
- Active Atlas
- Culture Close-up
- Data Discovery

Student Edition (print and online)
- Chapter Atlas

Student Journal (print and online)
- Section 1 Word Wise
- Section 1 Take Notes

21st Century Learning Online Tutor
- Read Special Purpose Maps
- Problem Solve

FOR THE TEACHER

my worldgeography.com Teacher Center
- Online Lesson Planner
- Presentations for Projection
- SuccessTracker

ProGuide: East and Southeast Asia
- Section 1 Lesson Plan, pp. T36–T37
- myWorld Activity Step-by-Step Instructions, p. T38
- Activity Support: Tokens and Questions, p. T39
- myWorld Geography Enrichment, p. T40
- Section Quiz, p. T41

Accelerating the Progress of ELLs
- Peer Learning Strategies, p. 46

3 Understand
Assess understanding

Review Review students' work in their **Student Journal.**

Assess Knowledge and Skills Use the Section Assessment and Section Quiz to check students' progress.

Assess Understanding Review students' responses to the Section Assessment Essential Question prompt.

Remediate Use these strategies to review and remediate.

If students struggle to . . .	Try these strategies.
Describe Japan's problem with limited space and earthquakes	Students put two items near the middle of their desks, and then shake their desks. How many fall off? Then have students repeat using ten items.
Problem solve	Assign additional practice with the **21st Century Online Tutor.**
Identify the purpose of special purpose maps	Students read the key of each map to see if it has a special purpose.

ELL Support

ELL Objective Students use Greek and Latin roots to understand geographic vocabulary.

Cultural Connections To connect students to natural disasters in Japan, have them discuss natural disasters that happen in their family's homeland and what they think are the causes.

ELL Early Advanced Tip Have students find Greek and Latin cognates in the section such as geography and volcano. Then map the words including a translation.

ELL Activity Have students pretend to be architects and build housing in a limited area. Ask students to draw a 3-inch square and cut out 18 tokens that are 1 inch square. Tell the students each token represents a housing unit. They have to fit all 18 tokens into the box. They can fold tokens to reduce the size of units or stack tokens as multistories. Students can draw in streets and parks in any free space. Connect the exercise to limited space in Japan and the Koreas. **(Kinesthetic/Visual)**

myWorld Activity   **Step-by-Step Instructions**

  40 min

Trade Off

OBJECTIVES

Students will

- trade with other countries to gain enough resources that meet their country's needs.
- attempt to solve the problem of scarcity of resources.

LEARNING STYLE

- Verbal
- Interpersonal
- Kinesthetic

21st Century Learning

- Solve Problems

MATERIALS

- Scissors
- Three hats or containers
- Activity Support: Tokens and Questions, p. T39

Activity Steps

1. Divide the class into three evenly distributed groups labeled Country A, Country B, and Country C.

2. Set up three containers. Label them raw materials, food, and manufactured goods. Have each student cut out the resource tokens from their *Activity Support: Tokens and Questions* and place them in the corresponding hat.

   ELL **Early Intermediate/Intermediate** Some ELL students might associate the word *resource* only with natural resources. Define the word *resource* as *a supply of something such as raw materials, manufactured goods, or people.*

3. Distribute unevenly all the raw materials tokens *only* to the students representing Country A. Make sure that each student in this group has at least five raw materials tokens. Then unevenly distribute the food

and manufactured goods tokens to students in all three groups. Each student should have at least one food token and one manufactured goods token.

   L2 **Extra Support** Explain to students that countries with less than five tokens of a resource have a scarcity of that resource, and countries with more than five tokens of a resource have a surplus of that resource.

4. Tell students that they have to get at least five tokens of each resource to fill the needs of their country. To do this, they have to trade tokens they have an excess of for tokens that they need. Students can trade tokens with other countries, but they cannot trade tokens with their own country.

5. After trading, have students complete *Activity Support: Tokens and Questions*. Discuss the activity.

More Activities From myWorld Teachers

 Local Connections Have students think about natural disasters they have experienced, such as earthquakes, hurricanes, tornadoes, blizzards, and thunderstorms. Then have them write about or make a work of art about this experience. **(Verbal/Visual)**

Climate Gallery Assign students to make large illustrations of their community showing typical weather during different seasons. Then assign other

students to illustrate scenes that show typical seasonal weather for Japan and the Koreas. Hang their work by season so that students can compare. **(Verbal/Visual)**

Taking a Hike Have pairs imagine that they will be taking a week-long hike into Japan's countryside. Have them create a hiking guide that describes the terrain they will cross, the supplies they should bring, and the clothes they should wear. **(Logical/Verbal)**

my worldgeography.com (Teacher Center) ➔   Find additional resources in the online Teacher Center.

Name ______________________ Class ______________ Date ____________

myWorld Activity Support **Tokens and Questions**

Trade Off

Directions Write the name of the country you have been assigned in the blank space. Use scissors to cut out the tokens, and then place the tokens in the corresponding container. Your teacher will then unevenly redistribute the tokens. You need to get at least five tokens of each resource to fill your country's needs. Trade extra tokens for tokens that you need with students representing other countries. Then answer the questions below.

Country: ______________________________

Resource Tokens

RAW MATERIALS	RAW MATERIALS	RAW MATERIALS
RAW MATERIALS	RAW MATERIALS	

FOOD	FOOD	FOOD
FOOD	FOOD	

MANUFACTURED GOODS	MANUFACTURED GOODS	MANUFACTURED GOODS
MANUFACTURED GOODS	MANUFACTURED GOODS	

1. If your country started out with a scarcity of raw materials, was getting enough raw materials through trade difficult? Explain.

____

2. If your country started with a surplus of raw materials, was trading for enough food and manufactured goods difficult? Explain.

____

Name _____ Class _____ Date _____

Enrichment: Japan's Temperatures

Directions Below is a graph that shows the average high temperatures for the cities of Sapporo on the northern island of Hokkaido, Tokyo on the central island of Honshu, and Fukuoka on the southern island of Kyushu. Study the graph and then answer the questions.

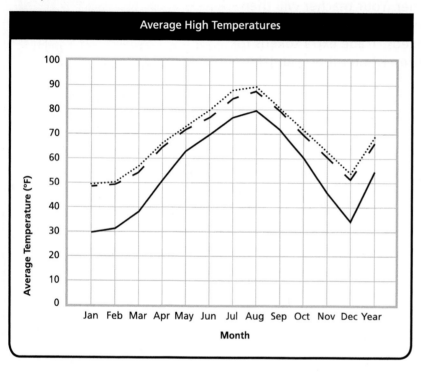

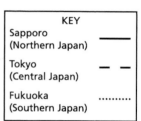

1. What is the highest average temperature shown on the above graphs? When and where did it occur?

_____

2. What is the lowest average temperature shown? When and where did it occur?

_____

3. Is there more of a difference between the average yearly temperature of Tokyo and Sapporo or Tokyo and Fukuoka? Explain your answer.

_____

_____

4. Activity Imagine that you are going to study for three months in Japan. Based on the above graphs, what city and during what three-month span would you like to visit? Explain.

Name _____ Class _____ Date _____

Section Quiz

Directions Answer the following questions using what you learned
in Section 1.

1. _____ Which of Japan's islands has the
largest level area?
a. Hokkaido
b. Honshu
c. Kyushu
d. Shikoku

2. _____ Tropical storms often hit Japan
during the
a. summer.
b. winter.
c. spring.
d. fall.

3. _____ What is the most important
agricultural product in Japan and the
Koreas?
a. corn
b. rice
c. soybeans
d. wheat

4. _____ In which of the following ways are
Japan and South Korea similar?
a. They both are peninsulas.
b. They both are made up of islands.
c. They both have dry summers.
d. They both have few mineral resources.

5. _____ Which of the following has made
flooding worse in the Koreas?
a. lack of tree cover
b. lack of crops
c. too many droughts
d. too many dams

6. In what ways do Japan's geographic features lead to a high
population density?

_____

_____

_____

_____

Chapter Atlas

- Model preparing to read by previewing the Key Ideas, Key Terms, headings, visuals, and captions. Have students make predictions about what they will learn. For ELL support, post the prompt, "I predict I will read about . . ."

- Preview and practice the reading skill, Label an Outline Map, by labeling a map of your town or city.

- Preteach this section's high-use Academic Vocabulary and Key Terms using the chart on the next page and in-text definitions. Have students practice Key Terms by completing the *Word Wise* page in their journals.

GUIDE ON THE SIDE

Physical Features

Identify Details Have students read to identify details about Japan and the Korea's physical features.

- How many large islands make up Japan? (four)

- On what type of landform are North and South Korea located? (peninsula)

Reading Skill

Label an Outline Map While they read, have students identify the Places to Know! on the outline map of the region in the **Student Journal**.

Section 1

Chapter Atlas

Key Ideas
- Mountains cover much of this region.
- A dense population requires careful use of resources.
- People have adapted to sudden natural disasters.

Key Terms
- foliage
- scarcity
- comparative advantage
- interdependent

Visual Glossary

Reading Skill: Label an Outline Map Take notes using the outline map in your journal.

A hiker at the base of Mt. Fuji in Japan ▼

Physical Features

Japan, at the far eastern edge of Asia, is sometimes called the "land of the rising sun." The Japanese see each day's sunrise before most parts of Asia. North and South Korea lie just to the west of Japan.

Japan is a 1,500-mile-long chain of islands made up of four large islands and about 3,000 smaller islands. The countries of North and South Korea together form the Korean peninsula.

Four tectonic plates are close to Japan and the Koreas. The plates are slowly moving together. The result is

ACADEMIC VOCABULARY

High-Use Word	Definition and Sample Sentence
occur	*v.* to take place; to happen *The parade occurs on the fourth of July.*
output	*n.* the amount of something produced *The industrial output of the nation increased last year.*

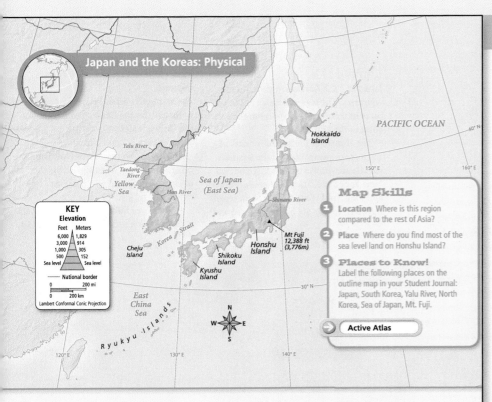

Japan and the Koreas: Physical

PACIFIC OCEAN

Hokkaido Island

Yalu River

Taedong River

Yellow Sea

Han River

Sea of Japan (East Sea)

Shinano River

Mt Fuji 12,388 ft (3,776m)

KEY
Elevation

Feet	Meters
6,000	1,829
3,000	914
1,000	305
500	152
Sea level	Sea level

— National border

0   200 mi
0   200 km
Lambert Conformal Conic Projection

Cheju Island

Korea Strait

Shikoku Island

Kyushu Island

Honshu Island

East China Sea

Ryukyu Islands

120° E   130° E   140° E   150° E   160° E

40° N   30° N

Map Skills

1 **Location** Where is this region compared to the rest of Asia?

2 **Place** Where do you find most of the sea level land on Honshu Island?

3 **Places to Know!** Label the following places on the outline map in your Student Journal: Japan, South Korea, Yalu River, North Korea, Sea of Japan, Mt. Fuji.

> **Active Atlas**

great pressure that causes earthquakes. Earthquakes that <u>occur</u> under the sea can make huge waves that slam into the towns along the shore. As the Pacific Plate sinks beneath Japan, it melts and is called molten rock. The molten rock then rises to Earth's surface, creating volcanic eruptions. Japan has 108 active volcanoes.

Both North Korea and South Korea are mountainous countries. In both countries, there are a wide coastal plain in the west and smaller plains in the east. South Korea has more flat land suitable for farming than North Korea.

Japan is more rugged than the Koreas. Mountains and hills cover about 70 percent of the country's surface. In Japan and the Koreas, most people live in the valleys and coastal plains. In Japan, the largest level area is on Honshu Island.

The mountains in these countries are popular sites for hiking. Mount Fuji, the highest peak in Japan, is particularly popular. The mountain is a volcano, but it has not erupted for centuries. Thousands of people climb Mount Fuji every year.

Reading Check Why are there earthquakes and volcanoes in Japan and the Koreas?

occur, *v.,* to take place; to happen

MAP SKILLS 1. This region is east of the rest of Asia. **2.** along the coast. **3.** Students should correctly label the outline map.

READING CHECK Three deep tectonic plates meet near Japan and the Koreas and press against each other with great pressure.

ANSWERS

- **Cause and Effect** What causes huge waves to slam into Japan's coastal towns? (earthquakes under the sea)
- **Infer** Why do you think most people live in the plains and the valleys of Japan? (Sample: The rest of Japan consists of rugged mountains. Building towns and cities in mountainous regions is difficult.)

Analyze Visuals Have students analyze the physical map on this page.

- What is the elevation of Mt. Fuji? (12,388 ft.)
- What is the elevation range of the land at the source of the Han River? (1,000 to 3,000 ft.)

 > **Active Atlas**

Have students go to myworldgeography.com to see more maps about Japan and the Koreas.

QUICK FACTS

Skiing in Japan Skiing has been a popular sport in Japan for many years. In fact, Japan has more ski resorts (about 700) than any other nation in the world. In 2005, one ski resort received 26,000 tourists, and other resorts are also very busy. The best skiing is found on the northern island of Hokkaido. The type of snow that this island gets is often very good for skiing. Hokkaido also gets a lot of snow. For example, the popular ski resort town of Niseko on Hokkaido gets about 46 feet of snow each year. This accumulation is more than the largest resorts get in North America.

GUIDE ON THE SIDE

Climate

- **Compare and Contrast** How is the climate of the northern Korean peninsula similar to the climate of New England? (They both have cool summers and long, cold winters.)

- **Cause and Effect** How do the winds from central Asia affect the climate of Japan and the Koreas during the winter? (The winds from central Asia carry little moisture during the winter. So when they blow on Japan and the Koreas, they bring little rainfall. As a result, this region has dry winters.)

Analyze Visuals Analyze the climate map on this page.

- What type of climate is found in Tokyo? (humid subtropical)

- What type of climate is found in most of the Korean Peninsula? (continental warm summer)

Active Atlas

Have students go to myworldgeography.com to see more maps about Japan and the Koreas.

Climate

Japan and the Koreas are mid-latitude countries. The seasonal range of temperatures in this region is similar to the east coast of the United States.

The climate of the northern parts of the Korean peninsula and the Japanese islands are similar to New England and New York State. They have cool summers and long, cold winters. In the fall, Japan's northern forests are bright with red and yellow foliage. **Foliage** is the leaves on the trees.

The southern part of Japan has a climate more like the southeast coastal region of the United States. Winters are mild, and summers are hot and humid.

During the winter, winds blow from central Asia into Korea and across the Sea of Japan. These cold winds are very dry, especially in North Korea.

About three fifths of North Korea's rain falls from June to September. By contrast,

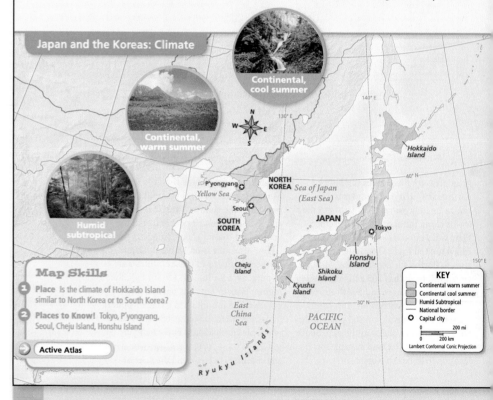

Japan and the Koreas: Climate

Map Skills

1. **Place** Is the climate of Hokkaido Island similar to North Korea or to South Korea?

2. **Places to Know!** Tokyo, P'yongyang, Seoul, Cheju Island, Honshu Island

Active Atlas

MAP SKILL 1. North Korea **2.** Students should correctly label the outline map.

GEOGRAPHY

Typhoons Each year, about 30 typhoons form in the Northwest Pacific Ocean. On average, about three of them hit Japan. Many of them have been very destructive. In 1959, a typhoon caused the deaths of 5,000 people. Recently, warning systems have helped to limit typhoon casualties. However, in 2002, a fierce typhoon hit South Korea, killing over 100 people. It was the worst typhoon in 40 years. Severe damage was done to the infrastructure, including roads and the telecommunications network. Tens of thousands of people went without electricity. North Korea also reported many casualties.

the sea brings some moisture all year to South Korea and Japan.

Summer seasonal winds, or monsoons, can drop as much as 80 inches of rainfall a year. They sometimes bring powerful tropical cyclones or hurricanes. In this part of the world, these storms are referred to as typhoons. Because of the warm, moist air, summers are humid in this region.

After a dry winter, the Koreas may experience a spring drought. The heavy summer rains that follow these droughts can cause flooding and mudslides. When this happens, houses are buried, and farmers may lose their crops.

Summer monsoon rainfall supports lush forests. As a result, most of the uplands of Japan and the Koreas are wooded. Particularly in Japan, people have worked hard to preserve their forests. It is one of the few industrialized countries that is heavily forested.

Reading Check Why are wind patterns important to climate in this region?

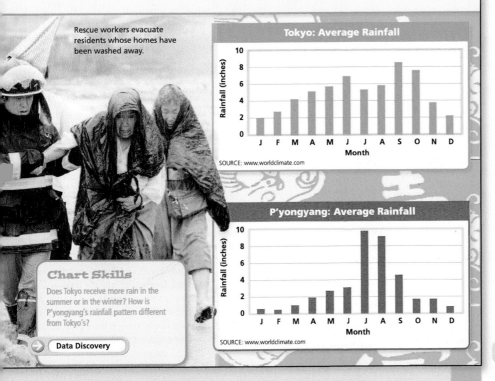

Rescue workers evacuate residents whose homes have been washed away.

Tokyo: Average Rainfall

SOURCE: www.worldclimate.com

P'yongyang: Average Rainfall

SOURCE: www.worldclimate.com

Chart Skills

Does Tokyo receive more rain in the summer or in the winter? How is P'yongyang's rainfall pattern different from Tokyo's?

Data Discovery

READING CHECK Wind patterns control the amount of rainfall in Japan and the Koreas.

CHART SKILLS Tokyo receives more rain in the summer. Tokyo has a steady amount of rainfall during the summer. P'yongyang has a sharp increase of rainfall during July and August.

GUIDE ON THE SIDE

- **Cause and Effect** What causes flooding and mudslides in the Koreas? (heavy summer rains after droughts)
- **Problem Solve** How did Japan prevent deforestation? (The Japanese worked hard to preserve their forests.)

Analyze Visuals Ask students to analyze the people in the photograph.

- Which person in the photograph seems to be helping the other two people? Explain. (The person on the left is helping. This person is dressed in protective clothing like a rescue worker.)
- Why do you think the people in the photo need to be helped? (Their homes have been washed away.)

Data Discovery

Have students go to myworldgeography.com to find data about Japan and the Koreas.

GEOGRAPHY

Rice and Japan's Government In an effort to maintain a high level of rice production, Japan's government subsidizes domestic rice farming. This policy is called the Rice Farming Income Stabilization Program. If the market value for domestic rice falls, the Income Stabilization Program pays rice farmers a certain amount to meet a predetermined standard. As a result, rice farmers are insured a strong income so they stay in agriculture, which has helped to increase rice production. The consumer price for domestic rice in Japan is high. However, the cost of imported rice is even higher. The reason for this is that Japan places steep tariffs on imported rice. By doing so, Japan's government has protected its rice farmers from the open market. Foreign governments, though, have been pressuring Japan to lower its tariffs.

Land Use and Natural Resources

- **Problem Solve** How have the Japanese solved the problem of farming on hilly terrain? (They use terraces to create flat fields on sloping ground.)

- **Draw Conclusions** What is one reason why North Korea's agricultural output lags behind South Korea's? (North Korea has a colder climate than South Korea.)

Analyze Visuals Analyze the land use map on this page.

- How is most of the land in western North Korea used? (to grow crops)

- What type of land use is found in most of Japan? (forest)

 myWorld Activity

Trade Off Find Step-by-Step Instructions and an Activity Support on pp. T38–T39. **(Verbal/Interpersonal/Kinesthetic)**

Special Purpose Maps Have students develop this skill by using this interactive online tutorial and activities. Students will learn how to read special purpose maps and apply that skill to various map challenges.

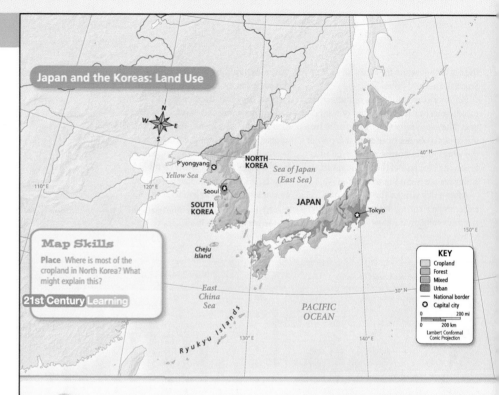

Japan and the Koreas: Land Use

P'yongyang ✪ NORTH KOREA Sea of Japan (East Sea)

Yellow Sea

Seoul ✪

SOUTH KOREA JAPAN Tokyo ✪

Cheju Island

East China Sea PACIFIC OCEAN

Ryukyu Islands

Map Skills

Place Where is most of the cropland in North Korea? What might explain this?

21st Century Learning

KEY
- ▢ Cropland
- ▢ Forest
- ▢ Mixed
- ▢ Urban
- — National border
- ✪ Capital city

0   200 mi
0   200 km
Lambert Conformal Conic Projection

 myWorld Activity Trade Off

Land Use and Natural Resources

With many hills and mountains, the countries of this region face a **scarcity,** or shortage, of flat land. This land is the best location for housing, but it is also needed for farming and industry. As a result, flat land is crowded. Japanese and Koreans must use their land carefully.

Farming the Land Rice is the most important crop in both Japan and the Koreas. With its cool, dry climate, North Korea's farm <u>output</u> lags behind that of South Korea and Japan. Yet, both South Korea and Japan are highly urbanized. Large cities in these two countries take up space. Less land is available for farming. Farmers often must work on difficult, hilly land. Terraces are used to create flat fields on sloping ground. Large tractors are too big to plow the narrow terraces. Instead, rice is planted and harvested by hand or with small machines. In some areas, farmers irrigate the land so that they can plant more than one crop per year on the same land. This type of small-scale rice farming takes a great deal of time and hard work. Farmers do this to make the most of limited land.

output, *n,* the amount of something produced

MAP SKILLS Most of the cropland in North Korea is in the western area. This land is probably flatter.

CORE CONCEPTS: LAND USE

Review Core Concept 4.2 before discussing land use in Japan and the Koreas. Review various ways that land can be used, including cropland, forests, industry, urban development, mining, and as an energy resource. Make sure that students understand the key idea of industrialization. Then have students identify various ways that Japan and the Koreas use land. Ask, How do geographic elements, such as terrain, influence how land is used in this region? Why is some of the land used to generate hydroelectricity? Does using land for mining in North Korea help industry in South Korea? Explain.

Food Imports and Exports Many other countries can produce farm goods more cheaply than Japan and the Koreas. These other countries have a comparative advantage over Japan and the Koreas in agriculture. **Comparative advantage** is the ability to produce goods at a lower cost than your competitors.

Because farming is costly in Japan and the Koreas, these countries import food. Still, people in this region continue to farm so that they will not be dependent on other countries for all their food.

The sea is also an important resource. Fish products are an important export for North Korea. The ocean currents near Japan create an environment that is good for many kinds of fish. Fish is also an important export for Japan as well as an important part of the Japanese diet.

Scarce Resources Mineral resources are not evenly spread across this region. Both Japan and South Korea have few mineral resources. North Korea, by contrast, is rich in mineral resources including coal, lead, iron ore, copper, gold, and salt.

Scarcity makes countries **inter-dependent,** which means they depend on each other. Japan and South Korea trade with each other to acquire some of the raw materials they need for industry.

In addition, all three countries need energy resources. Hydroelectricity is one source of energy. Because of the hilly land, there are many fast flowing rivers. These rivers are good for hydroelectric dams because the falling waters carry large amounts of energy that can be used to create electricity.

To meet their energy needs, South Korea and Japan have built nuclear power plants and also produce small amounts oil. Still, it is not enough. These countries must import oil and other resources to meet their energy needs.

Reading Check Which country is richest in mineral resources?

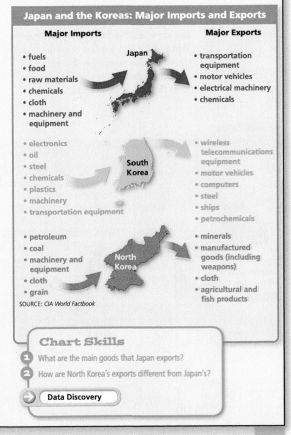

Japan and the Koreas: Major Imports and Exports

Major Imports

Japan
- fuels
- food
- raw materials
- chemicals
- cloth
- machinery and equipment

South Korea
- electronics
- oil
- steel
- chemicals
- plastics
- machinery
- transportation equipment

North Korea
- petroleum
- coal
- machinery and equipment
- cloth
- grain

Major Exports

Japan
- transportation equipment
- motor vehicles
- electrical machinery
- chemicals

South Korea
- wireless telecommunications equipment
- motor vehicles
- computers
- steel
- ships
- petrochemicals

North Korea
- minerals
- manufactured goods (including weapons)
- cloth
- agricultural and fish products

SOURCE: *CIA World Factbook*

Chart Skills

1. What are the main goods that Japan exports?

2. How are North Korea's exports different from Japan's?

 **Data Discovery**

READING CHECK North Korea

CHART SKILLS 1. transport equipment, motor vehicles, electrical machinery, chemicals **2.** Japan exports a lot of advanced technical equipment. North Korea exports more basic resources, such as minerals and agricultural products.

- **Identify Main Ideas** Why do many other countries have a comparative advantage over Japan and the Koreas concerning agriculture? (Many other countries can produce farm goods more cheaply than Japan and the Koreas.)

- **Infer** Why do you think Japan does not want to become completely dependent on other countries for food? (Sample: Other countries could take advantage and raise their food prices.)

Analyze Visuals Analyze the graphics on this page.

- What is one of the major imports of South Korea? (electronics, oil, steel, chemicals, plastics, machinery, transport equipment)

- What imports do North Korea and South Korea have in common? (oil/petroleum, machinery)

Data Discovery

Have students go to myworldgeography.com to find data about Japan and the Koreas.

GEOGRAPHY

Life Underground The skyscraper is the iconic image of densely populated cities in East Asia, but a lot is going on under the surface of many cities in Japan and South Korea. In both countries, much of the underground construction is shopping malls. Japan has more than 80 underground malls, which total over ten million square feet of retail space. During earthquakes, underground malls may actually be safer than structures on the surface. In the devastating 1995 Kobe earthquake, more than 100,000 buildings were destroyed yet the Santica underground mall received only minor damage. The mall became the disaster relief headquarters after the quake.

Adapting to Challenges

- **Problem Solve** How have the Japanese and the Koreans dealt with the problem of earthquakes?
  (building earthquake-resistant structures, using rubber pads under skyscrapers to absorb earthquakes, moving weights in buildings, warning systems)

Analyze Visuals Have students analyze the photographs on this page.

- Would you like to stay in a capsule hotel? Explain. (Sample: No, it seems cramped.)
- How is the furniture in the middle photograph different from the furniture you use? (Sample: Furniture in the photograph is smaller.)

→ **Culture Close-up**

Learn more about population and culture in Japan and the Koreas at myworldgeography.com.

---

my World IN NUMBERS

About **10** typhoons pass over Japan each year. Japan's typhoon season is **6** months long.

Adapting to Challenges

The people of the region have learned to live in a challenging environment. In the past, most buildings in Japan and the Koreas were made of wood. Fires, earthquakes, and floods might destroy them, but these wooden structures could be quickly rebuilt.

Today, the people of Japan and the Koreas use modern technology to build structures that can withstand the forces of nature. Rubber pads under skyscrapers dampen the shock waves of earthquakes. There are also computers that move weights in the base of the skyscrapers to keep the buildings balanced.

Safety Alerts Early warning systems also help people to take safety measures during earthquakes. One system developed in Japan can give people as much as 30 seconds warning. This might not seem like very much time. But every extra second is important when an earthquake is about to hit.

66 School children will be able to take shelter under their desks in classrooms if they have five seconds. In fact . . . if we have 10 seconds to prepare for major tremors, we can reduce the number of deaths caused by quakes significantly. 99
—Yoshinori Sugihara

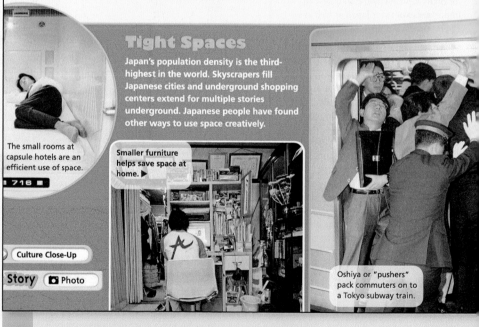

The small rooms at capsule hotels are an efficient use of space.

Tight Spaces

Japan's population density is the third-highest in the world. Skyscrapers fill Japanese cities and underground shopping centers extend for multiple stories underground. Japanese people have found other ways to use space creatively.

Smaller furniture helps save space at home. ▶

Culture Close-Up

Story 📷 Photo

Oshiya or "pushers" pack commuters on to a Tokyo subway train.

READING CHECK Sample: To deal with limited space, the Japanese and the South Koreans have built apartments and offices with multiple floors and have extended shopping centers underground.

ASSESSMENT 1. leaves on the trees **2.** a lack of something **3.** Sample: Because some countries have a comparative advantage over Japan concerning agriculture, Japan imports many food products. **4.** Since Japan is a mountainous country, it has limited flat areas where a large population can live and farm. As a result,

COMMON MISCONCEPTIONS

Japan and Urban Crowding Although Japan's urban areas are very crowded, they are not the most crowded in the world. The ten most densely populated urban areas in the world are:
(1) Mumbai, India, (2) Kolkata, India, (3) Karachi, Pakistan, (4) Lagos, Nigeria, (5) Shenzhen, China, (6) Seoul/Incheon, South Korea, (7) Taipei, Taiwan, (8) Chennai, India, (9) Bogota, Colombia, and (10) Shanghai, China. The most densely populated metropolitan area in Japan is Osaka/Kobe/Kyoto, which ranks thirty-eighth on the list of the world's most crowded cities.

Environmental Threats Managing resources is another challenge. With so many people crowded together, it is easy to use limited resources too quickly.

North Korea and South Korea have lost much of their forest land by cutting trees faster than they can grow back. Without tree cover, rain water washes quickly into rivers and streams and flooding becomes worse. As a result, soil needed for farming is washed away.

Overfishing is also a problem in the region. Near Japan, fish were taken from coastal waters too quickly. Now, ships must go far out to sea to find fish.

Intensive use of the land has resulted in serious pollution in all three countries. Factories, cars, and farms create air and water pollution.

While much remains to be done, the people in South Korea and Japan have pushed their governments to make changes. Their governments are working to reduce air and water pollution, find cleaner fuels, and recycle more waste.

The North Korean government has made less progress addressing these problems. The shortage of clean water for drinking and bathing is still a problem in that country.

Reading Check What are two ways people in Japan and the Koreas have adapted to their environment?

Overfishing threatens to drive the tuna fish into extinction. ▼

Section 1 Assessment

Key Terms

1. What is foliage?
2. What does scarcity mean?
3. Use the term *comparative advantage* to describe the products that Japan imports.

Key Ideas

4. How do physical features affect land use in this region?
5. How have Japan and the Koreas used technology to adapt to the forces of nature?
6. What environmental problems have Japan and the Koreas faced?

Think Critically

7. **Analyze Cause and Effect** How does scarcity make countries interdependent?
8. **Compare and Contrast** Why does North Korea have less agricultural production than Japan and South Korea?

Essential Question

How much does geography shape a country?

9. How much does geography affect the problems that countries in this region face? Are there other factors that influence pollution in these countries? Go to your Student Journal and record your answer.

GUIDE ON THE SIDE

- **Cause and Effect** What are some of the main causes of air and water pollution in Japan and the Koreas? (factories, cars, farms)
- **Identify Evidence** What is some evidence that shows that North Korea is dealing with serious water pollution? (shortage of clean water for drinking and bathing)

Analyze Visuals Ask students to analyze the photograph.

- Based on the photograph, do you think fishing is a successful industry in Japan and the Koreas? Explain. (Yes; the fisherman has caught a huge amount of fish.)
- Based on the photograph, do you think environmentalists are concerned about the fishing industry in Japan and the Koreas? (Sample: Yes, the huge amount of fish shown in the picture suggests that massive amounts of fish are caught daily in the region, which might lead to their extinction.)

History of Japan and the Koreas

OBJECTIVES

Students will know

- the history of Korea's dynasties and Japan's shogun system.
- foreign impact on Japan and the Koreas.
- the rise of Japan's economy after 1945.

Students will be able to

- identify the main ideas and details in the history of Japan and the Koreas.
- make decisions about significant events in the history of Japan and the Koreas.

SET EXPECTATIONS

In this section, students will

- read History of Japan and the Koreas.
- make decisions about important historical events.
- go On Assignment in Japan and the Koreas and get closer to the history of the region.

CORE CONCEPTS

You may wish to teach or reteach the following lessons from the Core Concepts Handbook:

- Economic Development, pp. 64–65
- Families and Societies, pp. 88–89
- Measuring Time, pp. 118–119

KEY

Differentiated Instruction

- **L1** Special Needs
- **L2** Extra Support
- **L3** On-Level
- **L4** Challenge

English Language Instruction

- **ELL** Beginner
- **ELL** Early Intermediate
- **ELL** Intermediate
- **ELL** Early Advanced
- **ELL** Advanced

1 Connect
Make learning meaningful

Make Connections Ask students if they think social classes, such as the lower class, exist in the United States. Then have them identify the various classes, including the largest and the smallest. Ask, In what ways do social classes in the United States affect people's lives? Do you think the class system should change? Why or why not?

ELL Intermediate/Early Advanced Ask students to list the social classes in their homeland using their native language. Then ask them to translate this list into English.

Activate Prior Knowledge Remind students that in the previous lesson, they learned that industrial development has caused severe pollution in Japan and the Koreas. Ask them to predict the ways in which the region's economy became industrial. Ask, Why would this change cause pollution?

L2 Extra Support Draw students' attention to the visuals in the previous lesson that show economic development and pollution in Japan.

Prepare Follow the steps in the section **Preview.** Preteach the Key Terms. Then have students complete *Word Wise* in their journals using in-text clues and the glossary for help.

2 Experience
Teach knowledge and skills

Read Use **Background** notes and **Guide on the Side** questions to model active reading. Have students use *Take Notes* in their **Student Journal** to identify foreign influences on Japan during the 1800s and 1900s. Have students complete **21st Century Online Tutor** *Main Ideas and Details,* and apply this skill to reading the section.

L2 Extra Support Have students read *Historical Roots.* Then ask them to create a two-column chart labeled *Main Ideas* and *Details* and take notes as they reread.

ELL Intermediate Post this model for writing sequence sentences: First the Civil War happened, and then the _____ happened. Next the _____ happened.

L4 Challenge Have students research the development of movable metal type by the Koreans and write a brief essay on how it improved printing.

 **Practice: myWorld Activity** Students will make a top-five list of the most significant events in the history of Japan and the Koreas. **Step-by-Step Instructions** and **More Activities** follow on p. T44.

SECTION 2 RESOURCE GUIDE

FOR THE STUDENT

my worldgeography.com Student Center
- Active Atlas
- Data Discovery

Student Edition (print and online)
- History of Japan and the Koreas

Student Journal (print and online)
- Section 2 Word Wise
- Section 2 Take Notes

21st Century Learning Online Tutor
- Identify Main Ideas and Details
- Make Decisions

FOR THE TEACHER

my worldgeography.com Teacher Center
- Online Lesson Planner
- Presentations for Projection
- SuccessTracker

ProGuide: East and Southeast Asia
- Section 2 Lesson Plan, pp. T42–T43
- 🏃 myWorld Activity Step-by-Step Instructions, p. T44
- Activity Support: Top Five List, p. T45
- myWorld Geography Enrichment, p. T46
- Section Quiz, p. T47

Accelerating the Progress of ELLs
- Reading Support Strategies, p. 42

3 Understand
Assess understanding

Review Review *Word Wise* and *Take Notes* in their **Student Journal.**

Assess Knowledge and Skills Use the Section Assessment and Section Quiz to check students' progress.

Assess Understanding Review students' responses to the Section Assessment Essential Question prompt.

Remediate Use these strategies to review and remediate.

If students struggle to . . .	Try these strategies.
Describe the shogun system in Japan	Ask one student to be the emperor's army, and five students to be the shogun's army. Is the shogun or emperor more powerful?
Identify Main Ideas and Details	In the text, tell students to look for which sentence describes what happens in the surrounding sentences.
Make Decisions	Show students how to make a pros and cons list.

ELL Support

ELL Objective Students will be able to use English to express main ideas and details.

Cultural Connections To connect students to the main ideas and details in the history of Japan and the Koreas, have students share what they think is the most important event in their personal history or their homeland's history.

ELL Early Intermediate/Intermediate Content Tip Remind students that when we refer to the "main" idea, we also mean the "most important" idea.

🏃 **ELL Activity** Say aloud the main idea: "Japan's economy got worse, but then it got better quickly." Then have students imagine that they are reporters who need to find out more details about this statement. Have them write five questions to find out this information. Remind them to think of *what, when, where, why,* and *how* questions. Then have students use the text to answer these questions. **(Verbal)**

myWorld Activity   Step-by-Step Instructions

  30 min

Best of the Best

OBJECTIVES

Students will

- evaluate the significance of events in the history of Japan and the Koreas.
- decide which events to include in a historical exhibit about Japan and the Koreas.

LEARNING STYLE

- Interpersonal
- Verbal

21st Century Learning

- Make Decisions

MATERIALS

- Activity Support: Top Five List, p. T45

Activity Steps

1. Tell the students to imagine that they are part of the research staff for an Asian history museum located in the United States. This museum is planning an exhibit about the history of Japan and the Koreas. In this exhibit, the museum wants to highlight the five most significant historical events in the history of this region.

2. Divide the class into four research teams. Have each team review History of Japan and the Koreas to look for events they consider most important. Students should take notes on why they should be included in the exhibit.

   ELL Beginner To help ELL students understand ranking, explain the significance of using numbers 1–5 and have them repeat the first 5 cardinal numbers after you.

L2 Extra Support To help students choose significant events, have them look for clues such as big historical changes or effects.

3. Each team should choose the five most significant events that they have found, rank them from 1 to 5, and then list them in *Activity Support: Top Five List.* Also, students should list the reasons why these events should be included in the exhibit. Remind students that this exhibit is for a U.S. audience. Then have students answer the questions at the bottom of the *Top Five List.*

4. Have each team present their top five events and argue persuasively for including them in the exhibit. Post all suggested events.

5. After the presentations, have students either vote or come to consensus by discussion on which five events should be included in the museum exhibit.

More Activities From myWorld Teachers

Local Connection Invite a local veteran from the Korean War to visit the classroom and talk about his or her experiences during the war. Ask students to prepare questions. **(Verbal/Visual)**

Samurai Armor Using the Internet or library, have students research samurai armor. Make sure they find out during what period the samurai wore armor and

why they stopped. Then have them draw a picture of this armor and write a paragraph that explains why the samurai stopped wearing this armor. **(Verbal/Visual)**

 Japan and Korea Lead a discussion about Japan's interaction with Korea from 1870 to World War II. Ask what effects Japan had on Korea. Have pairs of students role play a reflection on the past from both perspectives. **(Kinesthetic/Verbal)**

my worldgeography.com (Teacher Center) ➡ Find additional resources in the online Teacher Center.

Name _____ Class _____ Date _____

myWorld Activity Support   **Top Five List**

Best of the Best

Directions List and describe what your team thinks are the top five most significant historical events for Japan and the Koreas in the left column. Then state the reasons why your team chose each event in the right column. Answer the questions at the bottom of the page. Use extra paper if needed.

Events and Descriptions	Reasons
1. Event: _____ **Description:** _____	**1. Reasons:** _____ _____
2. Event: _____ **Description:** _____	**2. Reasons:** _____ _____
3. Event: _____ **Description:** _____	**3. Reasons:** _____ _____
4. Event: _____ **Description:** _____	**4. Reasons:** _____ _____
5. Event: _____ **Description:** _____	**5. Reasons:** _____ _____

1. Do you agree with your team that the first event listed above is more important than the other four? Why or why not?

_____

_____

2. What other events did your team discuss but leave out of the top five? Briefly explain why they were not included.

_____

_____

Name _____ Class _____ Date _____

Enrichment: Making Celadon

Directions Read the selection below. Answer the questions that follow and complete the activity.

Celadon is a type of pottery with a distinctive jade-green glaze. The Koreans significantly advanced the art of celadon making. For example, they were the first to use inlaid decorations, such as flowers or birds, beneath the glaze. The process of making this attractive pottery involves the following steps.

1. Gather the clay. Clay was usually gathered from riverbanks in certain regions in the Koreas.

2. Place the clay on a wheel, a device that spins the clay. As the clay spins, use your hands to mold it into the desired shape.

3. Engrave the clay with various designs.

4. Fire the shaped clay in a kiln. A kiln is an oven used for heating clay for pottery or bricks. This process hardens the clay.

5. Take the clay pottery out of the kiln. Check the piece for cracks and defects.

6. Dip the pottery into a glaze, which is often made of ground rice stalk mixed with ash. Allow the piece to dry.

7. Then place the glazed piece back in the kiln for the final firing.

This entire process can take days and, at times, weeks. Korean artisans are often perfectionists. They often destroy any pottery that does not meet their standards.

1. Give an example of how the Koreans advanced the art of celadon making.

_____

_____

2. What is a kiln?

_____

_____

3. **Activity** Draw a design for a piece of celadon. Decide what function your piece would have, such as a bowl or a pitcher. Then create a design to decorate it based on images of Korean pottery you research.

Name _____ Class _____ Date _____

Section Quiz

Directions Answer the following questions using what you learned
in Section 2.

1. _____ What dynasty ruled the Korean
peninsula from A.D. 668 to A.D. 935?
  a. Meiji
  b. Qin
  c. Silla
  d. Tokugawa

2. _____ Which of the following words best
describes Japan's foreign policy during
the Tokugawa?
  a. competitive
  b. isolation
  c. friendly
  d. open

3. _____ Which of the following countries did
Japan take control of in 1910?
  a. Korea
  b. Mongolia
  c. Russia
  d. China

4. _____ What type of government ruled
North Korea after World War II?
  a. communist
  b. democratic
  c. dictatorship
  d. oligarchy

5. _____ The Japanese government helped
Japan's economy to grow by supporting
  a. athletes and education.
  b. education and job training.
  c. the arts and job training.
  d. athletes and the arts.

6. In the table below, list the five levels of Japanese society during
medieval times, from top to bottom.

Five Levels of Medieval Society in Japan
1.
2.
3.
4.
5.

History of Japan and the Koreas

- Model preparing to read by previewing the Key Ideas, Key Terms, headings, visuals, and captions. Have students make predictions about what they will learn. For ELL support, post the prompt, "I predict I will read about . . ."

- Preview and practice the reading skill, Identify Main Ideas and Details, by using examples from a recent school assembly.

- Preteach this section's high-use Academic Vocabulary and Key Terms using the table on the next page and in-text definitions. Have students practice Key Terms by completing the *Word Wise* page in their journals.

Historical Roots

- **Identify Details** For about how many years have people lived on the Korean peninsula and the Japanese islands? (about 30,000 years)

- **Identify Main Ideas** Ideas from what country strongly influenced the Korean Kingdoms? (China)

Reading Skill

Identify Main Ideas and Details While they read, have students practice this skill by completing the *Take Notes* graphic organizer in the **Student Journal.**

Section 2

History of Japan and the Koreas

Key Ideas
- Japan and the Koreas all have long histories.
- Japan built an empire early in the 1900s but lost this empire at the end of World War II.
- Korea was divided into two countries, North Korea and South Korea, after the Korean War.
- Japan's economy grew rapidly after World War II.

Key Terms • shogun • samurai • Meiji Restoration • Korean War • constitutional monarchy   Visual Glossary

Reading Skill: Identify Main Ideas and Details Take notes using the graphic organizer in your journal.

The imperial palace in Seoul, South Korea ▼

he people of Japan and the Koreas have adapted to their environment by building skyscrapers that survive the tremors of earthquakes. These nations have also needed to survive political and cultural tremors, such as wars and invasions. Japan and the Koreas have changed since their beginnings, but they are still standing.

Historical Roots

People have lived in this region for about 30,000 years. Powerful kingdoms have influenced the history of these countries, but each has charted its own course.

Korean Dynasties For thousands of years, kingdoms rose and fell on the Korean peninsula. At times, Chinese empires controlled parts of the peninsula. Ideas from China, especially Confucianism and Buddhism, influenced the Korean kingdoms.

In A.D. 668, the kingdom of Silla conquered the other Korean kingdoms. They pushed the Chinese empire off the peninsula and created a strong government. This dynasty, rulers in the same family, lasted until A.D. 935. After that, a series of dynasties kept the peninsula united for centuries.

ACADEMIC VOCABULARY

High-Use Word	Definition and Sample Sentence
grant	*v.* to give *The government granted ten acres of land to the farmer.*
occupy	*v.* to take over, control *The army occupied the territory north of the river.*

Korean Achievements Under the various emperors, a unique society developed. Emperor Sejong called for a new writing system to be created in the 1400s. The system, called Hangul, is still used today. The Koreans also invented moveable metal type. This made printing easier. Korean potters also made delicate porcelain that is valued throughout the world.

Emperors and Shoguns in Japan
Around the time of the Silla dynasty in Korea, Japan became a unified country under an emperor. People believed the emperor was descended from a goddess.

For much of Japan's history, however, the emperors were not strong. Powerful military leaders called **shoguns** controlled Japan's government.

At times, neither the emperor nor the shoguns had complete control over all of the country. Some powerful landowners had their own armies. They granted land to **samurai**, or warrior lords, who supported them. These landowners fought each other to gain power. This created a lot of conflict in Japanese society.

In 1603, a shogun called Tokugawa Ieyasu (toh koo GAH wah ee yay AH soo) came to power. Ieyasu and the Tokugawa shoguns that followed him tried to bring peace to Japan. The Tokugawa brought the powerful landowners under the shogun's control.

The Tokugawa closed the country off from contact with most other countries. They wanted to keep outside forces from disrupting Japanese society.

grant, *v.,* to give

- **Problem Solve** How did the Koreans make printing easier? (They invented moveable type.)
- **Identify Details** What was the name of the shogun that came to power in 1603? (Tokugawa Ieyasu)

Analyze Visuals Have students analyze the graphic on this page

- How were samurai and knights similar? (They both were trained warriors who protected the lands of lords; they both followed a code of honor.)
- Do you think a samurai or a knight would more likely be able to read? Explain. (Samurai; the samurai valued education and many of them studied literature and poetry. Knights were generally not highly educated.)

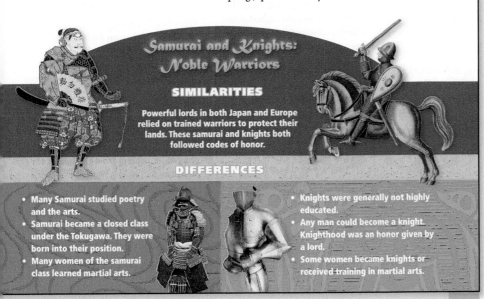

Samurai and Knights: Noble Warriors

SIMILARITIES

Powerful lords in both Japan and Europe relied on trained warriors to protect their lands. These samurai and knights both followed codes of honor.

DIFFERENCES

- Many Samurai studied poetry and the arts.
- Samurai became a closed class under the Tokugawa. They were born into their position.
- Many women of the samurai class learned martial arts.

- Knights were generally not highly educated.
- Any man could become a knight. Knighthood was an honor given by a lord.
- Some women became knights or received training in martial arts.

HISTORY

Perry's Treaty When four U.S. ships entered Edo Bay in 1853, the Japanese people who saw them were astounded. They had never seen steamships before, calling these vessels "giant dragons puffing smoke." Soon the Japanese realized that the vessels were a U.S. fleet commanded by Commodore Perry.

Perry wanted Japan's emperor to sign a treaty that would open trade between the United States and Japan. Usually, the Tokugawa officials decided on how to deal with foreigners. However, they knew that the United States had superior military power. Because of this, the officials asked feudal nobles for advice. The response was divided. Some nobles urged developing relations with the West. Doing this, they argued, would help strengthen Japan. Others wanted to throw the foreigners out. Later, Japan signed Perry's treaty.

- **Categorize** What were the classes of Japanese society under Tokugawa rule? List them in order from highest to lowest. (large landowners, samurai, peasants, craftspeople, merchants)

- **Compare and Contrast** How was Japanese culture similar to Korean culture? (Sample: Both cultures were strongly influenced by China.)

International Conflicts and Connections

- **Identify Details** When did the first Europeans arrive in Japan? (around 1600)

Analyze Visuals Have students analyze the picture on this page.

- Why do you think Western-style clothing became popular in the Meiji court? (Sample: The Meiji court wanted to make Japan as modern as nations in the West. Wearing Western-style clothing went along with this approach.)

myWorld Activity

Best of the Best Find Step-by-Step Instructions and an Activity Support on pp. T44–T45. **(Interpersonal/Verbal)**

▲ A dinner at the palace of Emperor Meiji. Western-style clothing became popular in the Meiji court.

myWorld Activity
Best of the Best

The Tokugawa created strict divisions between nobles and commoners. People were not allowed to move between these two groups. The nobles were mostly the large landowners and the samurai. The large landowners had the highest status. The highest-ranking commoners were peasants (or small farmers). Below them were craftspeople and merchants. Peasants made up 80 percent of the population.

Before the Tokugawa, Japan had close ties with other countries, particularly China and Korea. Buddhism had spread from Korea into Japan. Many Japanese studied Chinese literature and art. The Japanese writing system was based mainly on the Chinese writing system.

New forms of art developed during the Tokugawa period. The country was prosperous. Wealthy nobles and merchants supported artists who created new styles of theater and painting.

Reading Check How did The Tokugawa try to bring stability to Japanese society?

International Conflicts and Connections

Early in the 1800s, both Japan and Korea were largely cut off from the rest of the world. By the beginning of the 1900s, both nations had been pulled into international conflicts and trade networks.

Early Contact with Europeans Ships from Europe first arrived in Japan and Korea around 1600. Both kingdoms had decided to keep Western merchants and missionaries away. Korea allowed only Chinese and Japanese traders. It attacked American and French ships trying to enter its ports. This isolation, or lack of contact, continued until the mid-1800s in Japan and even longer in Korea.

Changes Come to Japan In 1854, the American commander Matthew C. Perry sailed into a Japanese port despite the Tokugawa ban on foreigners. The Japanese knew that Perry's ship carried powerful weapons. So they accepted the trade agreement that Perry brought from the United States. Soon other nations pushed Japan to sign similar treaties.

Many Japanese people thought that these trade agreements were unfair to Japan. They blamed the Tokugawa shogun for signing these treaties. Many Japanese people felt change was needed to make Japan a more powerful country.

In 1868, new leaders arose and pushed out the Tokugawa shogun. They brought back the emperor, but they told him what to do. This time in Japanese history is called **Meiji Restoration**. It marks the return to power of Emperor Meiji.

READING CHECK The Tokugawa created strict divisions between social groups.

QUICK FACTS

Kamikaze During World War II, some Japanese pilots were ordered by Japan's military to fly their planes into enemy ships. The pilots who went on these suicide missions were called kamikaze, or "divine wind." Kamikaze planes were often loaded with extra gasoline tanks and bombs, which made them more destructive when they crashed into a ship. In total, kamikaze attacks sank 34 ships. At the battle of Okinawa, kamikazes killed almost 5,000 U.S. soldiers. The best defense against a kamikaze was to surround the largest ship with smaller destroyers. When the kamikaze attacked a large ship, the destroyers would direct all of their fire on the approaching kamikaze.

The Rise of Japan Japan's new leaders expanded its industry and military. They also increased its power in the region.

In 1910, the Japanese took control over Korea. It was a difficult time for Koreans. They were forced to do hard work in new Japanese industries. They had to learn to speak Japanese, and many were forced to take Japanese sounding names. Japanese control of Korea was harmful to both the Korean people and culture.

Later Japan also invaded other countries. It took over large areas in the north of China as well as Formosa or Taiwan.

When World War II broke out, Japan joined on the side of Germany. Japan soon invaded Southeast Asia. The United States and Japan grew further apart. In 1941, Japan attacked the United States Navy at Pearl Harbor, Hawaii. As a result, the United States entered World War II.

In 1945, the United States dropped atomic bombs on the Japanese cities of Hiroshima and Nagasaki. The resulting casualties were huge, and Japan surrendered. It lost all the lands it had invaded, including Korea.

Reading Check How did Japan's empire grow and then shrink?

A Japanese fighter plane called a "Zero" ▼

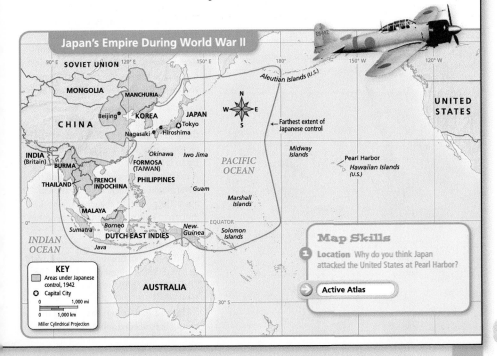

Japan's Empire During World War II

Farthest extent of Japanese control

Map Skills

1 **Location** Why do you think Japan attacked the United States at Pearl Harbor?

 Active Atlas

KEY
Areas under Japanese control, 1942
⊕ Capital City
0 — 1,000 mi
0 — 1,000 km
Miller Cylindrical Projection

READING CHECK Japan pushed China out of Korea and made Korea a colony. Japan then took over areas of China. Japan attacked Pearl Harbor. The United States declared war on Japan. The United States defeated Japan, causing Japan to lose the lands it had invaded.

MAP SKILLS Sample: Japan might have felt that Pearl Harbor threatened Japanese territories in the Pacific.

- **Cause and Effect** What caused the United States to enter World War II? (The Japanese attack on Pearl Harbor)

- **Identify Evidence** What evidence shows that Japan treated the Koreans harshly during the Japanese occupation of Korea? (The Koreans did the hard work in new Japanese factories and had to learn Japanese.)

Analyze Visuals Have students analyze the historical map on this page.

- What major Chinese city did Japan control in 1942? (Beijing)

- Japan conquered only a part of what large island? (New Guinea)

→ **Active Atlas**

Have students go to myworldgeography.com to see more maps about Japan and the Koreas.

CORE CONCEPTS: TYPES OF MAPS

Review Core Concept 1.5 before discussing the map on this page. Review the various types of maps, including physical maps, political maps, and special-purpose maps, and the characteristics of each. Then ask students what type of map is on this page.

(political map) What are some of the characteristics that identify this map? The map below shows the demilitarized zone located between North Korea and South Korea. Does this type of feature fit with this type of map? Explain.

Japan and the Koreas Since World War II

- **Summarize** How did the Korean War develop? (After World War II, the Soviet Union occupied northern Korea and the United States occupied southern Korea. A communist government developed in the north and a democratic government developed in the south. Both governments wanted to rule Korea. Soon North Korea invaded South Korea.)

- **Analyze Text** Do you consider a constitutional monarchy to be a democracy? Explain. (Yes, it is a type of democracy because the Japanese people are allowed to vote for their leaders).

Analyze Visuals Have students analyze the political map on this page.

- Based on the map, do you think North Korea or South Korea is more strongly influenced by China? Explain. (Sample: North Korea is more influenced by China since North Korea borders China to the north. South Korea does not border China.)

- Based on the map, what do the cities of P'yongyang and Seoul have in common? (Both are on the coast and both are situated at the mouth of a major river.)

Japan and the Koreas Since World War II

After World War II, Japan focused on rebuilding its government and its economy. In Korea, conflict quickly resumed. This conflict would divide a country that had been united for centuries.

The Korean War Japan's control of Korea ended after Japan surrendered at the end of World War II. At that time, the United States occupied the southern part of Korea. The Soviet Union occupied the northern part of the country. The United States and the Soviet Union disagreed about how to unite the two parts of Korea. They asked the United Nations to help, but they could not reach agreement.

Two new governments developed. One was a communist government in the north, which the Soviet Union supported. The other was a democratic government in the south, which the United States supported. Both governments claimed to rule Korea.

North Korea invaded South Korea in 1950. This marked the beginning of the **Korean War**. Hoping to limit the spread of communism, the United States led United Nations troops sent to defend South Korea. The Soviet Union and China aided North Korea.

Neither side won. Instead, they agreed to stop fighting in 1953. The two sides drew a new border. A strip along the border was declared a demilitarized zone, an area that neither army is allowed to enter. The peninsula was split into two countries: the communist Democratic People's Republic of Korea in the north—or North Korea, and the Republic of Korea in the south—or South Korea.

Japan's Recovery The United States occupied Japan after World War II. With the help of the United States, the Japanese created a new system of government. Japan is now a constitutional monarchy. A **constitutional monarchy** is a system of government in which the constitution limits the powers of the emperor or the monarch. Power lies in the hands of the voters, who elect their leaders.

Japan also needed to rebuild its economy after the war. Bombing had destroyed nearly all of the country's industry. The Korean War helped Japan's recovery get started.

U.S. and U.N. troops were based in Japan. They needed supplies and labor.

occupy, *v.,* to take over, control

South Korean soldiers patrol the border along the demilitarized zone. ▼

Two Koreas

125° E
130° E

CHINA

NORTH KOREA

Demilitarized Zone

P'yongyang

Seoul

SOUTH KOREA

35° N

Korea Strait

0   100 mi
0   100 km
Lambert Conformal Conic Projection

N W E S

READING CHECK Japan's economy industrialized.

CHART SKILLS 1970s

ASSESSMENT 1. A shogun was a military leader in Japan who strongly influenced the government. A samurai was a warrior in Japan who was hired by landowners to protect their land. **2.** The emperor was reestablished; industry expanded; military power expanded. **3.** The emperor or monarch of a nation is limited by that nation's

ECONOMICS

Zaibatsu After the Meiji Restoration in 1868, several cartels formed in Japan. Each cartel was organized around a single family. These groups came to be called zaibatsu. The four main zaibatsu included Mitsui, Mitsubishi, Sumitomo, and Yasuda. All of them owned banks, which they used to gain the money needed for their business ventures. The growth of the zaibatsu soared during the early 1900s. After World War II, the Allied forces ordered Japan to dissolve the zaibatsu. Technically, Japan did this by making individual companies independent from their parent companies. However, in the early 1950s, these individual companies formed enterprise groups that were similar in structure to the zaibatsu. These groups pooled their resources, which allowed them to make large enough investments in developing industries to make these industries competitive worldwide. In this way, the enterprise groups spurred Japan's economy.

The Japanese people went to work to meet those needs.

The Japanese built new factories to replace the ones destroyed during the war. These factories had the most modern technology. They produced goods better and cheaper than the old factories.

The Japanese government supported education and job training. It also encouraged people to work hard and save their money. Banks used these savings to make loans to businesses. This helped the economy to grow.

Japan had a well-educated workforce and modern equipment in its factories. Japan produced and exported well-made products such as cars, electronics, and cameras. Those products attracted buyers in many parts of the world. Exports helped Japan's economy grow very quickly for the following 30 years, and the Japanese people grew wealthier.

Reading Check How did the Korean War affect Japan?

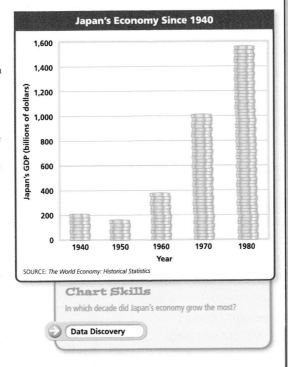

Japan's Economy Since 1940

Japan's GDP (billions of dollars)

SOURCE: *The World Economy: Historical Statistics*

Chart Skills

In which decade did Japan's economy grow the most?

▸ Data Discovery

Section 2 Assessment

Key Terms

1. Who were the shogun and the samurai?
2. What happened during the Meiji Restoration?
3. What is a constitutional monarchy?

Key Ideas

4. How did China influence the culture of Japan and Korea?
5. How did the Tokugawa change Japanese society?
6. Why was Korea divided after World War II?

Think Critically

7. **Draw Inferences** Why might the Koreans have wanted to create their own writing system rather than continuing to use the Chinese system?
8. **Analyze Cause and Effect** What factors helped the Japanese rebuild their economy after World War II?

? Essential Question

How much does geography shape a country?

9. Both Japan and Korea chose to limit contact with outsiders at certain times during their histories. How do you think their geography helped them to do that? Go to your Student Journal and record your answers.

constitution. **4.** Confucianism, Buddhism, Chinese writing system **5.** It created strict divisions between social groups. **6.** After World War II, the Soviet Union supported the communist government in North Korea and the United States supported the democratic government in South Korea. Soon a war started between North and South Korea. Neither side won, and the two countries remained separated. **7.** to develop a national identity **8.** supplying troops after the Korean War, government support of education, banks making loans to businesses **9.** Sample: Japan's chain of islands helped the Japanese to isolate themselves from foreigners.

Japan's Occupation of Korea

OBJECTIVES

Students will

- use primary sources to compare and contrast viewpoints about Japan's occupation of Korea.
- **21st Century Learning** synthesize information about Japan's occupation of Korea.
- **ELL** understand the terms *independence* and *liberty* and how they relate to each other.

SET EXPECTATIONS

In this lesson, students will

- read and analyze two documents about Japan's occupation of Korea.
- create a song, poster, or leaflet that protests Japan's actions in Korea during the occupation.

1 Connect

To help students understand *liberty* and *freedom,* have them recall times when they were told to do something they didn't want to do. Examples could include being grounded for doing something wrong or being told to do chores around the house. Ask students how they felt about being told to do these things. Did they think what they were told to do was fair? Did they have the desire for more freedom to choose their own activities? Would the situation be worse if a foreign government told them what to do instead of their own government? Have them explain.

L4 Challenge Students brainstorm reasons why one country would try to take over another and then write a fictional story about a foreign power that gained control of a nation and its people.

2 Learn

Preview Have students preview the two pages and identify the statue of the Korean independence activist. Ask them to predict why they think this statue was built. Read the Key Idea, glossary terms, and definitions. Clarify any questions about the meaning of these words.

Read Slowly read aloud the excerpt "Korea's Declaration of Independence" without stopping. Read the document again, this time stopping to read the questions at the left and prompting students to rethink and analyze the meaning of the words. Have students answer the questions using the location of the letters to provide clues. Do the same for the document "Nitobe Inazo's Argument." Lead a discussion starting with their responses to the questions. Ask, How do these documents help us to understand why the Koreans fought for independence against the Japanese? Do you think Koreans still honor this independence movement?

ELL Intermediate Define *independence* as freedom from control of another person or state. Then define *liberty* as freedom to think or act as one chooses. Ask students what these two terms have in common. Is independence possible without liberty?

myWorld Activity: A Call to Protest Divide the class into small groups. Tell the groups to pretend that they are a committee of Korean activists living during the Japanese occupation of their country. Then have them decide whether to compose a song, make a poster, or write a leaflet to voice their protest against Japan's occupation of Korea. **(Verbal/Visual/Rhythmic)**

30 min

3 Understand

Review Go back to the Key Idea. Discuss with students the similarities and differences between the two documents.

Assess Have each student complete **Analyze the Documents.** Review their answers to determine if students have met the lesson objectives.

Remediate If students struggle to synthesize, have them make a 2-column table with one column labeled *Like* and the other labeled *Dislike.* Then have them review the two documents and list what they think a Korean would like about each. Then have them list what they think a Korean would dislike. Tell them to express these likes and dislikes in a new way by making a song, poster, or leaflet.

Name _____ Class _____ Date _____

myWorld Activity Support   Guidelines

A Call to Protest

Directions Pretend you are Korean political activists working to change the way Koreans are treated under Japanese occupation. Decide as a group to make one of the following:

- a song that voices the Koreans' protest against Japan's occupation of their nation
- a poster that shows Japan's oppression of Korea and the struggle for Korean independence
- a leaflet that gives evidence of Japan's oppression and argues for Korean independence

Tips for Writing a Protest Song
• Choose a popular melody that you think would work well as a protest song.
• Review the two documents and pick out key points to use in your song.
• Try to write a chorus that rhymes.

Tips for Creating a Protest Poster
• Use images that convey the strong emotion that the Koreans feel against Japanese oppression and for Korean independence.
• Review the two documents and look for ideas that can be conveyed through images.
• Use a slogan that conveys in a few words the Korean cause of independence.

Tips for Writing a Protest Leaflet
• Gather evidence from the two documents about Japan's oppression of Koreans.
• Based on the two documents, make a list of rights that the Korean people are demanding.
• Use the evidence to write a description of Japan's oppression and then list the rights that the Korean people are seeking.
• Use a dramatic, attention-grabbing headline and image for the beginning of the leaflet.

Wrap-Up Share your song, poster, or leaflet with the class. Then explain, What were the common themes in the protest materials? Do these themes relate to oppression in today's world?

_____

_____

_____

How Japan Gained Control of Korea During the Russo-Japanese War (1904–1905), Korea declared neutrality. However, because of pressure by Japan, Korea eventually allowed Japanese forces to use the Korean peninsula for military operations against the Russians. After Japan won the war, the Treaty of Portsmouth gave Japan control of Korea. Then Japan forced Korea's emperor to sign a treaty that made Korea a protectorate of Japan. After this, the Korean emperor appealed to the international community to protect its independence. At a peace conference in 1907, the emperor attempted to convince powerful nations to prevent the Japanese takeover of Korea. This attempt failed. In 1910, Korea was forced to sign a treaty allowing Japan to annex the peninsula.

GUIDE ON THE SIDE

Synthesize Use the lettered prompts to help students synthesize information from the two documents into generalizations about the experiences of Koreans during the Japanese occupation.

ANSWERS

Ⓐ In the proclamation, Korea announces to the world its independence.

Ⓑ The Korean grievances against the Japanese include foreign oppression, the loss to the right to live, restriction of freedom of thought, damage to the dignity of life, and not being able to pursue the intelligent advances of the age in which we live.

Ⓒ Sample: It shows their desire for independence and the courage to state this desire while being oppressed by another country.

Primary Source

Japan's Occupation of Korea

Key Idea
- Koreans under Japanese rule wanted independence, but Japan's government refused to grant them freedom.

J apan took over Korea in 1910. Japanese rule was unpopular. Japan took large amounts of resources from Korea. On March 1, 1919, Korean nationalists released Korea's *Declaration of Independence*. They also protested against Japanese rule. Japan crushed these peaceful demonstrations and continued to rule Korea harshly. The *Declaration of Independence* gives voice to Korea's yearning for freedom. Nitobe Inazo was a Japanese official in Korea. His statement gives the Japanese government's justification for its rule over Korea.

▲ Independence Declaration Day celebration in Korea

Statue of a Korean independence activist ▼

Stop at each circled letter on the right to think about the text. Then answer the question on the left with the same letter.

Ⓐ **Main Idea** What does Korea announce to the world in the declaration?

Ⓑ **Summarize** What are the grievances, or charges, of the Korean people against Japan?

Ⓒ **Infer** The March 1, 1919, protests remain important to Koreans today. Why do you think this is the case?

proclaim, *v.,* announce
agony, *n.,* pain, torment
oppression, *n.,* harsh, unjust rule

Korea Proclaims Its Independence

❝ We herewith <u>proclaim</u> the independence of Korea and the liberty of the Korean
Ⓐ people. We tell it to the world in witness of the equality of all nations. . . . [W]e have come after these long thousands of years to experience the <u>agony</u> of ten years of foreign <u>oppression</u>, with every loss to the right to live, every restriction of the freedom of thought, every damage done to the
Ⓑ dignity of life, every opportunity lost for a share in the intelligent advance of the
Ⓒ age in which we live. ❞
—Korea's *Declaration of Independence,* March 1, 1919

BACKGROUND

ANSWERS

21st Century Learning SYNTHESIZE

To assist your students in synthesizing information from two sources, have students reread the two documents and paraphrase some of the sentences in their own words. Then have them answer the scaffolded questions at the left of each source. After this, have students make a list of the main ideas for each document. Then have them write at least two supporting details below each idea and one statement that uses information from both documents to draw conclusions about Japan's occupation.

GUIDE ON THE SIDE

Stop at each circled letter on the right to think about the text. Then answer the question on the left with the same letter.

D **Identify Bias** What does Nitobe Inazo think of the Korean people?

E **Paraphrase** In your own words, state Nitobe Inazo's reasons for Japanese rule in Korea.

F **Synthesize** Based on Nitobe Inazo's statement, what was Japan's attitude toward Korea during the colonial period?

tutelage, *n.,* instruction, guidance
conviction, *n.,* confidence, belief
steward, *n.,* guardian, supervisor
devolve, *v.,* to fall (to)
uplifting, *n.,* improvement, inspiration

Nitobe Inazo's Argument

❝ I count myself among the best and truest friends of Koreans. I like them . . . . I think they are a capable people who can be trained to a large measure of self-government, for which the present is a period **D** of <u>tutelage</u>. Let them study what we are doing in Korea, and this I say not to . . . boast of some of our achievements. In all humility, but with a firm <u>conviction</u> that Japan is a <u>steward</u> on whom **E** <u>devolves</u> the gigantic task of the <u>uplifting</u> of the Far East, I cannot think that the young Korea is yet **F** capable of governing itself. ❞
—Nitobe Inazo,
colonial administrator, 1919

Nitobe **Inazo**

Japanese troops invading Korea, around 1900 ▼

Analyze the Documents

1. **Compare Viewpoints** Would the Koreans who wrote the *Declaration of Independence* agree that Nitobe Inazo is "among the best and truest friends of Koreans"? Explain.
2. **Writing Task** How would a signer of the Korean declaration respond to Nitobe Inazo's statement? Use both documents to write a paragraph from the signer's viewpoint.

ANSWERS

D Inazo thinks that the Koreans are capable people who can be trained to govern themselves.

E Koreans must learn self-government by studying Japanese achievements in Korea.

F Japan viewed itself as a steward with the task of uplifting Korea and the rest of the Far East.

ANALYZE THE DOCUMENTS 1. No, Inazo views the Korean people as inferior to the Japanese, and that they must learn how to self-govern from the Japanese. **2.** Sample: Japan views itself as superior to Korea. The Japanese feel that they must teach us how to self-govern. Their teaching includes oppression. Such an approach is dictatorial; not a good model for self-government. Korea has a rich history of self-government, and the Korean people are perfectly capable of governing themselves.

ANSWERS

Japan and the Koreas Today

OBJECTIVES

Students will know

- the cultures of Japan and the Koreas.
- the economies of Japan and South Korea.
- the politics and economics of North Korea.

Students will be able to

- summarize Japan and the Koreas Today.
- compare viewpoints about limited and unlimited governments in Japan and the Koreas.

SET EXPECTATIONS

In this section, students will

- read Japan and the Koreas Today.
- compare manga cartoons about limited and unlimited governments.
- go On Assignment in Japan and the Koreas and gather data from charts.

CORE CONCEPTS

You may wish to teach or reteach the following lessons from the Core Concepts Handbook:

- Economic Development, pp. 64–65
- What Is Culture?, pp. 86–87
- The Arts, pp. 94–95

KEY

Differentiated Instruction
- **L1** Special Needs
- **L2** Extra Support
- **L3** On-Level
- **L4** Challenge

English Language Instruction
- **ELL** Beginner
- **ELL** Early Intermediate
- **ELL** Intermediate
- **ELL** Early Advanced
- **ELL** Advanced

1 Connect
Make learning meaningful

Make Connections Ask students to think about the type of art, music, sports, and food that they enjoy. Have them list examples on a sheet of paper. Then ask students to talk about how these preferences do or do not relate to their family, regional, or national culture.

ELL Early Intermediate/Intermediate Provide an English word bank relating to art, music, sports, and food that are popular with young people.

Activate Prior Knowledge Remind students that in the previous lesson, they learned about Japan's economic success after World War II. Ask them to predict if South Korea and North Korea also will have developed successful economies.

L2 Extra Support To help students make predictions about North Korea, have them think about China's command economy under communism. Ask, Is China's economy successful? We know that North Korea is communist too. What might this tell us about their economy?

Prepare Follow the steps in the section **Preview.** Preteach the Key Terms. Then have students complete *Word Wise* in their journals using in-text clues and the glossary for help.

2 Experience
Teach knowledge and skills

Read Use **Background** notes and **Guide on the Side** questions to model active reading. Have students use *Take Notes* in their **Student Journal** to help summarize Japan and the Koreas. Have students complete **21st Century Online Tutor** *Set a Purpose for Reading*, and apply this skill to reading the section.

L2 Extra Support Before reading each part, have students read and paraphrase the heading. After reading, use the headings as a structure for writing a section summary.

ELL Beginner To help English learners discuss Buddhism, have them make visual flashcards for the following words: *monk*, *temple*, and *bell*.

L4 Challenge Have students read and complete *Enrichment: Kim Jong-il* to learn more about the North Korean ruler. Then ask students to write a plot summary from the perspective of the filmmaker kidnapped by Kim Jong-il.

Practice: myWorld Activity Students will compare opinions about limited and unlimited governments. **Step-by-Step Instructions** and **More Activities** follow on p. T52.

SECTION 3 RESOURCE GUIDE

FOR THE STUDENT

my worldgeography.com Student Center
- Data Discovery

Student Edition (print and online)
- Japan and the Koreas Today

Student Journal (print and online)
- Section 3 Word Wise
- Section 3 Take Notes

21st Century Learning Online Tutor
- Set a Purpose for Reading
- Compare Viewpoints

FOR THE TEACHER

my worldgeography.com Teacher Center
- Online Lesson Planner
- Presentations for Projection
- SuccessTracker

ProGuide: East and Southeast Asia
- Section 3 Lesson Plan, pp. T50–T51
- myWorld Activity Step-by-Step Instructions, p. T52
- Activity Support: Brainstorm Guide, p. T53
- myWorld Geography Enrichment, p. T54
- Section Quiz, p. T55

Accelerating the Progress of ELLs
- Peer Learning Strategies, p. 46

---

3 Understand
Assess understanding

Review Review *Word Wise* and *Take Notes* in their **Student Journal.**

Assess Knowledge and Skills Use the Section Assessment and Section Quiz to check students' progress.

Assess Understanding Review students' responses to the Section Assessment Essential Question prompt.

Remediate Use these strategies to review and remediate.

If students struggle to . . .	Try these strategies.
Distinguish between South Korea and North Korea's standard of living	Practice reading the GDP graph that compares North Korea and South Korea.
Compare viewpoints	Assign additional practice with the **21st Century Online Tutor.**
Summarize Japan and the Koreas Today	Explain that a summary is a statement that applies to many things. *I like food* is a summary statement.

ELL Support

ELL Objective Students will be able to use English to compare viewpoints.

Cultural Connections Let students use their native language to describe the political systems in their homeland and in Japan. Have them compare systems.

ELL Advanced Content Tip Have students create a Venn diagram that compares and contrasts the economic development of Japan and South Korea. Then have them predict what a Korean or Japanese citizen might say about their economy.

ELL Activity Have pairs conduct an interview for a magazine about the culture of East Asia. Ask one student to imagine that he or she is a scholar from Japan. Have the other student interview the scholar about Japan's culture. Then have them switch roles and change the topic to South Korea. Both students will use captions, headings, and passages from the section to prepare questions and answers. **(Verbal/Interpersonal)**

myWorld Activity **Step-by-Step Instructions**

 30 min

Political Manga

OBJECTIVES

Students will

- draw manga cartoons that depict limited and unlimited governments.
- compare the viewpoints of limited and unlimited governments.

LEARNING STYLE

- Verbal
- Visual

21st Century Learning

- Compare Viewpoints

MATERIALS

- colored pencils or markers
- Activity Support: Brainstorm Guide, p. T53

Activity Steps

1. Pair students. Tell pairs that they will be drawing manga cartoons that depict limited and unlimited governments. Remind students what limited and unlimited governments are. Tell students that manga cartoons in Japan are often used to give information or opinions about a topic, similar to political cartoons in the United States.

   ELL Early Intermediate If ELL students have difficulty remembering the difference between *limited* and *unlimited*, explain that the prefix *un-* makes the root word mean the opposite. For example, *happy* means showing joy or pleasure; however, *unhappy* means showing sadness.

2. To prepare, have students review examples of manga shown in the text and sample political cartoons from the United States. Ask, How does a cartoon get across an opinion or message?

   L2 Extra Support Point out how these cartoons use facial expressions, actions, symbols, and captions to get across meaning.

3. Pairs should assign one student to draw a single frame cartoon depicting limited government and the other to draw a single frame cartoon showing unlimited government. Have them use the *Activity Support: Brainstorm Guide* to define limited or unlimited governments and to think of ideas.

4. Have each student draw his or her cartoon.

   L4 Challenge Have students create a multiframe manga cartoon about limited or unlimited government. Multiframe cartoons should tell a story.

5. Tell students to explain their cartoon to their partner. Volunteers can share their cartoons with the class.

 More Activities From myWorld Teachers

Local Connection Have students design a cultural exhibition about the religion, recreation, and arts in their region. Have students debate whether it is more important to show the diversity or the common ground of cultural practices in the region. **(Verbal/Visual)**

Interview Have students choose a partner. One person will be the reporter and the other will be an economic advisor for North Korea. Both students should research information about North Korea's economy and prepare to ask or answer questions. They should then conduct an interview. **(Logical/Verbal)**

Comparing Economic Reports Using data from the *CIA World Factbook*, have small groups research the economies of Japan and South Korea and create a presentation about their economic growth. Ask them to list similarities and differences. **(Logical/Verbal)**

 my worldgeography.com **Teacher Center** Find additional resources in the online Teacher Center.

Name _____ Class _____ Date _____

myWorld Activity Support   **Brainstorm Guide**

Political Manga

Directions Answer the questions below to help you brainstorm ideas for your manga cartoon. Then draw your cartoon on the back of this worksheet or on another sheet of paper.

1. What examples are given of a limited government and an unlimited government in the section? How did each type of government affect its citizens?

_____

_____

2. What type of government are you featuring in your manga? What is your opinion of this type of government?

_____

_____

3. What kind of characters do you want to use in your cartoon to get across your opinion? (You can use human and/or animal characters.)

_____

_____

4. A symbol is something that represents something else, like an idea. For example, a rabbit can be used as a symbol to represent a fast Internet connection. What symbol(s) do you want to use in your cartoon? What will the symbol(s) represent?

_____

_____

5. Manga cartoons often exaggerate the features of their characters, for example, ears or hands, to show emotions. What do you think would be an effective way to exaggerate your characters?

_____

_____

Name _____ Class _____ Date _____

Enrichment: Kim Jong-il

Directions Read the selection below. Answer the questions that follow.

Kim Jong-il is the ruler of North Korea. He was born in 1941 in Siberia, Russia (then the Soviet Union). However, the North Korean version claims that Kim Jong-il was born in a log cabin on Mount Paektu, the highest point on the Korean peninsula. In addition, they say that when he was born there was a double rainbow in the sky. Although this story is most likely not true, it shows how the North Korean government and Kim Jong-il have created a sense of mystery about the ruler. Doing this has made Kim Jong-il a mythic figure, and thus more awe inspiring in the eyes of the North Korean people. Also, because of this approach, foreigners have had a difficult time getting accurate information about this leader.

As a result, what is true about Kim Jong-il and what is made up cannot always be easily determined. The following information is most likely accurate. People believe that Kim Jong-il wears platform shoes to make himself appear taller. A lover of movies, he reportedly has a collection of about 20,000 films. Kim's favorite films supposedly include James Bond movies and any movie starring Elizabeth Taylor.

In 1978, Kim kidnapped a South Korean filmmaker and his actress wife and brought them to North Korea to improve filmmaking in his country. This report has been verified by the filmmaker and his wife, who eventually escaped and wrote a memoir about their kidnapping.

Also, experts know for a fact that he was trained by his father Kim Il-sung, the president of North Korea, to succeed him. Soon after his father's death in 1994, Kim Jong-il took control of the country. At first, he encouraged contact with other countries. However, in the 2000s, Kim's foreign policy became unfriendly.

1. Why do you think the North Korean authorities most likely made up a story about Kim Jong-il's birth?

_____

_____

2. Do you think Kim Jong-il has positive, negative, or mixed feelings about Western culture? Explain your answer.

_____

_____

Name _____ Class _____ Date _____

Section Quiz

Directions Answer the following questions using what you learned
in Section 3.

1. _____ Which of the following religions has
recently become very popular in South
Korea?
   a. Buddhism
   b. Christianity
   c. Daoism
   d. Shinto

2. _____ Which of the following caused a
severe economic crisis in Japan during the
1990s?
   a. Taxes were raised too high.
   b. Bad bank practices caused a recession.
   c. Too many workers went on strike.
   d. Trade embargos increased.

3. _____ Which of the following types of
government is found in South Korea?
   a. communism
   b. democracy
   c. dictatorship
   d. monarchy

4. _____ Which of the following pairs of
natural disasters has caused thirteen years
of food shortages in North Korea?
   a. drought and earthquakes
   b. earthquakes and disease
   c. flooding and drought
   d. flooding and earthquakes

5. _____ Which of the following did Japan
import from another country?
   a. anime
   b. karate
   c. tea ceremony
   d. baseball

6. Do you think North Korea and South Korea will ever reunify?
Give three reasons to support your answer.

_____

_____

_____

_____

Japan and the Koreas Today

- Model preparing to read by previewing the Key Ideas, Key Terms, headings, visuals, and captions. Have students make predictions about what they will learn. For ELL support, post the prompt, "I predict I will read about . . ."

- Preview and practice the reading skill, Set a Purpose for Reading, by using examples from your community.

- Preteach this section's high-use Academic Vocabulary and Key Terms using the table on the next page and in-text definitions. Have students practice Key Terms by completing the *Word Wise* page in their journals.

GUIDE ON THE SIDE

Prosperity and Democracy in South Korea

- **Draw Conclusions** What nation do you think had the strongest influence on the formation of a democracy in South Korea? (Sample: United States)

- **Identify Details** What exception did South Korea make concerning their limited government? (The leaders of South Korea did not have to follow these limits if the country faced serious economic or political problems.)

Reading Skill

Set a Purpose for Reading
While they read, have students practice this skill by completing the *Take Notes* graphic organizer in the **Student Journal.**

ANSWERS

Section 3

Japan and the Koreas Today

Key Ideas
- South Korea's economy has grown, and its democracy has become stronger.
- North Korea is a communist dictatorship.
- North Korea's nuclear program is a source of conflict in the region.
- Japan has struggled with economic problems in recent years.

Key Terms
- limited government
- recession
- unlimited government
- Shinto
- dictator

 Visual Glossary

Reading Skill: Set a Purpose for Reading Take notes using the graphic organizer in your journal.

◄ 63 Building, the tallest building in Seoul, South Korea

Japan and the Koreas have faced challenges in recent years. Yet, the people of South Korea and Japan have a good standard of living. These countries have become more influential in the world. By contrast, North Korea is largely isolated. Its people have suffered severe hardship.

Prosperity and Democracy in South Korea

South Korea has become more democratic over the years. It has also become a world economic power.

Growing Democracy The leaders of South Korea approved a constitution in 1948 and began building a new government. They created a **limited government**, that is, a government with powers that are limited by law. However, the constitution also stated that leaders did not have to follow those limits or protect individual rights if the country faced serious problems.

As a result, South Korea's political system was not always democratic. More than once, the military took over the country. Freedom of speech and freedom of the press was not always protected. In 1987, people began to call for change. Many South Koreans joined huge political protests. That year, the leaders changed the constitution.

Under the new constitution, the government cannot take away freedoms even when there are political or economic troubles. Citizens have more rights. The military is less powerful. It has not taken over the government since those reforms.

ACADEMIC VOCABULARY

High-Use Word	Definition and Sample Sentence
aid	*n.* help, assistance *The tornado victims received aid from the government.*

Economic Boom After the Korean War, the leaders of South Korea focused on producing industrial goods for export to other countries. The government supported a number of large companies. It helped them get the money and equipment they needed to make more products. The government also improved the education system.

Now, South Korea exports many high-technology goods, such as cell phones and computers. Its economy is one of the largest in the world. People now live more comfortably and have more belongings.

Still, the growth of South Korea's economy has not been stable. The government borrowed large sums of money from abroad. In the late 1990s, the country had too much debt. This hurt the economy. The economy improved, but the government will have to work to avoid this problem in the future.

Daily Life and Culture As the economy has grown, daily life for the people of South Korea has changed. In the past, most Koreans were farmers. Now, most people live in cities. In addition, South Korea now has contact with many countries. This has changed Korean culture. It has also introduced Korean culture to people throughout the world.

For example, the popular Korean sport of tae kwon do has become very popular outside the country. Tae kwon do became an official Olympic sport in 2000. At the same time, the Koreans have become fans of many sports from abroad. Soccer, in particular, is very popular. Almost every town has its own team. Other sports such

▲ Winner of a gold medal in tae kwon do, South Korea's Hwang Kyungseon (left) at the Beijing Olympics in 2008

as baseball, basketball, and volleyball have a wide following.

Religious life in South Korea has also changed. Christianity spread rapidly through the country after the Korean War. About one quarter of South Korea's population is Christian. In addition, about one quarter of the population is Buddhist. The Buddha's birthday is a national holiday in South Korea. More than ten thousand Buddhist temples dot the landscape. Both foreign visitors and Koreans study Buddhism at these colorful temples. South Koreans enjoy complete religious freedom.

Reading Check How has the South Korean government changed since the 1980s?

READING CHECK The government cannot take away freedoms even when there are political or economic problems. Also, the role of the military has been limited.

GUIDE ON THE SIDE

- **Summarize** How did the South Korean government help improve the economy of South Korea? (The government supported large companies. Also, the government spent money to improve education.)

- **Infer** Recently, the culture of South Korea has changed drastically. Do you think these changes have helped South Korea's economy? Explain. (Sample: Yes, more people are educated now than before. This means more people can do skilled jobs. Also, South Korea now has more interaction with other countries, which helps trade.)

Analyze Visuals Have students analyze the photograph on this page.

- How can you tell from the photograph that the martial artists are competing in a contest? (The coordinated colors of their helmets and jackets indicate that they belong to teams.)

- Based on the picture, why do you think tae kwon do is a popular sport? (Sample: because it has a lot of action and excitement)

QUICK FACTS

Eternal President Four years after the death of North Korea's ruler, Kim Il-sung, he was named the eternal president of the nation. What this means is that Kim Il-sung will always serve as the president of the country in spirit. Because of this, no other person can assume the office of president in North Korea. So when Kim's son, Kim Jong-il, became the leader of the country, he took the position of chairman of the National Defense Commission. The powers of this office were soon expanded.

Repression and Hardship in North Korea

- **Compare and Contrast** How are the governments of South Korea and North Korea different? (The South Korean government is a democratic, limited government. The North Korean government is an unlimited dictatorship.)

- **Predict** Based on the type of government that North Korea has, do you think this country has a successful economy? Explain. (Sample: Probably not. Tight government control does not motivate business people to think of creative ideas to make money.)

Analyze Visuals Have students analyze the chart on this page.

- Do you think North Korea or South Korea has better communications? (South Korea; it has more phone lines and cellphones.)

- What is the difference in life expectancy between North Korea and South Korea? (15 years)

 Data Discovery

Have students go to myworldgeography.com to find data about Japan and the Koreas.

STANDARD OF LIVING: NORTH AND SOUTH KOREA

	North Korea	South Korea
Economic output per person	$1,800	$27,100
Number of phone lines	1.2 million	24 million
Number of cell phones	0	43.5 million
Undernourished people	36%	1.6%
Life expectancy	64 years	79 years

SOURCE: CIA World Factbook, 2008, UN Common Database, 2001

A standard of living measures the health of a country by the goods and services its people can buy.

Chart Skills

From the information in this table, which country has a higher standard of living?

Data Discovery

Repression and Hardship in North Korea

North Korea is very different from South Korea. North Korea is one of the most isolated countries in the world. The people of North Korea face a hard life with little political freedom.

Dictatorship and Isolation North Korea is not a democracy. Its government is an example of an **unlimited government,** which is a government that, by law, may take any action it wants. Kim Jong-il is the country's leader. Kim is a dictator. A **dictator** has total control over the government. Kim Jong-il came to power when his father, Kim Il-sung, died in 1994.

Kim Il-sung rose to power in 1948. He was the leader of the Communist Party. Other parties were not allowed. Communist Party leaders tightly controlled the North Korean people. Like his father, Kim Jong-il is also a Communist and has kept this system.

The government controls the information reported by newspapers, radio, and television. The news supports Kim's policies. In addition, the leadership limits information from the outside world. Very few North Koreans have cell phones or Internet access.

People are not free to express their opinions. People who disagree with the leadership are punished. The North Korean government may have jailed up to 200,000 people for their political actions.

The North Korean government controls cultural and religious life. People cannot worship freely. Only a few churches and temples are allowed in the country.

The government promotes Korean culture by funding museums and the arts. Still, it controls the work of these writers, dancers, and musicians. It can ban any art that goes against the ideas of the leaders. North Koreans have few of the freedoms that South Koreans now enjoy.

CHART SKILLS South Korea

COMMON MISCONCEPTIONS

Korean Food Despite many cultural similarities between Korea, Japan, and China, these three countries have very different culinary traditions. Korean food is similar to Chinese and Japanese food in some ways. For example, all three cuisines include a lot of rice, soybeans, and fermented foods. However, in many ways, these three cuisines are very different. Korean cooking, for instance, often uses bold spices, such as red pepper and garlic. In contrast, Japanese food in general is more subtly flavored. Also, Korean cuisine seldom includes deep-fried food. Chinese cooking, though, often uses deep-frying.

▲ Kim Jong-il

Dancers in North Korea perform at a ceremony for the 95th anniversary of Kim Il-sung's birth.

A Crippled Economy North Korea is a communist country with a command economy. The government controls much of the economy and decides what goods are made. Often, it has not managed the economy well. As a result, the economy has not grown.

The leadership has focused on building a strong military. As a result, it does not spend enough to update machines on farms or in factories. Food production has fallen because of shortages of tractors, fertilizer, and fuel.

Natural disasters have added to these problems. Starting early in the 1990s, frequent floods and droughts damaged crops. More than two million people died of starvation in the late 1990s.

Foreign counties have given food aid to help North Koreans survive. Still, the population suffers. The government has focused on keeping control rather than solving its serious economic problems.

A Tense Border Many people in North and South Korea hope the Koreas can be reunited. In recent years, South Korea has given aid, in the form of food, to North Korea. In addition, leaders from North and South Korea have met and agreed to try to improve relations.

However, despite earlier promises not to develop nuclear weapons, North Korea has continued to build them. This has hurt North Korea's relationship with South Korea and many other countries around the world.

World leaders have met with North Koreans and tried to persuade the government to stop developing nuclear weapons. The United States and other countries have pressured North Korea to give up these weapons, but its leaders refuse. Peace and prosperity seem far away for North Korea.

aid, *n.,* help, assistance

Reading Check **Who is the leader of North Korea?**

GUIDE ON THE SIDE

- **Express an Opinion** Do you think North Korea produces many great artists? Explain. (Sample: No, great artists need the freedom to express new and creative ideas.)
- **Cause and Effect** What caused food shortages in North Korea? (natural disasters; old farm machinery; shortage of tractors, fertilizer, fuel)

Analyze Visuals Have students analyze the photographs on this page.

- What does the photograph of the festival tell us about the society of North Korea? (Sample: It is a society that values unity and strict control of the people.)
- Do you think Kim Jong-il would like the festival shown in the photograph? Explain. (Sample: Yes, Kim Jong-il seems to want his people to be united under his control. This festival shows that.)

READING CHECK Kim Jong-il

ANSWERS

CORE CONCEPTS: ECONOMIC PROCESS

Review Core Concept 5.2 before discussing Japan's economic problems. Review the key ideas of profit, revenue, competition, inflation, and recession. Then ask, why do you think Japan's economy has gone through a recession? Based on what you learned in Core Concept 5.2, why do you think bad bank practices might lead to a recession? Have the class brainstorm ways to recover from a recession. Post ideas and discuss. Make connections to current economic issues.

Challenges and Changes in Japan

- **Identify Main Ideas** What are two new challenges facing Japan? (slowed economic growth, aging population)

- **Cause and Effect** What were some effects of Japan's recession during the early 1990s? (Businesses produced less and many workers were laid off.)

Analyze Visuals Have students analyze the charts on this page.

- In 2000, what percent of Japan's population was younger than 64? (83 percent)

- What is the projected precent of Japan's population that will be 65 years old and older in 2030? (32 percent)

Data Discovery

Have students go to myworldgeography.com to find data about Japan and the Koreas.

---

my World IN NUMBERS

If there were

100 people in the world,

7 people would be **65** years old or older.

Challenges and Changes in Japan

Japan's growth in the decades after World War II made it an important economic power. Japan builds many high-technology goods, such as computers and video games. Today, Japan faces new challenges, including slower economic growth and an aging population.

Economic Woes Japan has one of the largest economies in the world. Still, the country's economy has not grown as quickly in recent years.

After the World War II, the Japanese sold more goods abroad. They invested the money they earned to make more advanced products. The Japanese people became wealthier.

At the start of the 1980s, the Japanese economy was doing very well. Each year stock prices went higher and higher. Then in the early 1990s, the Japanese economy started heading downward.

Due to bad bank practices, Japan's economy entered a **recession**, a time when the economy becomes weaker and does not grow. Businesses produced less. They laid off many workers. In 2003, Japan's economy began to improve. In 2008, however, it fell back into recession. Japan continues to face challenges that may make future economic growth difficult.

An Aging Population One of these challenges is supporting a large population of retired people. Japanese people, on average, live longer than people in any other country. They have healthy eating habits and a good healthcare system.

In addition, couples in Japan have fewer children now. As a result, there are

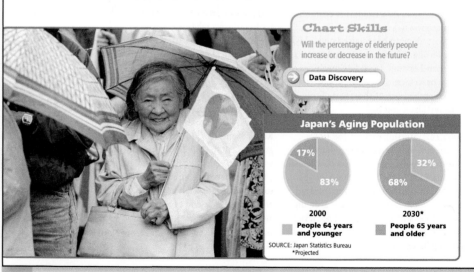

Chart Skills

Will the percentage of elderly people increase or decrease in the future?

Data Discovery

Japan's Aging Population

17% / 83%
2000

32% / 68%
2030*

People 64 years and younger

People 65 years and older

SOURCE: Japan Statistics Bureau
*Projected

CHART SKILLS increase

PRIMARY SOURCE

Elderly Crimes "Crimes by the elderly in Japan have surged to a record high, with many committed because of money worries, loneliness, and difficulty caring for sick relatives, a government report said on Friday. Japan has one of the lowest crime rates in the world, but an increasing number of them are committed by older people, the report revealed."
—*Sydney Morning Herald*, 2008

Ask students if they think the problem of rising crime with the elderly relates to the aging problem described on this page. If so, how?

fewer young people to support the elderly population. With fewer young people entering the workforce, Japan may not be able to produce as many goods. Its economy may remain weak.

Some companies in Japan are building new kinds of robots as one way to avoid a possible shortage of future workers. By taking over jobs that people currently do, robots may help keep Japan's economic production high. They can even care for the elderly:

> 66 There are robots [in Japan] serving as receptionists, vacuuming office corridors, spoon-feeding the elderly. They serve tea, greet company guests, and chatter away at public technology displays. 99
> —Associated Press

Changing Family Life Most Japanese people now live in cities. People are more likely to live in small family groups than with their extended families.

When the economy was growing quickly, many companies could provide excellent pay and benefits. Often only the husband worked. Wives generally stayed at home to care for children and older family members. Children were expected to study hard to get into college.

These family roles have changed in many families. During the recession, more women found jobs to help support their families. Also, some companies started hiring women as their older employees retired. These companies also encourage women to return to work after having children rather than becoming stay-at-home mothers.

Now, women have more job opportunities, but they still may not be treated equally to men. For example, women may find it difficult to be hired for the highest levels of management in a company.

School life has also changed in Japan. Many schools had classes six days a week to prepare students for difficult college entrance exams. Now, most schools have classes just five days a week.

Yet, the competition to get into the best colleges is as tough as ever. Many students attend extra classes during weekends and evenings in hopes of getting into one of Japan's best universities.

Reading Check How did economic problems change Japanese family life?

In an emergency, this security guard robot can put out a fire. *How might society change if robots could do many jobs that people now do?* ▼

- **Analyze Sources** Which of the robot functions listed in the quote do you think is the most important? Which do you think is the least important? Explain. (Sample: Spoon-feeding the elderly is the most important because it deals with taking care of basic needs. Chatting at technology displays is not important because it doesn't involve an important service.)

- **Summarize** How has the role of women changed in Japanese society? (Women used to stay at home and do domestic work. Now, women have more job opportunities.)

Analyze Visuals Have students analyze the photograph on this page.

- How could a robot like the one in the photograph save lives? (Sample: It could save the lives of firemen and people in fires.)

CAPTION Sample; People would have more free time to do leisure activities.

READING CHECK During the recession, more women found jobs to help support their families. Also, companies encouraged women to return to work after having children rather than become stay-at-home mothers.

CULTURE

Shinto Wedding Ceremonies About 60 percent of the weddings in Japan today use Shinto ceremonies. Most of these ceremonies are held in a Shinto sanctuary. A Shinto priest performs the ceremony. The bride wears a white kimono, which represents the beginning of her new life and the ending of her old one. The groom wears a black kimono. The bride and groom exchange many gifts. The most important gift given to the bride is the broad sash worn over a kimono called an obi. It represents female virtue. For the groom, the most significant gift he receives is the hakama skirt, which symbolizes fidelity. The bride and groom vow faithfulness and obedience to each other. Sometimes they exchange rings. The ceremony ends with the couple offering twigs to the Sakaki, or sacred tree.

Closer Look

Japan's Popular Culture

- **Identify Main Ideas** Why did Japan's entertainment industry grow after World War II? (more people had more time and money for entertainment)

- **Draw Conclusions** Do you think Japan's entertainment industry requires advanced technology? (Sample: Yes, creating anime and comics on such a wide scale probably involves advanced technology.)

- **Express Opinions** Would you be interested in watching an anime series? Explain. (Sample: Yes, the animation seems creative and expressive.)

- **Identify Evidence** Use the graph as evidence to prove that manga is becoming more popular. (Yes, manga sales have steadily increased from 2002 to 2006.)

myWorld Activity

Political Manga Find Step-by-Step Instructions and an Activity Support on pp. T52–T53. **(Verbal/Visual)**

Closer Look

JAPAN'S POPULAR CULTURE

Japan's entertainment industry grew after World War II. People had more time and money for entertainment, such as movies and video games. Japan now has the largest comic book industry in the world, and entertainment is one of Japan's major exports.

CRITICAL THINKING: **Why do you think Japanese entertainment has become popular in other countries?**

▲ Video games that started in Japan, such as the dancing game above, have become popular across the world.

Manga, or Japanese comics, are reaching a wider audience in the United States. ▼

Sales of Manga in the United States

Sales (millions of dollars) / Year

Year	Sales (millions of dollars)
2002	~55
2003	~100
2004	~135
2005	~170
2006	~200

SOURCE: Anime News Network

▲ An anime, or cartoon, character from the Japanese video game Dragon Ball Z

This character is from the famous anime series Yu Gi Oh! The show is popular in Japan and also Australia, Germany, and Britain. ▶

Shoppers in Tokyo browse manga. ▼

myWorld Activity
Political Manga

CRITICAL THINKING because Japanese entertainment is creative and fun

READING CHECK Buddhist funerals, Shinto marriage ceremonies, various traditions and holidays

ASSESSMENT **1.** Shinto is a traditional religion that originated in Japan. **2.** a government with powers that are limited by law **3.** Yes, he is a leader who has complete control over the government of his nation. **4.** North Korea has continued to develop and test nuclear weapons despite earlier promises not to. Other

ANSWERS

HISTORY

Japanese Tea The tea ceremony was first practiced in Japan by Zen monks during the Kamakura period (1192–1333). The monks drank tea to help them stay awake during long meditation sessions. Later, it became part of a Zen ritual that honored the first patriarch of Zen. During the 1400s, friends began to practice the tea ceremony at social gatherings. Here people would discuss paintings, calligraphy, and flower arrangements.

In the 1500s, Sen Rikyu, a member of the royal court, created rules for the ceremony called *wabi*. This ceremony is still popular in Japan today. *Wabi* emphasizes the qualities of harmony, respect, cleanliness, and tranquility.

A Rich Cultural Life

Most people in Japan belong to the same ethnic group and speak Japanese. There are not many immigrants. Yet, like South Korea, Japan is not cut off from the world. It influences and has been influenced by the cultures of many countries.

Spiritual Beliefs More than 80 percent of all Japanese people practice a combination of Buddhism and Shinto. **Shinto** is a traditional Japanese religion. In Shinto, kami are worshiped. Kami are gods or spirits that may live on earth in animals, trees, rocks, or other natural objects.

Today, many Japanese people practice both Buddhism and Shinto. For example, many Japanese people may have a Shinto marriage ceremony. Yet they will choose a Buddhist funeral.

Many traditions and holidays in Japan are connected to one of these two religions. At New Year's celebrations, Japanese people traditionally visit a Shinto shrine to pray to kami for a good harvest in the coming year.

Recent Cultural Borrowing In recent years, Japan has borrowed from the culture of many countries. Cultural imports, such as baseball and soccer, have been popular for many years in Japan.

At the same time, cultures around the world have borrowed from Japanese culture. Japanese martial arts, such as karate, are now popular around the world. So are Japanese foods such as sushi, or raw fish served with rice. Japanese artists have influenced artists in Europe, the United States, and other countries.

Japan has also had a big impact on the world of entertainment. It has had a large video-game industry for decades. Also, Japanese movies and television programs have a wide audience, especially in Asia.

More recently, Japanese anime—or cartoons—and manga—or comics—have attracted more and more fans throughout the world. Japan has added these products to its long list of successful exports.

Reading Check How have Shinto and Buddhism influenced Japanese culture?

GUIDE ON THE SIDE

A Rich Cultural Life

- **Infer** Do you think Shinto has a strong connection to nature? Explain. (Sample: Yes; in Shinto, people believe that gods called *kami* are found in elements of nature, such as animals and trees.)

- **Categorize** Group Japanese exports into three categories. Make sure that each category is broad enough to include many exports. (Sample: sports, food, entertainment)

Section 3 Assessment

Key Terms

1. What is Shinto?
2. What is a limited government?
3. Is Kim Jong-il a dictator? Explain.

Key Ideas

4. Why has North Korea's nuclear program created conflict in the region?
5. How did Japan's economy change beginning in the 1990s?
6. Why is Japan's aging population causing economic problems?

Think Critically

7. **Draw Inferences** Why does the North Korean government limit access to outside information?
8. **Analyze Cause and Effect** What caused South Korea's political system to become more democratic in recent years?

? Essential Question

How much does geography shape a country?

9. How important is geography to the differences between North Korea and South Korea? Go to your Student Journal and record your answers.

countries feel threatened. **5.** Due to bad bank practices, Japan's economy entered a recession. Businesses produced less. They laid off many workers. **6.** The increasing aging population requires more financial support. Also, there are fewer young people entering the workforce. **7.** Outside ideas might cause the North Koreans to rebel. **8.** South Korea revised its constitution. Also, the role of the military is now limited. **9.** Sample: North Korea has had severe floods and droughts, which has hurt their economy. South Korea has not been as badly affected by these disasters.

Governments and Citizens in Japan and the Koreas

OBJECTIVES

Students will

- learn about the governments of Japan and the Koreas.
- **21st Century Learning** identify evidence about what North and South Koreans consider to be a good citizen.
- **ELL** understand the word *activist* and that activism can cover a wide variety of causes.

SET EXPECTATIONS

In this case study, students will

- read Governments and Citizens in Japan and the Koreas.
- identify evidence about the governments of and citizenship in Japan and the Koreas.

1 Connect

Write the question "What is a democracy?" on the board. Then ask volunteers to answer this question. Answers might include having free choice, being able to vote, and electing a president. Then ask, If a country has elections, does that mean it is necessarily a democracy? Let the class discuss answers to this question. Then tell them that some countries, like North Korea, have elections but are not democracies.

ELL **Advanced** Have English learners share with the class the type of government in their family's homeland. Ask them if this government is different from the U.S. government and, if so, how?

2 Learn

Preview Have students preview Key Ideas, Key Terms, visuals, and headings. Ask them if they think the following statement is true or false: "Since Japan and South Korea are both democratic, the structure of their governments must be the same." Tell them they will return to this statement after reading.

Read While students read Governments and Citizens in Japan and the Koreas, ask questions found in **Guide on the Side** to build understanding of Key Ideas and lesson objectives.

 myWorld Activity: A Guide for Citizens Tell students to choose a partner. Then tell them that one student in each pair should list the top five qualities of a good citizen in North Korea, and the other should list the top five qualities of a good citizen in South Korea. They should take these qualities and make a guide for future citizens of each country, to teach them how a citizen in their countries is expected to act. When making the lists, students should not label their lists or include the name of their country in the lists. Then students should read aloud their list to their partners, get feedback, and make any needed corrections. Each pair should swap their guides with another pair and have this pair guess which guide is intended for citizens in which country. Finally, have students answer the questions at the bottom of the *Activity Support: Qualities List*. **(Verbal/Logical)**

30 min

L2 **Extra Support** Have students complete *Identify Evidence* in the **21st Century Online Tutor.**

3 Understand

Review Discuss the student partners' response to the questions, probing for understanding of key issues.

Assess Ask students to recall whether they thought that the statement they responded to earlier—"Since Japan and South Korea are both democratic, the structure of their governments must be the same"—was true or false. *(It was false).* Then ask students to explain the differences between the governments in the two countries.

Remediate To help students identify evidence about citizenship in Japan and the Koreas, have them create a table with two columns and two rows. Label one column Japan and South Korea and the other North Korea. Label the rows Voting and Political Involvement. Based on the text, have students describe voting and political involvement in these nations in the appropriate section.

Name _____ Class _____ Date _____

myWorld Activity Support   **Qualities List**

A Guide for Citizens

Directions List the most important qualities of a good citizen of either South Korea or North Korea. Use the list to write a guide for citizens.

1. Choose a partner. Decide with your partner which of you will make a list for a North Korean citizen and which of you will make a list for a South Korean citizen.

2. Review the information about citizenship in the case study. Based on this information, list in the chart what you think are the top five qualities of a good citizen in your chosen country.

3. Read aloud your list to your partner. Give each other feedback and revise your lists.

Top Five Qualities of a Good Citizen in _____
1. _____
2. _____
3. _____
4. _____
5. _____

4. On a separate sheet of paper, turn each list into a guide for citizens in each country with the title "A Guide to Citizenship." (DO NOT WRITE THE NAME OF THE COUNTRY.) Swap this guide with another pair. Have this pair guess which guide is for a North Korean citizen and which guide is for a South Korean citizen. Do the same for their guides. Then answer the questions below.

   1. What are some of the similarities and differences between your list and the list of your partner?

   _____

   2. What qualities does the North Korean government expect its citizens to have? What qualities are valued in South Korea?

   _____

GOVERNMENT

Japan's Emperor Japan's emperor is Emperor Akihito. He acceded to the throne in 1989, after the death of Emperor Hirohito. The emperor is the symbolic head of Japan. Because of this, the functions that he performs have a strong cultural significance for most Japanese. However, the emperor does not have political power. In state matters, he acts on the advice and approval of the cabinet. The emperor's duties include announcing new laws and treaties. In addition, he appoints the prime minister after the Diet has chosen this official. In addition, the emperor awards honors, receives foreign ambassadors, and makes official visits to foreign countries. Emperor Akihito is very interested in the conservation of wildlife. In fact, he has co-written several articles about the marine life of Japan. He has been married to Empress Michiko since 1959.

Two Democratic Systems, One Dictatorship

- **Infer** Why do you think the Japanese have kept the emperor as the head of state? (Sample: The Japanese value tradition.)

- **Identify Details** What is the legislature in South Korea called? (the National Assembly)

Analyze Visuals Point out the photograph on this page.

- Based on the photograph, what do you think are some of the personality traits of Emperor Akihito? (Samples: friendly, intellligent)

Case Study

Governments and Citizens in Japan and the Koreas

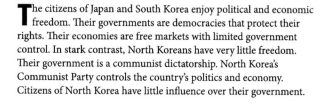

| Key Ideas | • Both South Korea and Japan are democracies. • South Korea has a presidential system, while Japan has a parliamentary system. | • Citizens in North Korea have very few rights. |

Key Terms • presidential system • parliamentary system

Emperor Akihito at the imperial palace in Tokyo ▼

The citizens of Japan and South Korea enjoy political and economic freedom. Their governments are democracies that protect their rights. Their economies are free markets with limited government control. In stark contrast, North Koreans have very little freedom. Their government is a communist dictatorship. North Korea's Communist Party controls the country's politics and economy. Citizens of North Korea have little influence over their government.

Two Democratic Systems, One Dictatorship
The organization of the Japanese and South Korean governments is different. However, in both systems, citizens actively choose their leaders. By contrast, Kim Jong-il and North Korea's Communist Party control the government of North Korea.

South Korea's political system is a **presidential system**. In this form of government, citizens elect the president, who heads the executive branch of government. The president also serves as the head of state, or the country's symbolic leader. The United States also has a presidential system. Citizens also vote for the members of the legislative branch of government. The legislative branch, much like Congress in the United States, makes the country's laws. In South Korea, the legislature is called the National Assembly.

Japan's government is a **parliamentary system**. In this system, people directly elect representatives to the legislative branch, or legislature. The legislature then selects the prime minister, who heads the executive branch. Since Japan is a constitutional monarchy, the emperor is the head of state. However, the emperor's powers are symbolic.

GOVERNMENT

North Korea's Local Government The government of North Korea has many local branches that serve the needs of various regions within the nation. In general, the local government has three levels: province, county/ city, and village/neighborhood. There are nine provinces. In addition, there are two cities and three special administrative regions that report directly to the central government. The provinces are divided into counties and ordinary cities that do not report directly to the central government. The counties are divided into villages and the cities are divided into neighborhoods. In addition, there are people's committees and people's assemblies. The assemblies are responsible for legislative functions, and the committees deal with administrative duties. All levels of the government must act under the approval of the central government, which is controlled by Kim Jong-il.

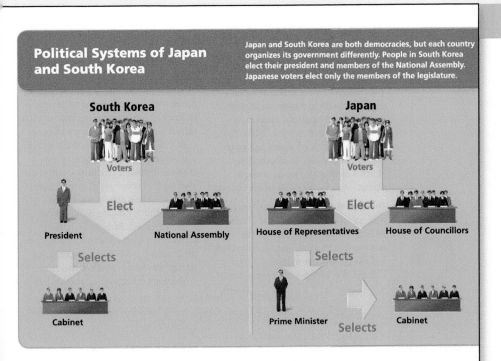

Political Systems of Japan and South Korea

Japan and South Korea are both democracies, but each country organizes its government differently. People in South Korea elect their president and members of the National Assembly. Japanese voters elect only the members of the legislature.

South Korea

Voters

Elect

President — National Assembly

Selects

Cabinet

Japan

Voters

Elect

House of Representatives — House of Councillors

Selects

Prime Minister — Selects — Cabinet

- **Compare and Contrast** How are Japan's and South Korea's governments different from North Korea's government? (Japan's and South Korea's governments are democratic. North Korea's government is a dictatorship.)
- **Identify Evidence** What evidence shows that North Korea is not a democracy? (North Koreans cannot vote for someone who is not supported by the Communist Party. One man controls the Party.)

Analyze Visuals Have students analyze the table on this page.

- How are the political systems of Japan and South Korea similar? (In both systems, citizens have the right to vote and the political leader of each nation selects the cabinet.)
- Do you think Japan's or South Korea's political system is more efficient? (Sample: South Korea, since it has a direct election for the president and fewer government bodies.)

Real power lies with the prime minister and the legislature. In Japan, the legislature is called the Diet. It has two parts, the House of Councillors and the House of Representatives. Japan's prime minister leads the Diet's largest party, so he also controls the Diet.

North Korea's citizens can also vote in elections, but they do not have a real choice. The Communist Party creates a list of candidates for each position in the government. No one runs against these candidates.

People cannot vote for someone else if they do not support the choice of the party. For example, no one ran against Kim Jong-il in the last election. He controls North Korea's Communist Party and makes sure that his supporters are chosen for the legislature.

In North Korea, the courts do not review the laws made by the government. In both South Korea and Japan, the highest levels of the court can review the laws. The courts can challenge laws that violate the constitutions of these countries. The courts help ensure that new laws do not violate the rights listed in the constitutions of these two countries.

Reading Check How are the political systems of Japan and South Korea different?

READING CHECK South Korea's political system is a presidential system, in which people directly elect the president. Japan's government is a parliamentary system. In this system, people directly elect representatives to the legislature. The legislature then selects the prime minister.

CORE CONCEPTS: CITIZENSHIP

Review Core Concept 8.5 before discussing citizenship in Japan and the Koreas. This core concept explains the rights and responsibilities of citizens of the United States. Review this information with the class. Make sure that students understand that the rights and responsibilities of citizens can vary depending on the country and type of government. Also, examine the various forms of civic participation. Then have students study the roles of citizens in Japan and the Koreas. In which of these countries are the rights and responsibilities of citizens the most different from U.S. citizens? Have students explain. Then ask, Do you think that the various types of civic participation are practiced by citizens of Japan and South Korea? Are they practiced by citizens of North Korea? Explain.

Rights and Responsibilities of Citizens

- **Summarize** How does North Korea's government control the economy of North Korea? (The government plans the economy and owns most businesses and lands. Also, citizens are assigned jobs by the government.)

- **Identify Details** What is the name of the dominant political party in North Korea? (Korean Worker's Party)

Analyze Visuals Have students analyze the photographs on this page.

- What impression do you think the candidate in the campaign poster gives? (Samples: businesslike, friendly, determined)

- Do you think the workers in the photograph on the left are making demands? Explain. (Sample: Yes, the worker in front has a clenched fist that is raised. This gesture shows that he is determined to get something done. All of the workers are wearing headbands with words on them. The words are probably demanding some type of change.)

Rights and Responsibilities of Citizens

The citizens of Japan and South Korea control their governments and enjoy many rights. By contrast, citizens of North Korea have very few rights. The government of North Korea has much greater control over its citizens' lives. North Korea's government controls almost every aspect of life in the country.

The Communist System Communism is both an economic system and a political system. The government plans the economy, owns most businesses and land, and assigns citizens to jobs.

People have fewer choices in a com-

A campaign poster for a candidate running for office in Japan ▼

munist system. For example, a person in North Korea cannot simply decide to quit his or her job and start a business of his or her own. That is because the government owns most businesses, and very few privately owned businesses are allowed.

In a dictatorship such as North Korea, opposition to the government is not allowed. Protesters risk their freedom and even their lives by speaking out. Organizing for change is almost impossible.

Many North Koreans belong to the Korean Worker's Party (KWP), North Korea's Communist Party. Kim Jong-il is the head of the KWP. This organization strengthens Kim Jong-il's dictatorship.

There are other political parties, but

Citizens Get Involved: Japan and South Korea

In South Korea and Japan, citizens are free to create organizations to express their opinions and protect their interests.

Labor Unions Workers may create unions to protect their interests. Unions often call for better wages and working conditions.

Environmental Groups The people in this photograph are celebrating the passage of an important environmental bill.

HISTORY

The 386 Generation Activism has been very influential in South Korea during the past 40 years. In the forefront of this movement has been the 386 generation. This term was first coined about 15 years ago. At that time, this generation was in their thirties, so the number "3" was used. The number "8" was used because they went to college in the 80s, and the number "6" was used because they were born in the 1960s. Many of the 386ers wanted a complete democracy. They helped to get rid of the dictatorial rule in South Korea during the 1980s. During the 1990s, many 386ers joined the Democratic Party and helped to elect a member of this party, Roh Moo Hyun, president. Critics, though, claimed that the 386ers have failed to live up to their promise. Roh's administration was divisive and did not improve life in South Korea. In 2007, the more conservative Lee Myung-bak won the presidency.

they must closely follow the policies of the KWP, and they cannot challenge the KWP leadership. In elections, North Koreans only have one choice—a KWP candidate. They can vote against this candidate but risk harsh punishment if they do so.

Democratic Systems In Japan and South Korea, there are several political parties. No political party in these countries holds powers like the KWP's. When the citizens of Japan and South Korea vote, they choose between candidates from different parties. Representatives must work hard on issues important to their voters if they want to win reelection.

Like the United States, political parties express the needs and points of view of different groups of people, but citizens can also form groups and speak out when they do not agree with their leaders. Unlike North Korea's dictatorship, these democracies have freedom of speech.

In South Korea, citizen organizations are growing in size and power. Human rights organizations, churches, and labor unions have worked for civil and economic rights.

Japan also has many activist groups. Labor unions have struggled there for years to improve working conditions and pay. Activists in both countries have rallied citizens in support of many causes. In a democracy, lawmakers must listen to citizens.

Reading Check Why don't citizen groups organize in North Korea?

Japanese voters in a recent election for members of the House of Representatives ▼

Assessment

1. Which officials do voters elect in South Korea's political system?

2. Which officials do voters elect in Japan's political system?

3. How does the Communist Party control elections in North Korea?

4. What kinds of citizen organizations influence politics in South Korea and Japan?

5. What kinds of things do unions struggle to improve for their members?

GUIDE ON THE SIDE

- **Draw Conclusions** In Japan and South Korea, why do you think lawmakers listen to their nation's activists? (Sample: In a democracy, lawmakers are elected by citizens. Since activists are citizens, lawmakers want their support.)

- **Express an Opinion** Do you think the activist groups in South Korea and Japan can help to improve the democracies of those countries? Explain. (Sample: Yes, activist groups can work to improve civil and economic rights and can influence laws.)

Analyze Visuals Point out the photograph on this page.

- Do you think the people in the photogaph take their political rights seriously? Explain. (Sample: Yes, they are using their right to vote.)

READING CHECK Groups that oppose the government are put down by the KWP. Their members would most likely go to jail.

ASSESSMENT 1. the president, members of the legislative branch **2.** legislative representatives **3.** The Communist Party controls the choice of candidates that citizens can elect. **4.** human rights organizations, churches, labor unions **5.** working conditions, job safety

ANSWERS

KEY TERMS AND IDEAS

1. Summer has the most rainfall since monsoons often hit Japan and the Koreas during this season. Monsoons can drop up to 80 inches of rainfall.

2. hydroelectricity, minerals, and oil

3. They invented a new writing system called Hangul. In addition, they invented a new technique for making porcelain and movable metal type.

THINK CRITICALLY

8. The Japanese have built structures that withstand earthquakes. Rubber pads under skyscrapers dampen the shock of earthquakes. Computers move weights in the base of skyscrapers to keep the buildings balanced. Also, warning systems help people get to safety during earthquakes.

9. There was only a small amount of good farmland. Also, during that time, Japan was very isolated. So it probably didn't import much food from other regions. Because of these reasons, growing food in Japan was very important.

10. North Korea's government strictly controls education in its nation. Only a certain type of cultural expression is allowed. Artistic expression is also strongly controlled by the government. Japan encourages education for its entire population. Many forms of cultural expression are encouraged.

11. The geography of this region tends to be mountainous. As a result, not much land is available for people to live on. To deal with this, nations in this region often build office and apartment buildings with multiple floors. Also, shopping centers are extended underground.

4. In 1868, new leaders in Japan pushed out the Tokugawa shogun. They brought back the emperor, but they told him what to do. This time is called Meiji Restoration since the Emperor Meiji was returned to power. The new leaders expanded Japan's industry and military.

5. South Korea has a democratic government that protects the rights of its people. North Korea has a dictatorship, which gives its people few rights.

6. Businesses produced less and many workers were laid off.

7. karate, sushi, anime, manga

Japan and the Koreas

Chapter Assessment

Key Terms and Ideas

1. **Explain** During what season do Japan and the Koreas get the most rain? Why is rain heaviest in this season?

2. **Recall** What are some of Japan's and the Koreas important natural resources?

3. **Summarize** What were some of the cultural achievements of the Koreans?

4. **Discuss** What was the Meiji restoration? What changes took place in Japan after this event?

5. **Compare and Contrast** How are the governments of North Korea and South Korea different?

6. **Recall** What were some of the effects of the recession in Japan during the 1990s?

7. **Summarize** What are examples of Japanese culture that have become popular in other countries?

Think Critically

8. **Solve Problems** How has Japan attempted to prepare for earthquakes?

9. **Making Inferences** Under Tokugawa rule, farmers had a higher social status than merchants. Why do you think farming was so highly valued?

10. **Comparing Viewpoints** How does North Korea view culture and the arts? How is this different from Japan?

11. **Core Concepts: Land Use** How does this region's geography create challenges for land use?

Places to Know

For each place, write the letter from the map that shows its location.

12. Japan
13. North Korea
14. South Korea
15. P'yongyang
16. Seoul
17. Mt. Fuji
18. **Estimate** Using the scale, estimate the length of the border between North Korea and South Korea.

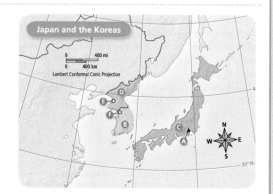

Japan and the Koreas

0   400 mi
0   400 km
Lambert Conformal Conic Projection

PLACES TO KNOW

12. C
13. D
14. B
15. E

16. F
17. A
18. about 200 miles

 **myWorld Chapter Activity**

Mission Earth Find Step-by-Step Instructions, Student Instructions and Rubric, and an Activity Support on pp. T33–T35. **(Visual/Verbal)**

 21st Century Learning

Search for Information on the Internet Students' reports should show a successful search of the Internet. If students need help with this skill, direct them to the 21st Century Online Tutor.

→ Online Assessment

Tailor review and assessment to each student's needs with an array of online assessments.

- Self-Test
- On Assignment Article or Slideshow
- Success Tracker

? Essential Question

How much does geography shape a country?

Demonstrate Understanding Plan a multimedia presentation that shows how Japan and the Koreas have adapted to and changed their environment. Make recommendations to the United Nations Environment Programme to help these countries solve environmental problems.

21st Century Learning

Search for Information on the Internet

Search for information on the culture of Japan, North Korea, or South Korea. Then write a report about that country's culture. Include pictures with your report. Be sure to include information on:
- religion
- the arts
- recreation
- food

WRITING TASK TIP

USING DATA Tell students that when using data to prove their thesis statement, they should try to find a pattern. To determine this, questions should be asked. Does the data span a period of time? If so, does the data increase, decrease, or stay the same over time? After a pattern is determined, a person should ask what this pattern indicates. For example, a steady increase in complaints about pollution indicates that pollution is getting worse.

Document-Based Questions

Success ⭐ Tracker™
Online at myworldgeography.com

Use your knowledge of Japan and Documents A and B to answer the questions below.

Document A

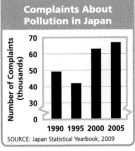

Complaints About Pollution in Japan

Number of Complaints (thousands)

70, 60, 50, 40, 30, 0

1990 1995 2000 2005

SOURCE: Japan Statistical Yearbook, 2009

Document B

" Japan's greenhouse gas emissions [releases] surged [increased rapidly] last year . . . Emissions of carbon dioxide and other greenhouse gases blamed for global warming spiked 2.3 percent to 1.37 billion tons in the 2007 . . ."

—CBS News, November 12, 2008

1. In Document A, which of the following years shows a drop in complaints about pollution?
   A 1990
   B 1995
   C 2000
   D 2005

2. Which of the following BEST describes the information presented in Document B?
   A Pollution decreased in 2007, which was encouraging.
   B Pollution stayed about the same in 2007.
   C Pollution increased a small amount in 2007, which is cause for some concern.
   D Pollution increased sharply in 2007, which is cause for alarm.

3. **Writing Task** Based on Document A and B, did Japan handle its pollution better in the 1990s or in the 2000s? Explain your answer.

DOCUMENT-BASED QUESTIONS

1. B

2. D

3. 1990s; According to the graph, the grievances against pollution actually lessened during the 1990s. However, they have increased during the 2000s. Also, the quote states that in 2007 emissions of carbon dioxide and other greenhouse gases surged.

Plan With Understanding by Design*

Chapter Objectives
Begin With the End in Mind

Students will demonstrate the following enduring understandings:
- Geography shapes culture and contributes to ethnic diversity.
- Geography can affect the diverse economies of a region.

- A region's resources can determine settlement patterns and economic life.

Connect
Make Learning Meaningful

Student Edition
- **Essential Question** What are the challenges of diversity?
- **myStory** Ridwan attends his cousin's wedding in Sumatra.

 **worldgeography.com**
myStory Online Learn about Minangkabau wedding traditions.

Student Journal
Essential Question Preview

Experience
Teach Knowledge and Skills

Student Edition
- Read Sections 1, 2, and 3.
- Answer Reading Checks and Section Assessment questions.

worldgeography.com
On Assignment myStory Video, Active Atlas, Data Discovery, Culture Close-up, and Language Lesson.

Student Journal
- Sections 1, 2, and 3 Word Wise
- Sections 1, 2, and 3 Outline Map and Take Notes

Teacher's Edition
myWorld Activities
- Section 1: Why Settle in Southeast Asia?, p. T66
- Section 2: Historical Cartoon, p. T72
- Section 3: Facing Challenges, p. T80

21st Century Learning Online Tutor
- Read Special Purpose Maps
- Ask Questions
- Sequence
- Compare Viewpoints
- Identify Main Ideas and Details
- Problem Solve

Understand
Assess Understanding

Assessment Booklet
- Chapter Tests • Benchmark Tests

Teacher's Edition
myWorld Chapter Activity
Students gather data on factors that have produced wealth in the region, evaluate their findings and dramatize them.

Student Edition
Chapter Assessment

worldgeography.com
On Assignment Students write and submit an online news article about the effects of economic differences in Southeast Asia.

Student Journal
Essential Question Writer's Workshop

Success ☆ Tracker™
Online at myworldgeography.com
Administer chapter tests and remediate understanding.

"Understanding by Design" is registered as a trademark with the Patent and Trademark Office by the Association for Supervision of Curriculum Development (ASCD). ASCD has not authorized, approved or sponsored this work and is in no way affiliated with Pearson or its products.

Connect to the Essential Question

Essential Question

What are the challenges of diversity?

Use the Essential Question poster and follow these steps to help students understand the Essential Question.

Connect to Their Lives

1. Ask students to define *diversity*. (If students have already studied this Essential Question, encourage them to note changes in the way they define or think about diversity.) Point out that this term refers to a wide range of differences that may exist among a group of people. Focusing on tastes and interests, encourage students to identify different tastes among friends, other students, or members of their community. Invite them to describe how people express these different tastes.

2. Have students list the ways people express differences in taste. Post the following chart for them to complete, or have students turn to the Essential Question Preview page in their **Student Journal:**

Category	Clothing	Food	Music	Interests
Expressions of Different Tastes				

3. Discuss students' responses. Ask, Do some differences in taste encourage or discourage interaction with other groups?

Connect to the Content

4. Now have students brainstorm types of diversity within a country or region. Examples might include the religious or ethnic differences within the population.

5. Ask students to identify the challenges of such diversity. Post the following chart for them to complete. (Help them to understand what might be included in each category, for example, one of the challenges of language diversity might be the inability to communicate with others.)

Type of Diversity	Ethnic	Religious	Political	Linguistic
Challenges				

6. After previewing the chapter, have students make chapter-related predictions on the *Essential Question Preview* page in the **Student Journal.**

7. Remind students that they will answer a prompt related to the Essential Question on each section's *Take Notes* page in the **Student Journal.**

Explore 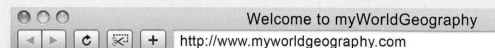 my worldgeography.com

---

Welcome to myWorldGeography

http://www.myworldgeography.com

ON ASSIGNMENT: Southeast Asia

For this chapter's assignment mission, students will

- take a digital trip to Southeast Asia.
- take on the role of a journalist.
- gather notes, images, and data throughout their journey for their story.
- write a compelling news article or make a multimedia slideshow on the Essential Question: *What are the challenges of diversity?*

ITINERARY

During their trip, students will make the following stops:

myStory Video

Learn more about Minangkabau wedding traditions.

Active Atlas

Study more maps of Southeast Asia.

Data Discovery

Gather data about the geography of Southeast Asia.

Culture Close-up

Explore to learn more about the culture and history of Southeast Asia.

Language Lesson

Learn greetings and other words in Bahassa, Ridwan's native language.

Self-Test

Assess their own knowledge of chapter content.

TIGed
TakingITGlobal for Educators

Extend the reach of every lesson by helping students connect to a global community of young people with common interests and concerns. Visit myworldgeography.com to

- explore Country Pages relating to Southeast Asia.
- delve deeper into this chapter's Essential Question: *What are the challenges of diversity?*
- find online alternatives to and solutions for the Unit Closer 21st Century Learning Activity.

---

my worldgeography.com

TEACHER CENTER

Preview and assign student materials, enrich your teaching, and track student progress with the following resources:

- Online Lesson Planning and Resource Library
- Presentations for Projection
- Online Teacher's Edition and Ancillaries
- Google Earth Links

Assess Enduring Understandings

myWorld Chapter Activity | **Step-by-Step Instructions** 1.5 hr

Gaining Wealth Through History

Teach this activity at the end of the chapter to assess enduring understandings.

OBJECTIVES

Students will demonstrate the following enduring understandings:

- Geography can affect the diverse economies of a region.
- A region's resources can determine settlement patterns and economic life.

Students will provide the following evidence of understanding:

- Economic Assessment Scale
- Character Skit

LEARNING STYLES

- Verbal
- Visual

MATERIALS

- Activity Support: Student Instructions and Rubric, p. T62
- Activity Support: Economic Assessment Survey, p. T63
- Blank Paper and Colored Pencils
- Activity Cards: #133–138
   - 133. Khmer king, Jayavarman VII—1200s
   - 134. Indian merchant—400s
   - 135. French explorer—1800s
   - 136. Mongol invader—1200s
   - 137. Portuguese soldier—1500s
   - 138. Electronics business owner—1900s

Activity Steps

1. **Set Expectations** Explain that some students will role-play the historical characters on the cards, while others will take the role of economic investigators. They will use their interviews with these characters to identify factors that have helped some characters gain wealth. Then they will assign the characters a rating on a scale. Finally, they will create a skit that dramatizes each character's success or failure.

2. **Field Research Jigsaw**
   - Divide the class into six small groups. Give each student a copy of the *Activity Support: Economic Assessment Survey* and each group one card.
   - Ask one volunteer from each group to role-play the character, while reading the activity card out loud. Have students discuss and record data on their Activity Supports to assess that character's success at gaining wealth in Southeast Asia.
   - Next, rearrange students, so that each new group has one person familiar with the information on

each card. Ask students to discuss their findings and compare the efforts of different characters to create wealth or growth.

L2 Extra Support Help students to create a web with *Economic Success* in the middle and, on the spokes, measures of success, such as *wealth*.

3. **Construct a Scale** Students should construct a scale from 1 to 10 and rate each character to show how successfully that character profited from the region's geography or resources.

ELL Early Intermediate Help students to create a picture graph showing the economic success of each character, drawing 0 to 10 treasure chests (low to high success) next to each name.

4. **Create a Skit** Have students return to their original groups. Ask each group to create a skit about their character's efforts to gain wealth.

Name _____ Class _____ Date _____

myWorld Chapter Activity Support   **Student Instructions and Rubric**

Gaining Wealth Through History

Activity Instructions: Read the following summary of your myWorld Chapter Activity. Follow your teacher's directions for more information.

1. Work with your classmates to collect information about how geography and resources have affected the economic growth of Southeast Asia through history.

2. Complete your *Economic Assessment Survey* of one historical character. Then share information with other group members.

3. Construct a scale from 1 to 10. Rate each of the six historical characters on the scale to assess each character's success in using the region's geography to gain wealth or produce economic growth.

4. Return to your original group and create a skit together about your character. Your skits should dramatize that character's efforts to use the region's geography and resources for economic growth.

myWorld Chapter Activity Rubric	3 Exceeds Understanding	2 Reaches Understanding	1 Approaches Understanding
Economic Assessment Scale	Reflects deep and accurate understanding of the relationship between geography and wealth; can support all ratings with detailed reasons	Reflects mostly accurate understanding of the relationship between geography and wealth; can support most ratings with clear reasons	Reflects some understanding of the relationship between geography and wealth; can support one or two ratings with some reasons
Character Skits	Contributes interesting and creative ideas to writing skit; participates in the skit	Contributes accurate ideas based on Activity Cards to writing skit; participates in the skit	Contributes a few ideas based on Activity Cards to writing skit; does not participate in the skit

Name _____ Class _____ Date _____

 myWorld Chapter Activity Support   **Economic Assessment Survey**

Gaining Wealth Through History

Directions Fill out this survey, collecting information from the Activity Card.

Name of Character _____

Home   Does the character come from Southeast Asia?   ☐ Yes ☐ No

Work   What does this character do? _____

Goals What does the character want?

Methods How does the character hope to achieve these goals?

Geography How does the region's geography help or hinder the character?

Climate:

Landforms or waterways:

Physical or human resources:

Other:

How much do you think the character will benefit economically from
the geography and resources of Southeast Asia?

_____

_____

_____

_____

Southeast Asia

- Introduce the Essential Question so that students will be able to understand the big ideas of this chapter (see earlier page, Connect to the Essential Question).

- Help students prepare to learn about Southeast Asia by looking at the chapter's maps, charts, and photos.

- Have students make and record chapter predictions with the Essential Question Preview in the **Student Journal.**

- Ask students to analyze maps on this page.

GUIDE ON THE SIDE

 Explore the Essential Question . . .

Have students complete the Essential Question Writer's Workshop in their **Student Journals** to demonstrate in-depth understanding of the question in the context of this chapter.

Analyze Maps Point out the political map.

- Which seas or oceans border the region? (Indian Ocean, South China Sea, Pacific Ocean)

- What country in the region is landlocked? (Laos)

- Where are the region's major cities located? (on large bodies of water and on rivers)

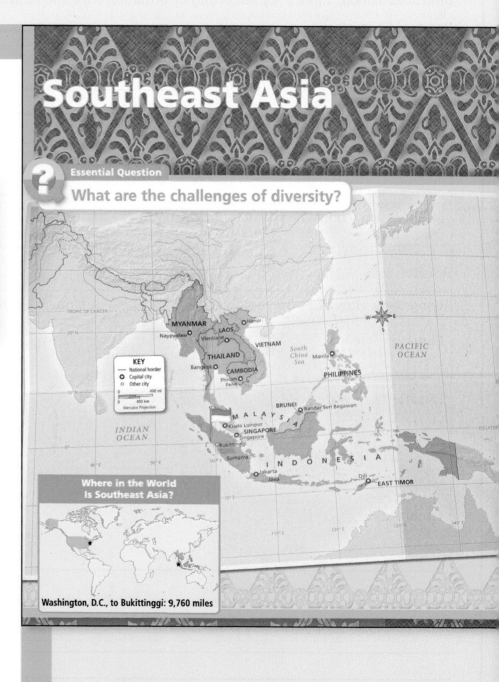

Southeast Asia

Essential Question

What are the challenges of diversity?

KEY
— National border
⊙ Capital city
○ Other city

0   400 mi
0   400 km
Mercator Projection

TROPIC OF CANCER

MYANMAR — Hanoi
Naypyidaw — LAOS
Vientiane
VIETNAM
THAILAND — South China Sea
Bangkok — CAMBODIA — Manila
Phnom Penh — PHILIPPINES
BRUNEI
MALAYSIA — Bandar Seri Begawan
Kuala Lumpur — SINGAPORE
Singapore
Bukittinggi
Sumatra — INDONESIA
Jakarta — Java — Dili — EAST TIMOR

INDIAN OCEAN
PACIFIC OCEAN

Where in the World Is Southeast Asia?

Washington, D.C., to Bukittinggi: 9,760 miles

INTRODUCE  my Story

Get students excited to learn about Southeast Asia by first experiencing the region through the eyes of Ridwan, a young man living in Sumatra.

- Read myStory and watch the myStory Video about his life.

- Have students complete *Minangkabau Wedding* in the Student Journal to prepare to learn about some interesting traditions of Ridwan's people.

my Story
A Minangkabau Wedding

In this section you will read about Ridwan, a young man helping his family and friends prepare for his cousin's wedding on the island of Sumatra in Indonesia. What does Ridwan's story tell you about the culture of Southeast Asia?

Explore the Essential Question
- at my worldgeography.com
- using the myWorld Chapter Activity
- with the Student Journal

Story by Millie Phuah for myWorld Geography Online

Laughing voices drift through the cool air as nineteen-year-old Ridwan works with the men. They are busily moving furniture and cleaning the house where a wedding ceremony will take place. Meanwhile, in the kitchen, dozens of women are preparing chili peppers, onions, garlic, ginger, and a host of other spices. The spices will go into the meat and vegetable dishes of the day-long wedding feast. Although it is still early in the morning, there is not a moment to lose. Soon hundreds of relatives, friends, and neighbors will start arriving to honor the happy couple getting married today.

Ridwan looks out over the rice fields and the sea that surround this village called Bukittinggi, a name meaning "high hill." He can't wait to see his cousin, Nentis, who is the bride, begin her life with Al, her groom.

"Weddings are happy and important events that everyone looks forward to because it's a time for relatives

my Story

A Minangkabau Wedding

- **Identify Details** What is Ridwan's family preparing on the morning of the wedding? (They prepare vegetable and meat dishes.)

- **Infer** What is the geography of Ridwan's community like? (coastal, hilly, mild)

ECONOMICS

Water Buffalo Power Asian water buffaloes were domesticated about 5,000 years ago. Unlike their wild relatives, domesticated water buffaloes are gentle. Water buffaloes supply at least 13 percent of the world's milk. Their milk is richer than cow's milk and is used to produce butter, oil, and cheese. These powerful beasts of burden have been compared to tractors. They supply 20 to 30 percent of Southeast Asia's farm power. They have the widest horn span of all cattle. Have students turn to Section 1 for an image of one of these animals. Then point out how the horns may have influenced the roof design of traditional Minangkabau houses, shown on the story opener page.

Preparing the wedding feast

Bride and groom in one pair of wedding costumes. The photo on the facing page shows them wearing another set of costumes.

- **Identify Details** Which countries outside Southeast Asia influenced the Minangkabau people? (China and India)

- **Compare and Contrast** In what way are Minangkabau families different from most other families? (Family homes are passed from mothers to daughters.)

and friends to get together. Today is especially meaningful to me, not only because my cousin is getting married, but it's also the first time I've attended a Minangkabau wedding," says Ridwan. (The Minangkabau are the main ethnic group in West Sumatra.) "And according to Minangkabau practice, Al is moving into Nentis' home, which belongs to the bride's grandmother."

Minangkabau culture is unique. Minangkabau houses often have upward-curved roofs that look like the horns of a water buffalo. The resemblance is not a coincidence. For centuries the Minangkabau depended on the buffalo for food and to help them plow the rice fields. In fact, the name *Minangkabau* means "winning buffalo." The Minangkabau are also one of the few ethnic groups in the world in which family homes are passed down from mothers to daughters, instead of from fathers to sons.

Nentis starts dressing early, because her wedding costume consists of layers of silk and other fabric woven with gold thread, gold jewelry, and a glittering Minangkabau headdress. Meanwhile, Al dons his suit. He looks like an Indian raja, or king, as he slips on a kris, an ornamental dagger. Such costumes reveal the Chinese and Indian influences that have helped shape Minangkabau culture.

QUICK FACTS

Family Lines Anthropologists describe societies as matrilineal when families trace their descent through females, or mothers. Patrilineal descent occurs when family identity is passed down from the father.

Some wedding guests visit the buffet outside.

Musicians entertain the guests.

Later in the day, as a band plays, the couple moves to the wedding dais, or platform. Everyone lines up to congratulate the smiling pair. It is a long day for the couple as they rise repeatedly to greet new arrivals. During the feast, long-separated relatives laugh and exchange news. Many have traveled from distant parts of Indonesia to be here today.

Traveling and moving away from home are common among the Minangkabau. In fact, Ridwan's parents left Bukittinggi years ago to run a textile shop in East Java. Ridwan helps at his family's textile business and lives in his maternal grandmother's house. The house will one day be passed down to Ridwan's mother and aunt, and then to his sister. When the time comes for Ridwan and his brothers to marry, they will move into their wives' homes. It is the Minangkabau way.

"This is part of Minangkabau culture and I totally accept it, just as all the other men do. It just makes me work harder at my vocation," says Ridwan. "I'd like to further my studies in the Indonesian language and be a theatre performer. My father, of course, hopes I'll take over his business one day, but I think I'll deal with that later," he smiles shyly.

Ridwan returns to his video camera, using modern technology to record an ancient tradition and the scenes that his family will enjoy throughout their lives.

 myStory Video

Join Ridwan as he shows you more about his life.

Meet the Journalist

Name Millie Phuah
Favorite Moment Talking to Ridwan's grandmother

GUIDE ON THE SIDE

- **Identify Main Ideas** Where will Ridwan move when he marries one day? (He will move into his wife's home.)

- **Identify Evidence** Which details support the idea that moving away from home is common among the Minangkabau? (Many relatives are coming from all over Indonesia for the wedding; Ridwan's own parents left their hometown to work with an uncle.)

myStory Video

Have students watch the video at myworldgeography.com about Ridwan's experience at his first Minangkabau wedding. Tell students to use their trackers to identify what Ridwan learns about his family's traditions.

Chapter Atlas

OBJECTIVES

Students will know

- the diversity of Southeast Asian landforms, vegetation, and resources.
- geographic influences on Southeast Asian settlement, culture, and history.

Students will be able to

- label outline maps of Southeast Asia.
- ask questions about the land and climate of Southeast Asia.

SET EXPECTATIONS

In this section, students will

- read the Chapter Atlas.
- interview a settler to Southeast Asia.
- work with the Active Atlas online.

CORE CONCEPTS

You may wish to teach or reteach the following lessons from the Core Concepts Handbook:

- Forces Inside Earth, pp. 24–25
- Water and Climate, pp. 36–37
- Land Use, pp. 50–51

KEY

Differentiated Instruction

- **L1** Special Needs
- **L2** Extra Support
- **L3** On-Level
- **L4** Challenge

English Language Instruction

- **ELL** Beginner
- **ELL** Early Intermediate
- **ELL** Intermediate
- **ELL** Early Advanced
- **ELL** Advanced

1 Connect
Make learning meaningful

Make Connections Ask students to write in their journals the three most distinctive features of their area, such as landforms, waterways, resources, or population. Make a list of their ideas, and have students briefly discuss their differences of opinion.

L4 Challenge Ask students to create a fact-opinion chart, listing information and opinions about the physical features in your locale.

Activate Prior Knowledge Remind students that they learned about China's varied landscape earlier in this unit. Ask them to predict one similarity and one difference between the lands of Southeast Asia and the southern part of China.

L2 Extra Support Invite students to review a physical map of China.

Prepare Follow the steps in the section **Preview.** Preteach the Key Terms. Then have students complete *Word Wise* in their journals using in-text clues and the glossary for help.

2 Experience
Teach knowledge and skills

Read Use **Background** notes and **Guide on the Side** questions to model active reading. Have students use *Take Notes* in their **Student Journal** to record important places to know in Southeast Asia on an outline map. Students should use the maps in the Chapter Atlas and the Active Atlas at myworldgeography.com, for assistance.

L1 Special Needs Have students use an eraser to trace the outline of mainland Southeast Asia on a map in the Chapter Atlas. Ask them to guess the number of islands in the archipelagoes of the region.

ELL Intermediate Help students to create a Venn diagram for comparing and contrasting the archipelagoes and mainland of Southeast Asia. At the top of one circle, they should write *Archipelagoes: differences;* at the top of the other circle *Mainland: differences.* In the intersection, they should write *similarities.* Have them use this diagram to track similarities and differences as they read.

 Practice: myWorld Activity Playing the role of settlers from India or China, students will ask and answer questions about their new home in Southeast Asia. **Step-by-Step Instructions** and **More Activities** follow on p. T66.

SECTION 1 RESOURCE GUIDE

FOR THE STUDENT

my worldgeography.com Student Center
- Active Atlas
- Data Discovery

Student Edition (print and online)
- Chapter Atlas

Student Journal (print and online)
- Section 1 Word Wise
- Section 1 Take Notes

21st Century Learning Online Tutor
- Read Special Purpose Maps
- Ask Questions

FOR THE TEACHER

my worldgeography.com Teacher Center
- Online Lesson Planner
- Presentations for Projection
- SuccessTracker

ProGuide: East and Southeast Asia
- Lesson Plan, pp. T64–T65
- 🏃 myWorld Activity Step-by-Step Instructions, p. T66
- Activity Support: Interview, p. T67
- myWorld Geography Enrichment, p. T68
- Section Quiz, p. T69

Accelerating the Progress of ELLs
- Peer Learning Strategies, p. 46

3 Understand
Assess understanding

Review Review *Word Wise* and *Take Notes* in the **Student Journals.**

Assess Knowledge and Skills Use the Section Assessment and the Section Quiz to check students' progress.

Assess Understanding Review students' responses to the Section Assessment Essential Question prompt.

Remediate Use these strategies to review and remediate.

If students struggle to . . .	Try these strategies.
Explain geographic influences on Southeast Asia's history and culture	Discuss the impact on their lives of local landforms or waterways.
Compare and contrast	Assign additional practice with the **21st Century Online Tutor.**
Understand terms, such as *volcanoes, monsoons,* and *cultural borrowing*	Direct them to photographs and other visuals in the Chapter Atlas related to these terms.

ELL Support

ELL Objective Students will be able to use English question words.

Cultural Connections To connect students to the physical features of Southeast Asia, encourage them to ask and answer questions about the landscape of their home countries.

ELL Intermediate Content Tip Model asking questions about geography, such as "What is the elevation?," "How do people get water?," or "Where do the people live?" Also model asking more complex investigational questions that use the conditional tense such as, "If a nation is an island, where would the people live?"

ELL Activity Ask students to locate India, China, and Southeast Asia on a world map. Then let them take turns tracing a route from India or China to the Southeast Asia mainland or islands. Have pairs ask questions about how to get from one location to another on the map. **(Visual/Kinesthetic)**

myWorld Activity   **Step-by-Step Instructions**

 20 min

Why Settle in Southeast Asia?

OBJECTIVES

Students will

- ask questions about the geography of different areas in Southeast Asia.
- recognize that cultural borrowing affected immigrants and their new homelands.

LEARNING STYLE

- Interpersonal
- Verbal

21st Century Learning

- Ask Questions

MATERIALS

- Activity Support: Interview, p. T67

Activity Steps

1. Remind students that many people from China and India settled in Southeast Asia over the centuries. Distribute copies of *Activity Support: Interview,* and tell them that they will be playing the role of a settler in Southeast Asia from India or China. Working in pairs, they will make decisions about their characters and the places where they settled.

2. After partners decide on details of the settler, they will answer questions related to the settler's new home and then ask and answer questions of their own. Students will record these responses on *Activity Support: Interview.* They should use their books for help.

   L1 Special Needs Use a timeline to help students place the settler and his or her mode of travel.

   L2 Extra Support Remind students to use the boldface headings in their books to lead them to information that might be helpful. They

may also want to turn a heading into a question to complete their worksheets. For example, the heading **Climate** could become a question: *What kind of climate did you find in your new home?*

3. Allow partners 15 minutes to complete their interviews.

4. Encourage partners to take turns role-playing the part of interviewer and settler, using their completed *Activity Support: Interview.*

5. If time allows, invite students to present their interviews to the class, and have the class guess where each settler made a new home.

 More Activities From myWorld Teachers

Local Connections Have students visit a local Southeast Asian restaurant or find and analyze a menu to research vegetables, fruits, and other ingredients that are native to the region. **(Kinesthetic/ Verbal)**

Map It Have students create a map showing the route that the settler took to Southeast Asia, including stops the settler may have made along the way. **(Visual)**

Round Table Have small groups discuss the difficulties of settling in a new land. What would be the greatest hardships in an undeveloped region: homesickness, unknown dangers, cultural or language differences with the local population, or other issues? **(Verbal)**

 my worldgeography.com (**Teacher Center**) → Find additional resources in the online Teacher Center.

Name _____ Class _____ Date _____

myWorld Activity Support   Interview

Why Settle in Southeast Asia?

Directions Fill out the description of a settler from India or China.
Then ask and answer questions from the settler's viewpoint.

This settler is from ☐ China   ☐ India

This settler arrived

☐ in ancient times   ☐ in the age of sailing ships   ☐ after 1800   ☐ in modern times

This settler traveled by

☐ foot   ☐ sailing ship   ☐ steamship   ☐ jet

This settler settled in

☐ Malaysia   ☐ Burma   ☐ Singapore   ☐ Vietnam   ☐ Bali   ☐ Sumatra

Question Why did you settle there?   **Answer**
Question In what ways did you change the environment of your new home?   **Answer**
Question   **Answer**
Question   **Answer**

T67

Name _____ Class _____ Date _____

Enrichment: Krakatoa

Directions Read the selection below. Answer the questions that follow and complete the activity.

It was early June 1883. People living in Batavia (present-day Jakarta) were puzzled. Something strange was happening on nearby Krakatoa. From Batavia they noted rumblings coming from the island. They saw puffs of ash over Krakatoa. What was going on? These odd events continued through the summer.

The mountainous island of Krakatoa sits in the Sunda Strait between Sumatra and Java. This channel links the Indian Ocean and the Java Sea. It was an important seaway for merchant ships.

On August 26, Krakatoa began to explode. One blast followed another. A black cloud rose 17 miles above the strait. Ships sailing nearby reported thick showers of black ash. Crews had to shovel it off their ships' decks. Choking winds tormented them. The blasts lasted all night. Sea waves burst onto shore. And then a strange quiet settled over the area. The calm didn't last. At 10:02 A.M., the next morning, the island blew up. The volcano collapsed in on itself, and most of Krakatoa sank with it. A giant tsunami followed. Coastal towns were washed away. An estimated 36,000 people lost their lives.

The 2009 World Almanac lists 18 notable volcanic eruptions in historical times. Of those, five occurred in Indonesia—including Krakatoa. Indonesia remains one of the world's top volcanic hot spots. Thankfully, great eruptions like the one at Krakatoa are rare.

1. Think about the description in this article about the months before Krakatoa burst. What does this information show about the state of volcanology (volcano science) in 1883?

_____

_____

_____

2. Right after the eruption of Krakatoa, scientists collected detailed information about the effects of this giant volcano on the rest of the world. What kinds of information were probably of interest? From where did they probably collect their data?

_____

_____

_____

_____

3. **Activity** Imagine that you watched the 1883 eruption of Krakatoa. Write an eyewitness account in your journal.

Name _____ Class _____ Date _____

Section Quiz

Directions Answer the following questions using what you learned
in Section 1.

1. _____ Mainland Southeast Asia is a wide
    a. island.
    b. archipelago.
    c. peninsula.
    d. delta.

2. _____ The archipelagoes of Southeast Asia
contain many
    a. major rivers.
    b. islands.
    c. plateaus.
    d. cordilleras.

3. _____ When do monsoon rains come to
mainland Southeast Asia?
    a. summer
    b. fall
    c. winter
    d. spring

4. _____ Typhoons are similar to
    a. earthquakes.
    b. floods.
    c. hurricanes.
    d. volcanoes.

5. _____ How do tsunamis cause destruction?
    a. by producing powerful winds
    b. by covering the land with huge waves
    c. by flinging hot rock and ashes into
       the air
    d. by rocking the earth severely

6. Complete the table below to show the influences of Southeast
Asia's geography on settlement and culture.

Characteristic	Influence on Southeast Asian Settlement and Culture
Tropical wet and dry climate	
North-south cordilleras	
Deltas with rich sediment	
Gentle seas	

Chapter Atlas

- Model preparing to read by previewing the Key Ideas, Key Terms, headings, visuals, and captions. Have students make predictions about what they will learn. For ELL support, post the prompt: "I predict I will read about . . ."

- Preview and practice reading special purpose maps by looking at the population density map of Southeast Asia. Help students to make predictions about the purpose of this map. Ask, What might you learn about Southeast Asia and its cities by studying a population density map?

- Preteach this section's high-use Academic Vocabulary and Key Terms using the chart on the next page and in-text definitions. Have students practice Key Terms by completing the *Word Wise* page in their journals.

GUIDE ON THE SIDE

Physical Features

- **Analyze Visuals** What does the background image tell you about the region? (Sample: There are active volcanoes here.)

- **Identify Details** How many countries make up Southeast Asia today? (11 countries)

- **Predict** Why do you think Southeast Asia's rivers are important to the region? (Sample: Rivers provide farmers with rich soil and water for their crops, transportation for trading, fishing stock, and an electricity source.)

Reading Skill

Label an Outline Map While they read, have students identify the Places to Know! on the outline map of the region in the **Student Journal.**

Section 1

Chapter Atlas

Key Ideas
- Southeast Asia is a region of varied landforms.
- Location and climate affect both agricultural production and natural resources.
- Geography has influenced Southeast Asian history and settlement patterns.

Key Terms • peninsula • archipelago • tsunami • monsoon • typhoon

(Visual Glossary)

Reading Skill: Label an Outline Map Take notes using the outline map in your journal.

Mount Mayon erupts in the Philippines.

Balinese dancers from Indonesia

Physical Features

Ridwan's cousin's wedding took place on the island of Sumatra in Indonesia. Indonesia is one of the 11 nations that make up Southeast Asia. The region has two parts: a mainland and an island area, part of which lies on the Equator.

The mainland of Southeast Asia is a **peninsula**—a land area almost surrounded by water. It extends from the Shan Plateau down to the narrow Malay peninsula. Among the major rivers are the Mekong, the Irrawaddy, and the Red River. These rivers carry rich soil to fertilize the deltas before they empty into the sea.

ACADEMIC VOCABULARY

High-Use Word	Definition and Sample Sentence
launch	*v.* to set in operation *They launched a new system.*
fertile	*adj.* rich, fruitful *The farmland was fertile.*

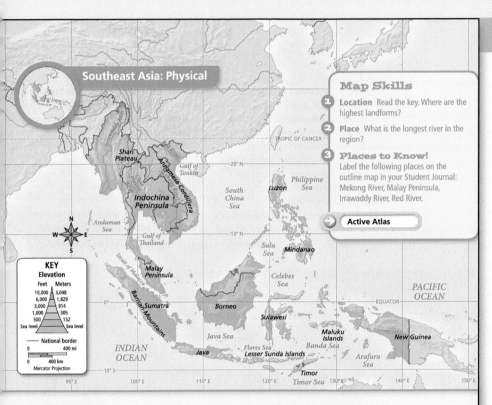

Southeast Asia: Physical

Map Skills

1. **Location** Read the key. Where are the highest landforms?
2. **Place** What is the longest river in the region?
3. **Places to Know!** Label the following places on the outline map in your Student Journal: Mekong River, Malay Peninsula, Irrawaddy River, Red River.

Active Atlas

GUIDE ON THE SIDE

- **Cause and Effect** What causes earthquakes in Southeast Asia? (They are caused by the shifting of underground plates.)

- **Draw Conclusions** Why is the string of active volcanoes in the Pacific called the "Ring of Fire"? (Fire and lava are associated with active, sometimes destructive, volcanoes.)

- **Infer** In what ways do the landscapes of Southeast Asian islands differ? (They differ in size, shape, soil, and origin.)

Analyze Maps Direct students to the physical map of Southeast Asia.

- Through which major Southeast Asian islands does the Equator pass? (Sumatra, Borneo, Sulawesi)

- Where are the Barisan Mountains? (on Sumatra)

The rest of the region is made up of **archipelagoes,** or groups of islands. The sizes of the islands vary greatly, from huge Borneo to tiny islands that may not even appear on some maps. Many island landscapes are breathtaking. Beyond beautiful sandy beaches, mountains and volcanoes tower over narrow coastal plains. Short, fast-flowing rivers run through rain forests filled with great biodiversity, or variety of living things.

Many islands in Indonesia and the Philippines are part of the Ring of Fire, a string of active volcanoes that encircles the Pacific Ocean.

Most of Southeast Asia is part of the Eurasian Plate, which is colliding with the Indo-Australian Plate. When these plates shift deep underground, destructive earthquakes can occur. In December 2004, an earthquake just 150 miles west of the island of Sumatra created a huge **tsunami,** or tidal wave. This tsunami killed more than 230,000 people living around the Indian Ocean. An early warning system has been <u>launched</u> to try to prevent such a disaster from happening again.

launch, *v.,* to set in operation

Reading Check What are the two main parts of Southeast Asia?

READING CHECK mainland and island area

MAP SKILLS **1.** northern mainland and New Guinea **2.** Mekong River **3.** Students should correctly label the outline map.

ANSWERS

 Active Atlas

Study more political maps of Southeast Asia online.

GEOGRAPHY

The Valley of Life Northeastern Thailand contains an area that has been called "The Valley of Life." The Mekong River runs through this region. It is a part of the Khorat Plateau that receives about 50 inches of rainfall each year. Many endangered species live there, including clouded leopards, pileated gibbons, Asian elephants, and sun bears. Rare birds, such as great thick-knees, river lapwings, and plain martins call the region home. Hunting, farming, intentional burning, fishing, and recreation are some threats to this valley of life.

Climate

- **Identify Details** Why do island temperatures remain fairly constant? (The islands are near the Equator.)
- **Compare and Contrast** How does the climate of the northern mainland differ from the climate of the region's islands? (The northern mainland has humid subtropical climate, whereas the islands have tropical wet climate.)
- **Cause and Effect** What are the effects of summer monsoons? (They bring heavy rain which causes river flooding.)

Analyze Maps Direct students to the climate map of Southeast Asia.

- Why are the islands so rainy? (They receive the effects of rain-producing wind, ocean, and temperatures.)
- In what direction does the monsoon wind blow in January and July? (It blows east to west in January; west to east in July.)

Climate

Southeast Asia is a region of hot temperatures and abundant rain—perfect conditions for the growth of rain forests. Parts of the mainland and most of the islands have a tropical wet climate. The climate in the northern part of the mainland is humid subtropical. The climate in the rest of the mainland is mostly tropical wet and dry.

Much of the mainland and the islands receive heavy rain. Although occasional dry conditions affect the mainland, most of the islands have no dry season. The islands are near the Equator, so temperatures are hot everywhere.

Every year **monsoons,** or seasonal winds, blow through the region. The summer monsoons carry heavy rain and cause flooding. These winds come in from the Indian Ocean. In the winter, monsoons blow from the Pacific.

Typhoons are storms much like hurricanes. They blow in from the western Pacific between June and November.

Reading Check What are typhoons?

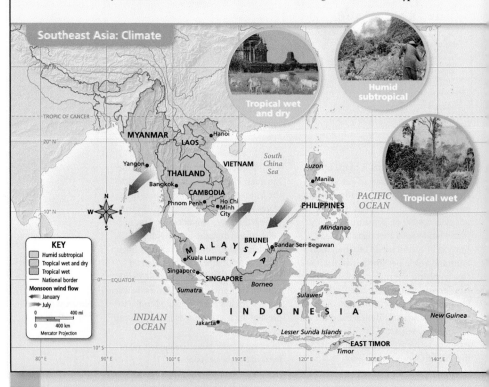

Southeast Asia: Climate

KEY
- Humid subtropical
- Tropical wet and dry
- Tropical wet
- National border

Monsoon wind flow
- January
- July

0   400 mi
0   400 km
Mercator Projection

Tropical wet and dry
Humid subtropical
Tropical wet

READING CHECK Typhoons are giant storms similar to hurricanes.

PRIMARY SOURCES

Malacca on the Strait "Observers [during the 1400s] reported that the town of Malacca [on the southwest coast of Malaysia] boasted 15,000 merchants and more ships in the harbor than any port in the known world, induced by stable government and a free trade policy."
—Craig A. Lockard, *Southeast Asia in World History*

"[Malacca] is a city that was made for merchandise, fitter than any other in the world . . . . Commerce between different nations for a thousand leagues on every hand must come to [Malacca]."
—*Portuguese visitor of the early 1500s*

People and Geography

Geography has shaped the history and culture of Southeast Asia. In the north, mountains separated mainland Southeast Asia from the rest of Asia. Within the region itself, north-south cordilleras, or parallel mountain ranges, isolated early societies. Later, the cordilleras helped define national borders. The rivers that carried rich sediment to the deltas also played an important role, for it was in the <u>fertile</u> river valleys that the first civilizations emerged.

The mostly gentle seas of Southeast Asia allowed trade, much of which traveled through the narrow Malacca Strait. For centuries pirates and kings fought to control the riches of this waterway. Another rich prize lay to the east in the Maluku Islands. Here, in the volcanic soil, grew rare spices such as nutmeg and cloves. At one time, these spices could be found nowhere else on Earth. The spice trade attracted Europeans—who came first to trade and then to colonize.

Reading Check Where did spices grow?

fertile, *adj.*, rich, fruitful

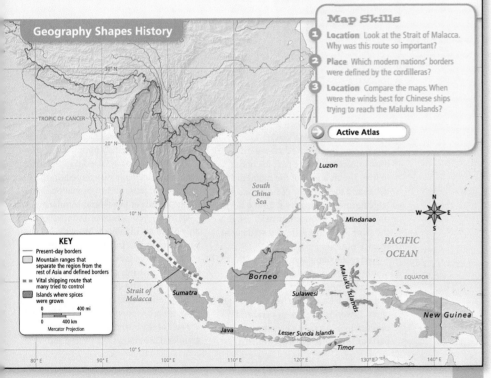

Geography Shapes History

Map Skills

1. **Location** Look at the Strait of Malacca. Why was this route so important?
2. **Place** Which modern nations' borders were defined by the cordilleras?
3. **Location** Compare the maps. When were the winds best for Chinese ships trying to reach the Maluku Islands?

→ **Active Atlas**

KEY
— Present-day borders
▢ Mountain ranges that separate the region from the rest of Asia and defined borders
▪▪▪ Vital shipping route that many tried to control
▢ Islands where spices were grown

0 — 400 mi
0 — 400 km
Mercator Projection

GUIDE ON THE SIDE

People and Geography

- **Cause and Effect** What caused many early cultures of Southeast Asia to develop independently? (Parallel mountain ranges isolated early societies.)

- **Cause and Effect** What effect did mountain ranges have on national boundaries in the region? (Mountains acted as natural borders.)

- **Summarize** Why did so many groups fight for control of the Malacca Strait? (The gentle seas gave access to rich trade; traders desired the valuable spices of the Maluku Islands.)

→ **Active Atlas**

Learn more about the history of Southeast Asia through historical maps online.

READING CHECK Spices grew in the Maluku Islands.

MAP SKILLS 1. It shortens the journey for ships traveling along the coast. 2. Vietnam, Laos, Cambodia, and Myanmar 3. winter months

QUICK FACTS

Population Density Singapore is the world's second-most densely populated country with more than 17,000 persons per square mile.

Settlement and Land Use

- **Identify Details** What fraction of the Indonesian islands are populated? (6000/17000, or 6/17, or about one third)

- **Cause and Effect** Why do farmers live near river deltas and on volcanic islands? (The soil is richer there.)

- **Draw Conclusions** Why is population thinnest in mountainous and rain forest areas? (Growing crops, traveling, or setting up communications is harder.)

- **Analyze Maps** Which island nations are heavily populated? (the Philippines and parts of Indonesia)

21st Century Learning

Using the 21st Century Online Tutor, students can get more tips about reading a special-purpose map.

myWorld Activity

Why Settle in Southeast Asia?
Find Step-by-Step instructions and an Activity Support on pp. T66–T67. **(Interpersonal/Verbal)**

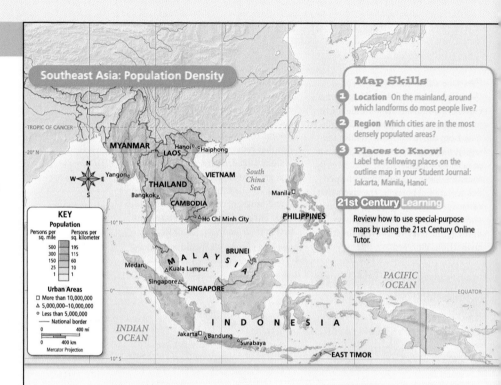

Southeast Asia: Population Density

Map Skills

1. **Location** On the mainland, around which landforms do most people live?
2. **Region** Which cities are in the most densely populated areas?
3. **Places to Know!** Label the following places on the outline map in your Student Journal: Jakarta, Manila, Hanoi.

21st Century Learning

Review how to use special-purpose maps by using the 21st Century Online Tutor.

myWorld Activity
Why Settle in Southeast Asia?

Settlement and Land Use

The natural resources of the region have influenced where people choose to live. The rich soils of the mainland deltas and the volcanic islands attracted large farming populations. Today, large populations are concentrated in roughly the same areas that attracted settlement in ancient times.

Today the population density of Southeast Asia is very uneven. On the mainland, most people live on coastal plains and deltas, or in river valleys and cities. Fewer people live in rural and mountainous areas, such as the northern parts of Myanmar (formerly Burma),

Thailand, Vietnam, and Laos. Some areas of rain forest are hardly populated at all.

The populations of island nations are even more unevenly distributed. In the Philippines, most of the population live on the islands of Luzon and Mindanao.

Of the 17,000 islands in Indonesia, only 6,000 are inhabited. More than 60 percent of Indonesia's population resides on the island of Java. Nearly all the rest lives on the islands of Sumatra, Borneo, and Sulawesi. The easternmost province of Indonesia, Irian Jaya (IRH ee ahn JAH yuh), is hardly populated at all.

Most of the farming areas on the mainland are along river valleys and

MAP SKILLS 1. river deltas and coastal areas **2.** Haiphong, Hanoi, Ho Chi Minh City, Bangkok, Yangon, Kuala Lumpur, Singapore, Jakarta, Bandung, Surabaya, and Manila **3.** Students should correctly label the outline map.

COMMON MISCONCEPTIONS

Rice Tales When it comes to rice, many Americans think only of white and brown rice. In fact, there are more than 100,000 cultivated and wild species of rice. Scientists hope to preserve as many kinds as possible in special rice "gene banks." Many Americans might also be surprised to learn that rice is the main food of over 3 billion people—about one half of the world's population.

deltas where plentiful water and good soil allow people to grow rice. Thailand's rice is some of the best in the world. Because Southeast Asia has very little land that is level enough for farming, the peoples of this mountainous region have cleverly altered their landscape to meet their needs. By sculpting the hillsides into steps, or terraces, they have turned mountain slopes into farmland for rice crops. On the higher slopes, cool temperatures provide the perfect conditions for growing tea.

Southeast Asian forests are a great natural resource. Exported lumber from the rain forests is a major source of income for some nations. The lumber is exported mainly to Japan and the United States.

Reading Check Why did large populations develop in the deltas?

Urban Problems

Even though there are many large cities, the region as a whole is mainly rural. However, more people are moving to urban areas in search of jobs and higher living standards. This migration has turned Jakarta, Bangkok, Manila, and Phnom Penh into huge cities with growing urban problems.

The increase in population places great strains on the cities' infrastructures, such as water supplies, electricity, and sewage facilities. Housing, healthcare, and other services also suffer. There are many environmental problems, such as air pollution and traffic congestion. The monsoon rains bring floods that cause sewage overflow and water contamination.

Reading Check What urban problems can be traced to population increases?

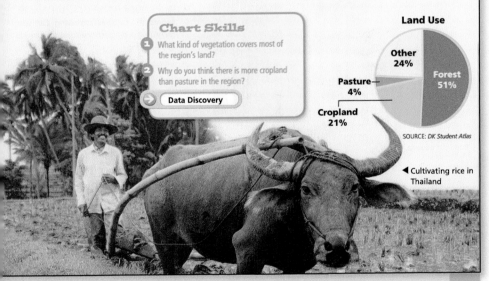

Chart Skills

1 What kind of vegetation covers most of the region's land?

2 Why do you think there is more cropland than pasture in the region?

Data Discovery

Land Use

Other 24%

Pasture 4%

Cropland 21%

Forest 51%

SOURCE: *DK Student Atlas*

◀ Cultivating rice in Thailand

READING CHECK Farming in deltas with rich soil and water supplies led to surpluses, which could support more people and more complex groupings.

READING CHECK air pollution, traffic congestion, water contamination, strain on infrastructures

CHART SKILLS 1. forest 2. Pasture requires more space and would not be the best use of limited farmland.

GUIDE ON THE SIDE

Urban Problems

- **Identify Main Ideas** Why are Southeast Asian cities growing? (People move there hoping for jobs and opportunity.)

- **Summarize** What problems do large Southeast Asian cities face today? (Large population puts pressure on the environment [pollution, water contamination] and on social services, public works, health, and housing.)

- **Analyze Graphs** What land use does "Other" probably refer to? (cities, industry, mountains, highlands)

- **Analyze Visuals** What does the photograph suggest about rice farming in the region? (Farmers still use traditional methods.)

 Data Discovery

Have students go online to discover more Southeast Asia land use statistics.

CULTURE

Overseas Chinese People of Chinese descent who live outside the Republic of China are considered *hua chiao,* or overseas Chinese. According to the Overseas Chinese Affairs Commission, about 35 million Chinese were living outside the mainland in 2000. Over 27 million of them reside in Asia, especially Thailand, Hong Kong, Malaysia, and Singapore.

As one Chinese blogger, Bing Ma Yong, writes, "In Chinese culture, hometown, people of hometown and motherland are always be loved no matter where we go no matter our home town are mountain or plain, rich or poor. Chinese say, 'Falling leaves come back to root.' The root is our home town and mother land."

A History of Diversity

- **Identify Details** Which area in Southeast Asia has the highest Chinese population? (Singapore)

- **Draw Conclusions** Why does the region have great religious diversity? (The influence of immigrants and traders from China, India, and other areas resulted in great religious diversity.)

- **Predict** What religions do you think can be found in Southeast Asia? (Possible answers: Buddhism, Hinduism, Islam)

Analyze Visuals Ask students to study the photograph of the Cao Dai temple.

- What features from other religious buildings can you identify in this temple? (columns and pointed arches like a mosque; curved roofs like a pagoda; two towers at the entrance like a church)

- What other features do you see? (balconies; roof with several levels; varied windows and openings)

A History of Diversity

Southeast Asia has a history of cultural and religious diversity. Waves of migrations from the north have brought Burmese, Thai, and Lao peoples onto the mainland. Other ancient migrations brought settlers to the region by sea. Today, Chinese, Indians, Malays, Burmese, Indonesians, Vietnamese, Filipinos, Thai, Khmer, and Hmong all call the region home. In addition, there are indigenous peoples who live in remote, isolated rain forest communities.

There has always been a strong Chinese presence in Southeast Asia. In ancient times, China was ruling parts of what is now Vietnam by 100 B.C. This started a long history of Chinese involvement in Vietnam.

Today, Chinese communities thrive in every country in the region. Many Chinese immigrated into the region in the 1800s when demand for labor was high. The Chinese population ranges from less than 1 percent in East Timor to 77 percent in Singapore. There are also large Indian communities in Malaysia and Myanmar.

Cultural Borrowing

Southeast Asia's location on the international trade routes has created a lively cultural exchange. In Vietnam the Cao Dai religion mixes elements of several major religions. Cao Dai temples express this cultural borrowing. *Can you identify the different cultural features in this building?*

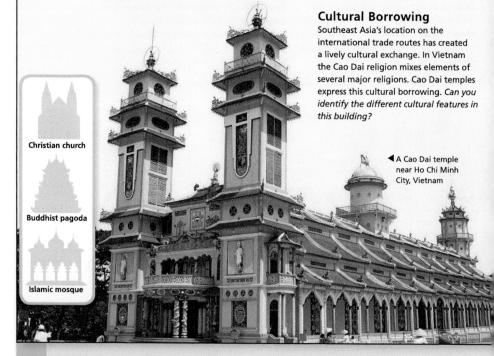

◄ A Cao Dai temple near Ho Chi Minh City, Vietnam

Christian church

Buddhist pagoda

Islamic mosque

READING CHECK Merchants and travelers, first from Asia and then from Europe, brought new traditions and faiths. People from different islands intermarried and absorbed new ideas.

SECTION 1 ASSESSMENT 1. Sample: Mainland Southeast Asia is a peninsula. The rest of the region is composed of archipelagoes. Monsoons blow in heavy summer rains. Earthquakes cause tsunamis. Typhoons hit from the western Pacific in June through

QUICK FACTS

Muslim Communities Marco Polo made the first Western reference to Muslim communities in Southeast Asian islands when the famous trekker stopped in Sumatra in 1292.

Indonesia has the largest Muslim population of any country in the world—over 200,000,000 people (about 86 percent of the country's population).

In a region of such ethnic diversity, it is not surprising that there is much religious diversity as well. Most of mainland Southeast Asia was influenced by two different forms of Buddhism that spread from India and China.

Islam became the major religion in large parts of island Southeast Asia. On most of the islands it replaced Buddhism and Hinduism. However, islands such as Bali remained Hindu. Today Bali is part of Indonesia, a country that has the largest Muslim population in the world.

While most people of the islands are Muslim, the majority of people in the Philippines are Roman Catholic due to Spanish colonization in the 1500s. However, there are Muslims in the Philippines as well, especially on the two islands of Mindanao and Palawan.

Many religious communities blend customs and traditions from more than one faith. This cultural mixing is a feature of Southeast Asian life. Ridwan's Minangkabau are a good example of this cultural openness, which began in ancient times. From their homeland in the mountains of Sumatra, the Minangkabau traveled downriver to trade. In time they became merchants and travelers, pursuing the knowledge and wealth of the wider world. Along the way they absorbed Indian, Chinese, and Western customs and beliefs. They married their old traditions to the new ways of Islam that they embraced. Later, they enthusiastically adopted the educational system of the Dutch. Their openness to other cultures has served them well. Today the Minangkabau are among the wealthiest, most educated, and most powerful groups in Indonesia.

Southeast Asia's location, which attracted international trade, helped the Minangkabau achieve economic success. In the next section you will see how the story of the Minangkabau connects with Southeast Asia's history of economic trade and cultural exchange.

Reading Check Why is Southeast Asia populated with such a great diversity of ethnic groups?

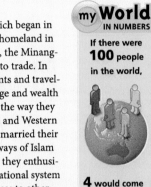

my World IN NUMBERS

If there were **100** people in the world,

4 would come from Indonesia.

GUIDE ON THE SIDE

- **Summarize** Which religious traditions are found in Southeast Asia? (Buddhist, Hindu, Muslim, Catholic)
- **Infer** Why did trading help produce cultural diversity in the islands of the region? (Traders brought new ideas and traditions that the native population absorbed.)
- **Express an Opinion** Do you think that the success of the Minangkabau is a result of their ability to absorb influences of other ethnic groups? Explain your answer. (Sample: Yes, they became more educated and more successful because of their interactions with other groups.)

Section 1 Assessment

Key Terms	Key Ideas	Think Critically	Essential Question
1. Use the following terms to describe the geography and climate of Southeast Asia: peninsula, archipelago, tsunami, monsoon, typhoon.	**2.** What are some differences between the landscapes of the mainland and the islands? **3.** Where do most Southeast Asians live? **4.** How have Southeast Asians adapted the landscape to meet their needs?	**5. Synthesize** Compare the population density map with the physical map. What patterns do you see? **6. Draw Conclusions** Why might the coastal areas and islands have had more contact with the outside world?	**What are the challenges of diversity?** **7.** Why did the geography of the region help create such a diverse population? Go to your Student Journal to record your answer.

2. The mainland has mountain ranges and long rivers; the islands have rain forests, beaches, volcanoes, coastal plains, and short rivers. **3.** On the mainland, they live on coastal plains, deltas, river valleys, and cities. On the islands, they live on Java, Sumatra, Borneo, and Sulawesi. **4.** They terraced hills and mountains to create farmland. **5.** Population is concentrated in the lowlands. **6.** These regions were visited by people traveling by sea to other parts of the world. **7.** Sample: Rich soil and spices attracted traders from Asia and beyond.

ANSWERS

The History of Southeast Asia

OBJECTIVES

Students will know

- merchants' and invaders' influence on Southeast Asian culture.
- effects of nationalism and ideological conflict.

Students will be able to

- recall the sequence of events in Southeast Asian history.
- compare viewpoints of colonizers and people from Southeast Asia.

SET EXPECTATIONS

In this section, students will

- read the history of Southeast Asia.
- create a graphic story based on Southeast Asian history.
- discover data and work with the Visual Glossary Online.

CORE CONCEPTS

You may wish to teach or reteach the following lessons from the Core Concepts Handbook:

- Migration, pp. 78–79
- Cultural Diffusion and Change, pp. 96–97
- Measuring Time, pp. 118–119

KEY

Differentiated Instruction

L1 Special Needs **L2** Extra Support
L3 On-Level **L4** Challenge

English Language Instruction

ELL Beginner **ELL** Early Intermediate **ELL** Intermediate
ELL Early Advanced **ELL** Advanced

1 Connect
Make learning meaningful

Make Connections Ask students to check out local memorials to the veterans who fought in Vietnam during the 1960s and 1970s or interview their parents or grandparents about their memories of that period. Have students share a journal entry about their findings.

L4 Challenge Have students create a poster about the local impact of the Vietnam War, using photographs, drawings, and their interviews.

Activate Prior Knowledge Remind students that they learned about Southeast Asia's rich resources, including spice crops. Invite them to predict how these resources might have affected Southeast Asia's interaction with other parts of the world.

L2 Extra Support Review the Geography Shapes History map and the Cultural Borrowing feature in Section 1 with students.

Prepare Follow the steps in the section **Preview.** Preteach the Key Terms. Then have students complete *Word Wise* in their journals using in-text clues and the glossary for help.

2 Experience
Teach knowledge and skills

Read Use **Background** notes and **Guide on the Side** questions to model active reading. Have students use *Take Notes* in their **Student Journal** to sequence important events in Southeast Asian history. Have them complete **21st Century Online Tutor** *Sequence*, and apply this skill to the section.

L1 Special Needs Help students to list the events of a day at school in correct sequence.

ELL Intermediate Post a timeline with 100-year intervals, beginning with A.D. 1200 and ending with A.D. 1980. Help students to place the following dates on the timeline: A.D. 1287, A.D. 1407, A.D. 1511, and A.D. 1975. Then have them copy the timeline and identify each date, as they read the text.

 Practice: myWorld Activity Students will create sets of cartoons that show historical events from two points of view. **Step-by-Step Instructions** and **More Activities** follow on p. T72.

FOR THE STUDENT

my worldgeography.com **Student Center**
- Timeline
- Active Atlas

Student Edition (print and online)
- The History of Southeast Asia

Student Journal (print and online)
- Section 2 Word Wise
- Section 2 Take Notes

21st Century Learning **Online Tutor**
- Sequence
- Compare Viewpoints

FOR THE TEACHER

my worldgeography.com **Teacher Center**
- Online Lesson Planner
- Presentations for Projection
- SuccessTracker

ProGuide: East and Southeast Asia
- Lesson Plan, pp. T70–T71
- myWorld Activity Step-by-Step Instructions, p. T72
- Activity Support: Viewpoints, p. T73
- myWorld Geography Enrichment, p. T74
- Section Quiz, p. T75

Accelerating the Progress of ELLs
- Organizing Information Strategies, p. 48

3 Understand
Assess understanding

Review Review *Word Wise* and *Take Notes* in the **Student Journal.**

Assess Knowledge and Skills Use the Section Assessment and the Section Quiz to check students' progress.

Assess Understanding Review students' responses to the Section Assessment Essential Question prompt.

Remediate Use these strategies to review and remediate.

If students struggle to . . .	Try these strategies.
Understand the sequence of events in Southeast Asian history	Have students categorize events by period of rule. Then order those periods using dates.
Compare viewpoints	Assign additional practice with the **21st Century Online Tutor.**
Recall the impact of colonization on Southeast Asia	Have groups take notes on one area of impact, such as politics or culture, and present to the class.

ELL Support

ELL Objective Students will be able to use English to compare viewpoints.

Cultural Connections To connect students to the sequence of Southeast Asia's history, encourage them to name three events in the recent history of their hometown and list them in order from least recent to most recent.

ELL Early Intermediate Content Tip For each key term, write a phrase using it in context: *reservoir* full of water; *surplus* of food; *maritime* trading; *exploit* workers. Then have partners create a picture illustrating one of these phrases.

ELL Activity Review pronouns and the conjugation of the verb *think*: I think; He thinks, We think; They think; etc. Use the example of parents and children to come up with different viewpoints on the topics of bedtime, meals, and clothes. Have students role-play children and parents' different viewpoints. **(Kinesthetic/Verbal)**

myWorld Activity   **Step-by-Step Instructions**

 20 min

Historical Cartoons

OBJECTIVES

Students will

- Compare viewpoints of different members of Southeast Asia's population.
- Identify challenges that Southeast Asians faced in different time periods

LEARNING STYLE

- Visual

21st Century Learning

- Compare Viewpoints

MATERIALS

- Activity Support: Viewpoints, p. T73
- Blank paper
- Colored pencils

Activity Steps

1. Remind students that important historical figures and events have changed the course of history in the region. Tell them that they will work in groups to create sets of cartoons showing two competing viewpoints, or ways of seeing, the same event.

2. Groups of four will choose one of the following events to illustrate: The Mongol invasion of the Khmer Empire (1287); the Portuguese conquest of Malacca (1511); or the Vietnamese overthrow of the French (1954). Next, they identify the two sides of this conflict and use the Activity Support to write their ideas about how each side would see this event. Finally, they break into pairs, with each pair taking one side of the event to illustrate as a cartoon. Students may refer to their books or other resources.

   L2 Extra Support To help students understand the idea of comparing viewpoints, ask them whether teachers and students have the same ideas about homework and television. Have them compare these viewpoints.

3. Allow partners 15 minutes to create their cartoons showing the story from one viewpoint. Make sure that students understand that, for this activity, their ideas are more important than their artistic skills.

   L3 On Level Students should write a description or make a simple sketch of what they want in each frame, before drawing their final cartoons.

4. Post students' cartoons for the class to view. If time allows, encourage students to discuss the similarities and differences in the cartoons' viewpoints.

More Activities From myWorld Teachers

Local connections Like Southeast Asia, the United States has a history of people arriving from many lands. Have students learn more about the home countries of their extended family. **(Verbal)**

Time It Have students create an illustrated timeline of important events in Southeast Asian history.

Encourage students to use online research to find images. Consider making a giant timeline to fill a wall. **(Visual)**

Role Play Have students create a skit, based on their cartoons, showing different viewpoints of characters from a given time period. Have students make symbolic props for their characters. **(Kinesthetic)**

my worldgeography.com (**Teacher Center**)   Find additional resources in the online Teacher Center.

Name _____ Class _____ Date _____

myWorld Activity Support   **Viewpoints**

Historical Cartoons

Directions With your group, choose one of the following events from Southeast Asian history: The Mongol invasion of the Khmer Empire (1287); the Portuguese conquest of Malacca (1511); or the Vietnamese overthrow of the French (1954). Think about the two sides of the event. Describe each side by explaining the viewpoint and the person who holds this viewpoint. Work with a partner from your group to illustrate one side's viewpoint of this event in a cartoon.

Event: _____

Viewpoint	**Viewpoint**
Person 1:	**Person 2:**

Name _____ Class _____ Date _____

Enrichment: Angkor, City of Temples

Directions Read the selection below. Answer the questions that follow and complete the activity.

King Jayavarman II founded the Khmer capital in A.D. 802. Located in northwest Cambodia, this area became known as Angkor. It continued to be a rich center of trade and power for about 600 years. Eventually Angkor contained over 100 temples. It also had palaces and other buildings made of wood—as well as a three-mile moat.

The most famous temple in the "City of Temples" was Angkor Wat. Built in the first half of the 1100s, this temple was enormous. It was decorated in fabulous stone sculptures and religious scenes from Hinduism.

During the next three hundred years, the Khmer kings gradually lost power. Over time, the world mostly forgot about Angkor.

In 1860, Henri Mouhot, a French explorer, came upon the ruins of Angkor. He compared its temples to the greatest Greek and Roman buildings. During the 1900s, the French began the first serious efforts to save Angkor. Fighting in the region stopped their work. Angkor continues to be an important site today. Tourists can visit its ruins. Angkor's wooden buildings, however, disappeared long ago. The United Nations agency, UNESCO, has recognized the significance of Angkor. The old Khmer capital has been declared a "World Heritage" site. Efforts are now in progress to help preserve Angkor for future generations.

1. Why do you think Henri Mouhot compared Angkor with Greek and Roman buildings?

_____

_____

2. Why do you think the wooden buildings of Angkor disappeared?

_____

_____

3. Activity After 1860, some French expeditions removed Angkor sculptures to Paris. Write a letter to the prime minister of France saying what you think he should do with the statues today.

_____

_____

_____

_____

Name _____ Class _____ Date _____

Section Quiz

Directions Answer the following questions using what you learned
in Section 2.

1. _____ The Khmers built reservoirs to
   a. protect their farms from invaders.
   b. show respect to their ancestors.
   c. make their cities look beautiful.
   d. store water for irrigation.

2. _____ What was the effect of the Khmer
   farmers' surplus?
   a. They bought many slaves.
   b. They earned great wealth.
   c. They enjoyed rainwater all the time.
   d. They explored the Pacific Ocean.

3. _____ Maritime trade took place by
   a. land.
   b. river.
   c. sea.
   d. roads.

4. _____ How did the Europeans exploit
   Southeast Asia?
   a. by helping common people get wealthy
   b. by bringing in new inventions
   c. by curing terrible diseases
   d. by using the resources for their own
     gain

5. _____ Why is the Khmer empire called a
   "seed culture"?
   a. Many Southeast Asian traditions grew
     out of that culture.
   b. Many new crops grew during that time
     period.
   c. Southeast Asia's population grew during
     that period.
   d. Southeast Asian trading grew
     dramatically during that period.

6. Complete the web below to show the cultural influences of
many foreign lands on Southeast Asia.

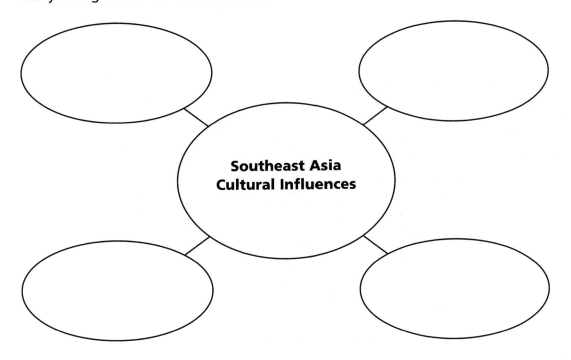

Southeast Asia
Cultural Influences

  T75

History of Southeast Asia

- Model preparing to read by previewing the Key Ideas, Key Terms, headings, visuals, and captions. Have students make predictions about what they will learn. For ELL support, post the prompt: "I predict I will read about . . ."

- Preview and practice the reading skill, sequence, by listing the steps you take to get onto the Internet

from a computer and find a particular kind of information.

- Preteach this section's high-use Academic Vocabulary and Key Terms using the table on the next page and in-text definitions. Have students practice Key Terms by completing the *Word Wise* page in their journals.

GUIDE ON THE SIDE

Ancient Southeast Asia

- **Identify Details** What ancient city drew the Chinese into Southeast Asia? (Co Loa, in present-day Vietnam)

- **Identify Evidence** What evidence shows us that societies of Southeast Asia were becoming more complex after 500 B.C.? (Rice surpluses, development of crafts; and trade provide evidence.)

- **Draw Conclusions** Why did civilizations grow up in Southeast Asia's river valleys? (The rivers supplied water. Farmers could grow enough food to support large populations and to develop wealth for building and cultural activities.)

- **Analyze Visuals** What does the photograph suggest about why the Angkor civilization was mostly forgotten after its decline? (After the people left, the rain forest covered up much evidence of its existence.)

Reading Skill

Sequence While they read, have students practice this skill by completing the *Take Notes* graphic organizer in the **Student Journal.**

Section 2

History of Southeast Asia

Key Ideas
- Southeast Asia's location encouraged trade and cultural and ethnic diversity.
- Europeans transformed the cultural geography of the region.
- Wars of independence were followed by civil wars on mainland Southeast Asia.

Key Terms • reservoir • surplus • maritime • exploit

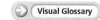
Visual Glossary

Reading Skill: Sequence Take notes using the graphic organizer in your journal.

If the history of Southeast Asia were a video, it would show you a story of migrations and trade. First you would see people living on the volcanic island of Java tens of thousands of years ago. Running the video forward would show newcomers migrating to the region by land and sea. Soon you would notice Indonesian boats carrying the earliest trade goods between India and China.

Ancient Southeast Asia

As the video reached 500 B.C., you would see fields of rice growing in the lowlands of Cambodia and Vietnam. Everywhere you would notice populations increasing because of plentiful harvests. Soon you would see villages specializing in particular crafts and trading goods with one another as societies became more complex.

More than 2000 years ago, civilizations grew up in the river valleys, where rice crops kept the populations well fed. In the north of what is now Vietnam, the city of Co Loa grew rich. Its wealth attracted the Chinese, who conquered the city by 100 B.C. In the south, port cities bustled with foreign merchants, traders, and traveling priests. The famous ethnic diversity of Southeast Asian cities had emerged.

Reading Check Why did populations increase in ancient times?

◀ A strangler fig tree creeps over the ruins of Angkor Thom, Cambodia. Culture Close-up

READING CHECK Populations increased where food supplies were plentiful.

ACADEMIC VOCABULARY

High-Use Word	Definition and Sample Sentence
invader	*n.* a person who enters a place by force *Invaders attacked the village.*
resource	*n.* something that a country can use to its advantage *Spices were a costly resource.*

The Great Kingdoms

Between A.D. 500 and 1500 kingdoms grew and trade expanded. Southeast Asians blended foreign influences into their own culture.

Controlling the Strait The region's location on international trade routes led to contact with India and China. Local kingdoms adopted religions from India, such as Hinduism and Buddhism.

Commerce created such wealth that coastal states fought to control trade. One of the busiest trade routes went through the Strait of Malacca. Srivijaya, a Hindu-Buddhist kingdom on Sumatra, controlled the strait from A.D. 600 to 1300.

Agricultural Empires On the mainland, a civilization rose in what is now Cambodia. The Khmers (kuh MEHRZ) used the landscape to meet their needs.

They built **reservoirs,** or storage pools, of rainwater to irrigate rice fields. This produced huge harvests. They grew rich by selling their extra, or **surplus,** food.

The Khmer empire was a kind of "seed culture" from which many Southeast Asian traditions grew. The Khmers had a strong influence on the culture of Cambodia and Thailand.

As the Khmer empire declined, fierce <u>invaders</u> entered the region. In 1287 the Mongols destroyed the Burmese empire of Bagan (Pagan). But the invaders suffered from the tropical heat and rains. They were also startled by Southeast Asian war elephants, which hurled enemy soldiers into the air with their trunks! During their invasion of Java, the Mongols lost three thousand men.

Reading Check Which civilizations influenced culture in Southeast Asia?

invader, *n.,* person who enters a place by force

Ancient Trade Routes

In ancient times, goods from the Mediterranean, China, India, and Southeast Asia were exchanged along the trade routes. Southeast Asia occupied an important position on these routes.

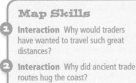

Map Skills

1. **Interaction** Why would traders have wanted to travel such great distances?
2. **Interaction** Why did ancient trade routes hug the coast?
3. **Interaction** Where might you have seen the busiest shipping lanes in ancient times?

Active Atlas

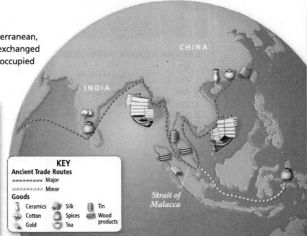

CHINA

INDIA

KEY
Ancient Trade Routes
▬▬▬▬▬ Major
▬ ▬ ▬ ▬ Minor
Goods
Ceramics   Silk   Tin
Cotton   Spices   Wood products
Gold   Tea

Strait of Malacca

READING CHECK India and China

MAP SKILLS 1. Spice trade was highly lucrative. **2.** Knowledge of island geography was limited; sailors wanted to stay near known areas; they wanted to be closer to land if storms picked up. **3.** Malacca Strait, along the coasts

GUIDE ON THE SIDE

The Great Kingdoms

- **Cause and Effect** What effect did trade have on religion in the region? (Trade brought Hinduism and Buddhism.)

- **Analyze Text** What does it mean when the text says that the Khmer empire was a "kind of 'seed culture'"? (A seed culture is the origin of practices, beliefs and arts.)

- **Compare and Contrast** In what ways were the Mongols different from the Chinese and Indian intruders in Southeast Asia? (Sample: The Mongols wanted to destroy Southeast Asian societies. By contrast, the Chinese and Indians blended their cultures.)

Analyze Maps Direct students to the trade routes map.

- What products did Chinese merchants bring to other lands? (silks, tea, ceramics)

- What products did Indian merchants bring to other lands? (spices, cotton)

Culture Close-up

Have students go online to explore the ancient cultures of Southeast Asia.

ECONOMICS

Rubber Industry Manufacturers use two kinds of rubber, natural and synthetic. Southeast Asia supplies over 90 percent of the world's natural rubber. Before World War II, most rubber was natural. During the war, Japan cut the United States off from rubber supplies in Southeast Asia.

As a result, production of synthetic rubber rose from 8,000 tons in 1941 to 820,000 tons in 1945. Nearly three quarters of all rubber is synthetic today.

The Age of Commerce

- **Summarize** Why did Islam spread rapidly through the islands of Southeast Asia? (Traders from India brought their religion with them and converted an important ruler of Malacca.)

- **Compare and Contrast** Why did the Europeans come later to Southeast Asia than the Indians and Chinese? (Europe is much farther from Southeast Asia than India or China.)

- **Synthesize** In 1511, what possible routes could Europeans use to reach Southeast Asia? (They could travel by sea [around Africa past India and through the waterways of Southeast Asia]; by land [across Asia into Southeast Asia]; or by land and sea.)

Closer Look

Analyze Graphs Direct students to the colonial export graph.

- How many thousands of metric tons of coffee were exported from Dutch Indonesia in 1900? (50)

- How many thousands of metric tons of rubber were exported from British Malaya in 1920? (about 125)

Closer Look

EFFECTS OF COLONIZATION

Between the 1850s and the 1950s, Southeast Asia was colonized first by Western nations and then occupied by Japan. During that hundred-year period the region changed forever. Large plantations replaced small farms. The demand for cheap labor attracted workers from India and China.

THINK CRITICALLY **Study the graph. Which export increased dramatically around 1910?**

The Dutch built plantations like this one in Indonesia. ▼

Western governments introduced export crops such as rubber and coffee. The region still exports these goods.

Colonial Exports, 1900–1930

Thousands of Metric Tons

Rubber from British Malaya

Coffee from Dutch Indonesia

1900   1910   1920   1930
Year

SOURCE: *International Historical Statistics*

The Age of Commerce

By the 1400s, the old agricultural empires of Bagan and the Khmer had declined. New regional powers had emerged, based on **maritime,** or sea, trade. Meanwhile, the religion of Islam was spreading along the trade routes, carried by Muslim merchants. After the ruler of the rich port of Malacca converted to Islam in 1414, the religion spread through the islands. Ridwan's Minangkabau ancestors were some of the people who converted to the faith.

The famous wealth of Malacca and its control of the spice trade excited the envy of Europeans. For centuries, Europeans had been trying to gain control of the trade in spices, many of which grew on the Maluku Islands. Then, in 1511, the Portuguese conquered Malacca.

During the following centuries, Western powers tightened their grip on Southeast Asia and **exploited,** or took advantage of, the region's resources. The Spanish, Dutch, British, French, and Americans all founded colonies there. Only Thailand managed to resist colonization.

Reading Check **How did Western powers change Southeast Asia?**

Independence, War, and Recovery

During the early 1900s, independence movements in the region grew. Then, during World War II, Japan took control of most of Southeast Asia. After Japan lost the war, European powers tried and failed to regain control of the region. By 1957 the countries of Southeast Asia had won independence.

THINK CRITICALLY Rubber from British Malaya

READING CHECK They colonized and exploited resources and land.

READING CHECK Japan invaded the region; Southeast Asian nations resisted Japanese efforts to colonize.

HISTORY

Heroic Sisters The Vietnamese still revere two sisters who lived nearly 2,000 years ago—Trung Trac and Trung Nhi. Around the year A.D. 40, they led a successful, though brief, rebellion to oust the Chinese who controlled Vietnam. Soon a Chinese army suppressed them and re-established control. Despite this defeat, the story of the two sisters inspired Vietnamese women during the Vietnam War.

Mainland Conflicts For some nations, the fight for independence was long and bloody. In Vietnam, communist forces under Ho Chi Minh fought the French. War lasted until 1954, when France gave up control. Vietnam was divided into two republics: a communist north and a non-communist south.

However, fighting soon developed between north and south. The United States first sent advisers and then troops to South Vietnam to stop the spread of communism. The fighting spread to neighboring nations. This war dragged on until 1975, when the country was united under communist rule, following the departure of United States troops from the area.

Cambodia, which gained independence in 1953, also suffered conflict. As the Vietnam War heated up, Cambodia was dragged into the fight. This led to years of suffering. Under the brutal communist government of the Khmer Rouge, people who lived in the cities were forced into the countryside, where millions of them were murdered.

Southeast Asia Recovers The 1900s had been a violent century for Southeast Asia. The communist nations of Vietnam, Laos, and Cambodia all suffered terribly from the wars of the mainland. In addition, some communist economic policies had been disastrous. In the late 1980s Vietnam, Laos, and Cambodia adopted some capitalist practices that finally turned their economies around. However, today the communist countries of Southeast Asia remain the poorest nations in the region.

The capitalist countries such as Indonesia and Malaysia approached the new century in better shape. They marketed their <u>resources</u> and varied their economies. Rather than relying on agricultural exports, these economies now include manufacturing. Some Southeast Asian nations, like Singapore, were so successful that by the 1990s they were called "Asian Tigers." In the next section, you will read more about Southeast Asia today.

Reading Check What changes did World War II bring to Southeast Asia?

resource, *n.,* something that a country can use to its advantage

myWorld Activity
Historical Cartoon

- **Identify Main Ideas** Why didn't the partition of Vietnam end the battle for independence? (The United States intervened to stop the spread of communism.)

- **Express an Opinion** Why do you think it took so long for Southeast Asian nations to win independence? (For financial and military reasons: European nations did not want to let go of their lucrative holdings or strategic positions in Southeast Asia.)

- **Inference** Why have some Southeast Asian nations been called "Asian Tigers"? (They were given this name because of their strong, dynamic economies.)

 myWorld Activity

Historical Cartoons Find Step-by-Step Instructions and an Activity Support on pp. T72–T73. **(Visual)**

Section 2 Assessment

Key Terms
1. Use the following terms to describe the history of Southeast Asia: reservoir, surplus, maritime, exploit.

Key Ideas
2. Why was there so much trade in Southeast Asia?
3. How did Europeans transform Southeast Asia?
4. How did Southeast Asians gain independence?

Think Critically
5. Draw Conclusions Why did different states want to control the Strait of Malacca?
6. Make Inferences Why are the communist countries the poorest in the region?

Essential Question
What are the challenges of diversity?

7. How did Southeast Asians react to contact with many different religions? Go to your Student Journal to record your answer.

SECTION 2 ASSESSMENT **1.** Sample: Khmer used reservoirs for irrigation and producing surpluses. Maritime traditions led to invasion. Intruders exploited the area's resources. **2.** Spices and other resources encouraged trade. **3.** They established plantations; exploited resources; attracted immigrants; set up new nations. **4.** Nationalism grew in the early 1900s; they resisted Japanese efforts during World War II; they fought successful battles for independence. **5.** for access to trade, spices, and resources **6.** exploitation, communist economic policies, harsh government **7.** They absorbed new religions and blended them with old traditions.

Southeast Asia in the 1200s

OBJECTIVES

Students will

- recognize the importance of early travel writers to our understanding of the past.
- **ELL** use gestures to understand difficult key terms.

SET EXPECTATIONS

Students will

- read and analyze excerpts about Southeast Asia by two travel writers from the 1200s.
- write a short essay using details from the documents.

1 Connect

Point out to students that travel writing is a genre of nonfiction that is very popular today. Ask them if they have ever written long e-mails, letters or journal entries while taking a trip. Ask, What about the experience made you want to write it down? Why do you think people enjoy reading other people's travel writing? Responses might include,

"I was amazed by how different everything was, and I wanted to remember it. Some readers like to learn about and imagine places that they will probably never visit. Other readers may plan trips based upon information they learn from travel writers."

2 Experience

Preview Have students preview the two pages with the travel writers' documents. Invite them to respond to the images of Marco Polo and Angkor Wat. Read the Key Idea, glossary terms, and definitions. Clarify any questions about the meaning of these words by providing examples. Invite a volunteer to read the introduction.

L1 Special Needs For students who need frequent movement, incorporate the travel theme by letting students change seats after each document is read.

Read Slowly read aloud the excerpt from *The Travels of Marco Polo*. Then read the document a second time, stopping to read the questions at the left. Also ask questions that require using the glossary terms, such as, Why might the Kaugigu kings have paid the Great Khan a yearly tribute? (They hoped that the Great Khan would leave them in peace.) Repeat this procedure with the Zhou Daguan excerpt. Use their responses to the questions as a starting point for discussion. Ask, Why are the writings of these travelers important to our understanding of early civilizations?

ELL Early Intermediate Use visual images to help students understand the glossary terms, such as a simple picture of a deer for *game*; or gold coins for *tribute*. Have students act out trying to erase something that is *indelible*.

ELL Early Advanced Point out that *indelible* contains the prefix *in-* meaning "not" and *del* as in *delete*.

myWorld Activity: Khmer Justice
Have students analyze a third primary source excerpt in order to draw conclusions about Khmer ways of thinking about right and wrong. Distribute *Activity Support: Source Analysis,* and have students determine its importance to our understanding of Khmer justice.

20 min

ELL Beginner Allow students to work with a partner with more advanced English skills. **(Verbal/Logical)**

3 Understand

Review Return to the Key Idea, and have a student read it aloud. Then ask students to find examples in the documents of the region's rich resources.

Assess Have students complete **Analyze the Documents.** Review their answers to determine if students have met the lesson objectives.

Remediate If students struggle to find details that show impressions of each civilization, write an impression, for example: *Kaugigu was rich in resources desired by traders*. Then have students find details that show the land's rich resources (gold, spices, and game).

Name _____ Class _____ Date _____

 myWorld Activity Support   **Source Analysis**

Khmer Justice

Directions Read the excerpt from Zhou Daguan's description of Khmer justice in the case of a dispute, or argument, between two men. Keep in mind that Daguan's diary is the only account of life in that ancient kingdom. Then answer the questions.

Excerpt from Zhou Daguan's Diary

"Take the case where two men are in dispute and no one knows who is right or who is wrong. In front of the royal palace, there are twelve small stone towers. Each of these two men is made to sit inside a tower, and the two men are watched over by their family members. They stay one or two days, or even three or four. When they come out, the person who is in the wrong is certain to have caught some sickness; either he has ulcers, or catarrh, or a malignant fever. The innocent person has nothing wrong with him. Thus they decide who is in the right and who the wrong."

1. Where would the Khmer send two men having a dispute?

_____

2. How long would the men stay there?

_____

3. Who would watch over the two men?

_____

4. How would they decide which man was wrong?

_____

5. Why might disputes have been settled near the royal palace?

_____

_____

6. What does this excerpt teach us about ideas of fairness in Khmer society? Do you agree with these ideas? Explain why or why not.

_____

_____

_____

Marco Polo Marco Polo (1254–1324) may be the most famous travel writer of all time. He was born in Venice (in present-day Italy) to a noble family involved in trade. In 1271, Polo joined his father and uncle on a voyage to China. His travels took him across Asia to the East China Sea. He returned home traveling by ship as far south as Sumatra, where he was detained for a long period, and along the coast of India to Persia, where he took a land route to the Black Sea. He reached Venice again in 1295, twenty-four years after his departure. Marco Polo's experiences were not recorded for several years, until he landed in an enemy prison after a naval battle. There, he dictated his stories to another captive, Rusticiano (Rustichello of Pisa). Before that time, Marco Polo had shared his experiences with friends only.

GUIDE ON THE SIDE

Identifying Details Use the lettered prompts to help students analyze the documents and identify details to support the main idea or thesis of their essays.

ANSWERS

(A) China is more powerful and controls them to some degree.

(B) There is an abundance of many kinds of spices.

(C) They are tattoos.

Primary Source

Southeast Asia in the 1200s

Key Idea
• The people of Southeast Asia developed sophisticated civilizations that grew rich from natural resources.

▲ Marco Polo

Marco Polo traveled widely in Asia, and his accounts include descriptions of life in the many lands that he visited. On a mission for Kublai Khan, he visited Southeast Asia. The first text comes from his description of a Southeast Asian kingdom.

Zhou Daguan was a member of a diplomatic mission from China to the Khmer empire in the late 1200s. Upon his return, Zhou Daguan wrote a book, *Notes on the Customs of Cambodia*, describing the land and the people.

An ancient pagoda in Laos ▼

Read the text on the right. Stop at each circled letter. Then answer the question with the same letter on the left.

(A) **Summarize** What is the relationship between Kaugigu and China?

(B) **Draw Conclusions** What other valuable goods does Kaugigu produce?

(C) **Infer** What are the body decorations described?

submitted, *v.,* gave in to another country's power

tribute, *n.,* payment a weaker nation makes to a stronger one

game, *n.,* animals hunted for food

The Travels of Marco Polo

❝ Kaugigu has its own king. The people . . . have <u>submitted</u> to the Great Khan and pay him a yearly **(A)** <u>tribute</u>. . . . This province is rich in gold. It also abounds in precious **(B)** spices of many sorts . . . There are plenty of elephants and animals of many other kinds and no lack of <u>game</u>. The people live on meat, milk, and rice. . . . All the people alike, male and female, have . . . their flesh covered all over with pictures of lions and dragons and birds and **(C)** other objects. . . . ❞
—Marco Polo, *The Travels of Marco Polo*

ANALYZE THE DOCUMENTS 1. Both passages give some information about the king; Marco Polo's passage also describes common people. Daguan's excerpt describes the royal entourage, including the military. **2.** Sample: Marco Polo's account gives the impression that the Kaugigu, though subjugated to the Khan, were an organized and highly developed society ruled by a king. He uses many details about their food, gold, animals, and spices to show that the people were well fed and comfortable. His description of

21st Century Learning IDENTIFY DETAILS

To assist your students in identifying important details that support their impression of ancient Kaugigu and Cambodia, encourage them to begin with their most important ideas about each place. Remind them that paragraphs should always include a main idea and supporting details to back it up. Ask what idea or impression Marco Polo gives about the king and society of Kaugigu. What idea does Daugan give about the Khmer king and society? Then ask them to find details to support each idea.

Read the text on the right. Stop at each circled letter. Then answer the question with the same letter on the left.

D **Summarize** Who leads the procession?

E **Analyze** Who is the procession meant to honor?

F **Infer** What does the gold on the elephants' tusks and the parasols show?

procession, *n.*, group of people moving in a slow, formal manner

tapers, *n.*, tall, thin candles

sovereign, *n.*, ruler

parasols, *n.*, umbrellas that protect from strong sunlight

The Customs of Cambodia

❝ When the King leaves his palace, the <u>procession</u> is headed by the **D** soldiery; then come the flags, the banners, the music. Girls of the palace, three or five hundred in number, gaily dressed, with flowers in their hair and <u>tapers</u> in their hands, are massed together in a separate column. . . . Finally **E** the <u>Sovereign</u> appeared, standing erect on an elephant and holding in his hand the sacred sword. This elephant, his tusks sheathed in gold, was accompanied by bearers of twenty white <u>parasols</u> with golden shafts. All around was a bodyguard of elephants drawn **F** close together. ❞

—Zhou Daguan, *Notes on the Customs of Cambodia*

▲ Khmer carving showing the king in procession

ANSWERS

D Soldiers lead the procession.

E It honors the king.

F They show the wealth of the kingdom and power of the king.

The Khmer temple of Angkor Wat in Cambodia ▼

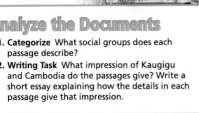

Analyze the Documents

1. **Categorize** What social groups does each passage describe?
2. **Writing Task** What impression of Kaugigu and Cambodia do the passages give? Write a short essay explaining how the details in each passage give that impression.

their tattoos shows that they were a unique and creative group of people. Zhou Daguan gives the impression that the Khmer king was powerful, holding a position of great respect. He focused on many details of the monarch's wealth: the great parade with hundreds of prettily dressed girls and a bodyguard of many elephants as well as people carrying parasols. The king's own appearance, standing on an elaborately decorated elephant and holding a sacred sword, adds to this strong impression that the king was very powerful.

Southeast Asia Today

OBJECTIVES

Students will know

- cultures and religions of Southeast Asia.
- issues of environment and economics.

Students will be able to

- identify main ideas about the region's cultures.
- suggest solutions to problems facing Southeast Asia.

SET EXPECTATIONS

In this section, students will

- read Southeast Asia Today.
- create a chart of challenges confronting Southeast Asia and offer solutions.
- learn to speak phrases in Bahasa and complete the On Assignment.

CORE CONCEPTS

You may wish to teach or reteach the following lessons from the Core Concepts Handbook:

- Population Growth, pp. 74–75
- What Is Culture?, pp. 86–87
- Political Systems, pp. 106–107

KEY

Differentiated Instruction
- **L1** Special Needs
- **L2** Extra Support
- **L3** On-Level
- **L4** Challenge

English Language Instruction
- **ELL** Beginner
- **ELL** Early Intermediate
- **ELL** Intermediate
- **ELL** Early Advanced
- **ELL** Advanced

---

1 Connect
Make learning meaningful

Make Connections Ask students to write in their journals one challenge or problem that their town or their state is facing today. Invite them to share their ideas. Discuss why the problems in their community might be similar to or different from Southeast Asia's challenges.

Activate Prior Knowledge Remind students that in Section 2 they learned how people from all over the world were attracted to Southeast Asia's geography and resources. Ask students to predict how modern Southeast Asian societies might take advantage of the geography and resources of the region.

L2 Extra Support Review the Trade Routes map in Section 2, having students trace each route with an eraser and identify important points on each route.

Prepare Follow the steps in the section **Preview.** Preteach the Key Terms. Then have students complete *Word Wise* in their journals using in-text clues and the glossary for help.

2 Experience
Teach knowledge and skills

Read Use **Background** notes and **Guide on the Side** questions to model active reading. Have students use *Take Notes* in their **Student Journals** to identify the most important ideas and details on the topics of culture, religion, population, and environment in Southeast Asia. Have them complete **21st Century Online Tutor** *Identify Main Ideas and Details*, and apply this skill to the section.

L1 Special Needs Direct students to the photos in the Closer Look feature. Ask them what they would like to learn about traditions in Southeast Asia.

ELL Intermediate Post a Main Idea-Details chart with four rows. The first row should have space for writing a main idea. The next three rows should provide space for three details. Have students identify three details that support the main idea of the text about religion: *Southeast Asia is a region of diverse religious traditions.*

 Practice: myWorld Activity Students will create a chart of challenges facing Southeast Asia today, rate how pressing each one is, and offer solutions. **Step-by-Step Instructions** and **More Activities** follow on p. T80.

SECTION 3 RESOURCE GUIDE

FOR THE STUDENT

my worldgeography.com Student Center
- Language Lesson
- Culture Close-up

Student Edition (print and online)
- Southeast Asia Today

Student Journal (print and online)
- Section 3 Word Wise
- Section 3 Take Notes

21st Century Learning Online Tutor
- Identify Main Ideas and Details
- Solve Problems

FOR THE TEACHER

my worldgeography.com Teacher Center
- Online Lesson Planner
- Presentations for Projection
- SuccessTracker

ProGuide: East and Southeast Asia
- Lesson Plan, pp. T78–T79
- 🏃 myWorld Activity Step-by-Step Instructions, p. T80
- Activity Support: Problem-Solution Rating, p. T81
- myWorld Geography Enrichment, p. T82
- Section Quiz, p. T83

Accelerating the Progress of ELLs
- Reading Support Strategies, p. 42

3 Understand
Assess understanding

Review Review *Word Wise* and *Take Notes* in the **Student Journal.**

Assess Knowledge and Skills Use the Section Assessment and the Section Quiz to check students' progress.

Assess Understanding Review students' responses to the Section Assessment Essential Question prompt.

Remediate Use these strategies to review and remediate.

If students struggle to . . .	Try these strategies.
Understand uneven development in Southeast Asia today	Use the GDP chart as a starting point for reviewing economic differences among the different countries in the region.
Identify main ideas and details	Have students read the topic in each boldface head and state the most important point of the following text.
Analyze the varied cultural elements of the region	Direct students to the pie charts and photographs that focus on Southeast Asia's cultural diversity.

ELL Support

ELL Objective Students will use English words relating to culture.

Cultural Connections To connect students to Ridwan's experience of a wedding in his ancestral homeland, have them describe a wedding or other important ceremony in their culture.

ELL Early Advanced Content Tip Have students copy each of the following words: *insurgency* and *international*. Ask them to circle the prefixes *in-* and *inter-*. Explain the difference between the meanings of the two. Discuss how the prefixes help them to understand the meaning of the terms.

ELL Activity Have students work in small groups to make a word wall on culture. Assign groups an area of culture (religion, food, clothes, ceremonies, language) and have them brainstorm words in a concept web. Then make placards for the word wall and define terms as necessary. **(Verbal)**

myWorld Activity   **Step-by-Step Instructions**

  30 min

Facing Challenges

OBJECTIVES

Students will

- identify social, economic, environmental, and political issues confronting Southeast Asia today.
- offer solutions to challenges facing Southeast Asia today.

LEARNING STYLE

- Verbal
- Kinesthetic

21st Century Learning

- Problem Solve

MATERIALS

- Activity Support: Problem-Solution Rating, p. T81

Activity Steps

1. Point out to students that Southeast Asia's great diversity has contributed to a variety of challenges. Tell them that they will be asked to consider four problems facing the area today and to rate these problems on a scale of 1 to 5, from most difficult to solve to least difficult to solve. Students will work in pairs.

2. Allow partners 15 minutes to fill out *Activity Support: Problem-Solution Rating* and to give a suggested solution for the most pressing problem.

   L2 Extra Support Have students rate a personal study issue, such as remembering to write down assignments or leaving a book at school, on a scale from 1 to 5 (small problem to big problem).

   ELL Early Intermediate Help students to create a mini-glossary of challenging vocabulary on the

problem-solution worksheet: *income, inequalities, overpopulation, underpopulation, pollution,* and *terrorist.* Post the glossary for reference.

3. Post a scale from 1 to 5. Have students cut out each problem from the chart and tape it to a point on the continuum, from most to least difficult to solve. If time allows, have students volunteer to give reasons for their ratings on the scale.

4. Then have partners join groups of other students who wrote a solution for the same problem. Allow 5 minutes to list solutions.

5. Post their lists. If time allows, have a member of each group present their solutions and answer questions from other groups.

More Activities From myWorld Teachers

Local Connections Have students identify challenges facing them at school today, such as passing state tests or finding enough time to finish homework thoroughly. Ask what they do to face their own challenges. **(Verbal)**

Create a Collage Have students each bring in one or more pictures of Southeast Asia today from magazines, newspapers, Web sites, or their own

drawings. Have groups use these pictures in a collage of Southeast Asia today. **(Visual)**

Conference Convene a conference to discuss one or more of the problems facing Southeast Asia today, and possible solutions. Consider having students form a panel of "experts" to present at the conference. **(Verbal)**

my worldgeography.com (Teacher Center) ➔ Find additional resources in the online Teacher Center.

Name _____ Class _____ Date _____

myWorld Activity Support   **Problem-Solution Rating**

Facing Challenges

Directions Facing a challenge is like solving a problem. Use the
chart below to rate the difficulty of facing each problem or challenge,
1 being the easiest to solve and 5 being the most difficult to solve.
Then write a solution for the most difficult challenge.

Challenges	How difficult is it to face this challenge?				
Income inequalities	1	2	3	4	5
Overpopulation or underpopulation	1	2	3	4	5
Air pollution	1	2	3	4	5
Terrorist attacks	1	2	3	4	5
Other	1	2	3	4	5

Evaluating Issues

Which challenge do you think is most difficult to face? Why?

_____

What solution or solutions do you think would work best for facing
this challenge?

_____

_____

_____

_____

_____

_____

Name _____ Class _____ Date _____

Enrichment: Southeast Asia's Amazing Fruits

Directions Read the selection below. Answer the questions that follow and complete the activity.

Most Americans have tasted bananas and pineapples. But how many have tried durians? All three fruits grow in Southeast Asia. All are considered "major fruits," because of their economic importance to the region. Nearly one third of the world's pineapples grow in Southeast Asia. More than 15 percent of the world's bananas are produced there.

At least 400 kinds of fruits and nuts grow in the region. Most cannot be found in American grocery stores. However, the global marketplace is changing and growing. Someday soon, you may find the durian in a grocery store near you.

In case you were wondering, the durian is known as "the king of fruits." It can reach 40 cm long and usually weighs 1 to 5 kilograms. It is famous for its strong smell which carries long distances. Many people do not find this odor appealing. However, it attracts a variety of forest animals, such as orangutans, squirrels, and even tigers.

Some Major Fruits	World's Top Producers From the Region
Bananas	Indonesia, Malaysia, Philippines, Thailand, Vietnam
Durian	Thailand
Jackfruit	Thailand
Mango	Indonesia, Philippines, Thailand
Pineapple	Indonesia, Philippines, Thailand
Rambutan	Indonesia, Malaysia, Thailand

1. Why do you think so many different kinds of fruit grow in the region?

_____

2. What percentage of the world's bananas and pineapples are grown in the region?

_____

3. Activity Use the information from the table above to draw a product map to show where major fruits grow in the region.

Name _____ Class _____ Date _____

Section Quiz

Directions Answer the following questions using what you learned
in Section 3.

1. _____ Deforestation is taking place because of
   a. monsoon flooding.
   b. global demand for products.
   c. volcanic eruptions.
   d. dry conditions.

2. _____ The leaders of Myanmar's military
   junta are
   a. soldiers.
   b. priests.
   c. business people.
   d. artists.

3. _____ How would the Philippine
   government respond to an insurgency?
   a. The government would try to work with
      their members.
   b. The government would want to support it.
   c. The government would ignore it.
   d. The government would fight it fiercely.

4. _____ A separatist group is a group
   that wants
   a. "separate but equal" institutions.
   b. to give religious leaders more power.
   c. an independent state.
   d. to win an election.

5. _____ What is the purpose of ASEAN?
   a. to promote Islamic ideals in the world
   b. to give Southeast Asian leaders more
      power in the world
   c. to protect Southeast Asia from Western
      influence
   d. to encourage economic and social
      development

6. Complete the chart below to explain issues facing Southeast Asian
   countries today.

Issue	Effects	Countries Affected
Political unrest		
Overpopulation		
Underpopulation		
Pollution		
Poverty		

Southeast Asia Today

- Model preparing to read by previewing the Key Ideas, Key Terms, headings, visuals, and captions. Have students make predictions about what they will learn. For ELL support, post the prompt: "I predict I will read about . . ."

- Preview and practice the reading skill, identify main ideas and details, by using an example of a main idea about culture in your community.

- Preteach this section's high-use Academic Vocabulary and Key Terms using the chart on the next page. Have students practice Key Terms by completing the *Word Wise* page in their journals.

Southeast Asian Culture Today

- **Cause and Effect** What effect did merchants and immigrants have on Southeast Asian culture? (They brought in new customs and religions.)

- **Identify Main Ideas** Why did Chinese religions change after they came into Vietnam? (They were influenced by local beliefs in spirits.)

- **Analyze Sources** Reread the quote by poet Rabindranath Tagore. What does he mean? (After Indian culture entered Southeast Asia, it was transformed into a uniquely Southeast Asian culture.)

 Reading Skill

Identify Main Ideas and Details While they read, have students practice this skill by completing the *Take Notes* graphic organizer in the **Student Journal.**

Section 3

Southeast Asia Today

Key Ideas
- Southeast Asia is a culturally diverse region.
- Southeast Asian countries have differing political goals, human rights records, and economies.
- Population and environmental issues affect economies throughout the region.

Key Terms • secular • military junta • insurgency • separatist group • ASEAN

 Reading Skill: Identify Main Idea and Details Take notes using the graphic organizer in your journal.

Southeast Asia is one of the world's most diverse regions. Its wide range of governments and income levels sets it apart from other places in the world. Its varied geography is home to many cultures and ethnic groups, such as Ridwan's Minangkabau. Today this diverse region is developing new industries and has an important role to play in international trade.

Southeast Asian Culture Today

Southeast Asia's culture was formed by geography and history. The region's location on international trade routes attracted merchants and immigrants, new customs, and new religions. Southeast Asia's unique culture astonished a famous Indian poet during his visit to Indonesia. He observed,

❝ I see India everywhere, but I do not recognize it. ❞
—Rabindranath Tagore

Today, the culture of Southeast Asia is still being shaped by a diversity of peoples and the environment they share.

Religion

Over the centuries, Indian traders from the East brought Hinduism and Buddhism from India and Sri Lanka. From China to the north, Mahayana Buddhism and Confucian thought entered Vietnam. These religions and ideas mixed with the local beliefs in spirits.

◀ The Petronas Towers, Kuala Lumpur, Malaysia

ACADEMIC VOCABULARY

High-Use Word	Definition and Sample Sentence
convert	*n.* a person who changes from one religion to another *Their leader is a convert to Hinduism.*
considerable	*adj.* large *He left his considerable wealth to charity.*

Later, Arab and Indian traders brought Islam, which took root in Malaysia and most of Indonesia. As the region came under European influence, Christianity gained <u>converts</u>, especially in the Philippines and Vietnam.

Religious traditions are woven through Southeast Asian culture. On most of the mainland, Buddhism is the main religion. However, Islam dominates on most of the islands and on the Malay Peninsula. In Malaysia, there are two systems of justice. One system is **secular,** or nonreligious, and the other is Islamic. Some Malaysian Muslims prefer to seek justice in courts that use Islamic, or Sharia, law.

Indonesia has the world's largest Muslim population. However, its mixed population of Muslims, Buddhists, Hindus and Christians has created a tolerant society. Through the region there is also much cultural blending, as customs and ideas from different religions are fused.

convert, *n.,* a person who changes from one religion to another

Reading Check What religion is most popular on the mainland of Southeast Asia?

GUIDE ON THE SIDE

- **Identify Main Ideas** What is cultural blending? (It is the mixing of customs and ideas from many areas.)

- **Compare and Contrast** How do religious traditions on the mainland differ from those on the islands? (The mainland is mostly Buddhist, while the islands are Islamic or mixed.)

- **Synthesize** Why does Indonesia have a tradition of tolerance? (This tradition resulted from the mix of religious groups.)

Closer Look

LAND AND CULTURE

The environment shapes the culture of Southeast Asia in many ways. In a region of monsoon flooding and long coastlines, water plays a central role in people's lives.

THINK CRITICALLY How have people adapted to the environment of Southeast Asia?

Floating markets are a common sight in the watery lowlands. ▶

Many religious rituals, such as the Buddhist festival of Phaung Daw U in Myanmar, take place on water.

Water puppets entertain children in Hanoi, Vietnam.

Closer Look

Analyze Visuals Ask students to study the photographs in the **Land and Culture** feature.

- In what ways do the people of Southeast Asia depend on water? (They depend on water for farming, drinking, travel, and trade.)

- Why might floating markets be common? (Sample: Merchants can bring in goods by water and trade them without leaving their boats; merchants don't need a store or middleman; space for anchoring a boat is plentiful.)

READING CHECK Buddhism

THINK CRITICALLY They hold ceremonies on the water and have floating markets.

ANSWERS

BIOGRAPHY

Aung San Suu Kyi Aung San Suu Kyi was born in present-day Myanmar (formerly Burma). Her father was the commander of the Burma Independence Army. Aung San Suu Kyi received her education overseas. In 1988, she returned home, when her mother became ill. At that time, Burma was in the midst of a popular uprising against the government. Aung San Suu Kyi became involved in politics, supporting the demonstrators.

A year later, Aung San Suu Kyi was placed under house arrest by the newly formed goverment of Myanmar. In 1991, she was awarded the Nobel Peace Prize for her efforts. The government of Myanmar offered to free her, if she agreed to leave the country; she refused. In 1995, the government released Aung San Suu Kyi from house arrest, only to place her under house arrest again in 2000.

Governments and Citizens

- **Identify Details** Which Southeast Asian nations have constitutional monarchies? (Thailand, Malaysia, Cambodia, and Brunei)

- **Connect** Which Southeast Asian nations have three branches of government like the United States? (Indonesia, Philippines, Singapore, and East Timor)

- **Draw Conclusions** Why did the government of Myanmar arrest Aung San Suu Kyi? (They would not tolerate her political dissent.)

Analyze Graphs Direct students to the pie graphs of ethnic groups.

- About what fraction of Malaysia's population is of Chinese background? (about one quarter)

- About what fraction of Singapore's population is Chinese? (about three quarters)

Data Discovery

- Have students go online to find more data on ethnic groups in Southeast Asia.

Governments and Citizens

The governments of Southeast Asia are as diverse as the region's population and religions. Citizens' rights also vary.

considerable, *adj.*, large

Types of Governments Republics such as Indonesia, the Philippines, Singapore, and East Timor have constitutions that provide citizens with some protections and freedoms. Like the United States, these countries have legislative, executive, and judicial branches of government. In Indonesia, democracy has been growing stronger ever since the fall of the dictator Suharto in 1998.

Chinese festival in Singapore ▼

Ethnicities

Malaysia*

7.8%
7.1%
11%
23.7%
50.4%

*2004 estimate

Singapore*

7.9%
1.4%
13.9%
76.8%

*2000 census

Malay	Indian
Chinese	Other
Indigenous	

SOURCE: CIA World Factbook Online, 2008

Chart Skills

1. In which country are Malays the largest ethnic group?
2. Where might Chinese cultural influence be strongest?

Data Discovery

Malaysia, Cambodia, the kingdom of Thailand, and the sultanate of Brunei are all constitutional monarchies in which one person rules as head of state. Yet, there is a <u>considerable</u> degree of democracy in some of these nations.

In other nations governments allow much less democracy. The Communist nations of Laos and Vietnam are one-party states ruled by an oligarchy, or a small group of people. Myanmar is ruled by a brutal **military junta,** a committee of military leaders. The junta punishes its critics and has placed the political leader Aung San Suu Kyi under house arrest. In 2008 the junta blocked disaster relief intended for victims of a cyclone.

Political Tensions In Myanmar, political frustration sometimes erupts into demonstrations. However, political tensions afflict every nation in the region.

In the Philippines, the government is fighting an **insurgency,** or rebellion, from a Muslim **separatist group** on islands in the south and east. A separatist group is a group of people who want to establish an independent state.

In Thailand, the Constitutional Court brought down the government in 2008, after months of anti-government protests.

Even in more democratic countries, such as Malaysia and Indonesia, disputes rage over economic issues, corruption, election fraud, and crime rates. In this ethnically diverse region, there are also constant concerns over income inequalities between ethnic groups.

Reading Check Which nations are one-party states?

READING CHECK Laos, Vietnam, and Myanmar

GRAPH SKILLS 1. Malaysia **2.** Singapore

GEOGRAPHY

Forest Change The Food and Agriculture Organization has tracked changes in forest area worldwide. The statistics for Southeast Asian countries show an overall loss of forest (1990–2005) in most countries. Only Vietnam has had a significant gain of forest. Change for this period by country is as follows:

Brunei: −0.7 percent; Myanmar: −1.2 percent; Cambodia: −1.3 percent; Indonesia: +0.6 percent; Laos: −0.5 percent; Malaysia: −0.4 percent; Philippines: −2.2 percent; Singapore: ±0.7 percent; Thailand: −0.6 percent; East Timor: −1.2 percent; Vietnam: +2.5 percent.

Air Pollution

In 1997 an environmental disaster struck Southeast Asia as fires meant to clear land burned out of control. The fires created a huge cloud of smoke that threatened economies and public health. The fires were stopped by a certain Southeast Asian weather pattern. *Can you identify the weather pattern?*

◀ People in cities like Jakarta and Bangkok wore breathing masks.

▲ The fires of 1997 destroyed millions of acres of forest.

Population and Environment

Some environmental problems in Southeast Asia have emerged when there are too many people living in an area for its resources to support.

Population Issues Countries with higher rates of population growth must worry about feeding a growing population. Countries with low population growth are also concerned about the future. If there are not enough younger people in the work force, who will pay the taxes that support social security and medical benefits for the elderly? Singapore's population is hardly growing at all. To encourage growth, the government has offered citizens tax rebates of thousands of dollars for every child that is born.

In contrast, Indonesia is dealing with overcrowding on the island of Java, where 60 percent of Indonesians live. Overpopulation strains resources. It also damages the environment.

The government of Indonesia encourages families to migrate to the outer islands such as Sulawesi by providing money and land. However, there are no jobs or social services on the islands. The land must be cleared and the soil is poor.

The Environment Today Because of the global demand for wood products, Southeast Asian forests are disappearing. Countries such as Indonesia are having difficulty stopping this destruction. A weak central government has been unable to enforce regulations.

Reading Check **What are some environmental problems in Southeast Asia?**

Population and Environment

- **Cause and Effect** Overpopulation causes what problems in Java? (It strains resources and damages the environment.)
- **Infer** Why does the government of Singapore pay citizens to have children? (They want to ensure a sufficient workforce in the future.)

Analyze Visuals Direct students to the air-pollution photographs.

- What do the face masks in the photos show about the fires? (They show how damaging the smoke from the fires was.)
- What public health hazard would such fires cause? (They would cause breathing problems.)

ECONOMICS

Technology Super Corridor To make Malaysia a global high-tech center, the government established the Multimedia Super Corridor (MSC) at the end of the 1900s. This high-tech center is located south of Kuala Lumpur, Malaysia's capital. The MSC is 50 km long and 15 km wide, making its area larger than Singapore. The government offers many incentives to foreign investors in the MSC.

Diverse Economies

- **Identify Main Ideas** Why do Singapore and Brunei have the most successful economies? (They have stable governments, resources, skilled workers, banks, and transportation and communication systems.)

- **Infer** Why might the government of Myanmar resist globalization? (The government may be attempting to maintain power by restricting outside influences.)

Chart Skills Direct students to the GDP chart.

- What was Thailand's GDP per capita in 2008? ($7,900)

- Did any Southeast Asian nations have a larger per capita GDP than the United States in 2008? Explain. (Yes; Brunei and Singapore did.)

- What might cause Brunei's GDP per capita to change dramatically from year to year? (Its most important resource is oil, and the demand and price may change.)

Data Discovery

- Have students go online to find more data on Southeast Asian economies.

Diverse Economies

Southeast Asia includes some of the richest and poorest nations in the world. There are many factors that can hinder economic growth. As you have read, the poorer nations all suffered wars in recent times.

Uneven Development A successful economy depends on certain conditions. There must be a stable government, natural resources, skilled workers, banks, and transportation and communication systems. Singapore and Brunei meet these conditions and are the most successful countries economically. More than half of Brunei's income comes from oil and natural gas production. Singapore's economy is based on exports of consumer electronics and information technology.

The economies of Southeast Asia are as diverse as other aspects of the region. Although international trade is bringing changes to countries such as Indonesia, nations such as Myanmar and Cambodia continue to resist globalization.

Countries without transportation networks, stable government, or freedom for their citizens—such as Myanmar—have difficulty in attracting foreign investments. Nations with oil and natural gas such as Indonesia are more attractive to investors.

Southeast Asian Economies
This graph shows the gross domestic product (GDP) for most countries in Southeast Asia.

Below: Searching through trash in Phnom Penh, Cambodia
Lower right: The modern skyline of wealthy Singapore

Chart Skills

1. Which country has the highest GDP in the region?

2. Which countries have the lowest?

Data Discovery

GDP per Capita of Selected Southeast Asian Nations

Nation	GDP per Capita
Brunei	$51,000
Singapore	$49,700
Malaysia	$13,300
Thailand	$7,900
Indonesia	$3,700
Philippines	$3,400
Vietnam	$2,600
East Timor	$2,500
Laos	$2,100
Myanmar	$1,900
Cambodia	$1,800
United States (for comparison)	$45,800

SOURCE: CIA World Factbook Online, 2008

READING CHECK One half of the world's oil supplies and one third of its trade pass through the Strait.

CHART SKILLS 1. Brunei 2. Cambodia and Myanmar

SECTION 3 ASSESSMENT 1. Sample: Some governments' policies are secular rather than religious; a military junta rules Myanmar; the government of the Philippines must fight insurgency by an Islamic separatist group. 2. Southeast Asia is a center of international trade, with the Strait of Malacca as a global

QUICK FACTS

Linguistic Diversity People speak an estimated 7,000 languages worldwide. In Southeast Asia, about 1,000 of these languages are spoken.

Southeast Asia and the World Today Southeast Asia is once again a center of international trade. The Strait of Malacca is a major global shipping lane. The ports of Singapore, Malaysia, and Indonesia benefit greatly from such traffic. But there are also enormous dangers along the strait. Modern-day pirates have attacked merchant ships. And since the al-Qaeda attack on September 11 and later attacks in Indonesia, there is a new fear. Attacks by militant groups on shipping could endanger the world's oil supply. In the words of one writer,

> With 60,000 vessels transiting through the Strait each year, carrying half of the world's oil supplies and a third of its trade, the stakes are high in maintaining stability along these sea lanes.
>
> —Chietigj Bajpaee

All the countries in the region have the potential for economic growth. Tourism is an important source of income in all of Southeast Asia. Malaysia is developing a high-technology complex near its capital, Kuala Lumpur. This complex is called the Multimedia Super Corridor. Thailand is attempting to develop high-technology industries, but the lack of skilled labor may be an obstacle.

ASEAN, the Association of Southeast Asian Nations, is a trade group working to promote growth and social progress. The organization has reduced regional tariffs and has created a free-trade area.

Today Southeast Asia's problems and strengths are tied to its geography and history. Many of its people, such as the Minangkabau, continue to welcome foreign culture and new ideas. With its ancient traditions of cultural diversity and international trade, Southeast Asia is well positioned to play an important role in the modern world.

Reading Check Why is the Strait of Malacca so important to the world's economy?

my World IN NUMBERS

In 2007, Thailand had a labor force of about **37** million people. In 2008, this figure rose to about **38** million.

myWorld Activity
Facing Challenges

Section 3 Assessment

Essential Question

?

Key Terms

1. Use the following terms to describe Southeast Asia today: secular, military junta, insurgency, separatist group.

Key Ideas

2. What role does Southeast Asia play in the world economy?

3. What kinds of governments exist in Southeast Asia?

4. Why are Southeast Asian rain forests under threat?

Think Critically

5. **Draw Conclusions** Why is religious tolerance valued in Indonesia, where there are so many religious faiths?

6. **Synthesize** Why is it so difficult for Southeast Asian nations to solve environmental problems?

What are the challenges of diversity?

7. Why has "Unity in Diversity" become the motto of Indonesia? Go to your Student Journal to record your answer.

shipping lane for one half of the world's oil and one third of the world's trade. **3.** Southeast Asia is a mix of constitutional republics, constitutional monarchies, and communist dictatorships. **4.** Global demand for lumber and weak enforcement threaten forests. **5.** Tolerance eases tension and allows diverse groups to get along. **6.** Economic concerns are often considered more important than efforts to solve environmental problems. **7.** Everyone's success depends on varied groups working together and respecting differences.

myWorld Activity

Facing Challenges Find Step-by-Step Instructions and an Activity Support on pp. T80–T81. **(Verbal/Kinesthetic)**

Geography of a Disaster

OBJECTIVES

Students will

- understand the causes and effects of a tsunami.
- **21st Century Learning** summarize texts of first-hand accounts.
- **ELL** analyze word choice in a first-hand account.

SET EXPECTATIONS

In this case study, students will

- read Geography of a Disaster.
- analyze first-hand accounts of the 2004 tsunami.

1 Connect

Explain that different kinds of natural disasters occur throughout the world. Have students share stories that they have seen or read in the news in recent years about floods, hurricanes, tornadoes, or other natural disasters. Ask, Did national, state, or local governments help victims of the disaster? What kind of relief efforts did charitable groups provide? Point out that young people sometimes help with relief efforts. Ask, What kind of relief effort could a school organize?

L2 Extra Support Explain that *relief* in the context of natural disasters has a specific meaning: help for those affected by the disaster such as distributing food, drinking water, clothes, and shelter.

2 Learn

Preview Have students preview Key Ideas, Key Terms, visuals and headings. Use Core Concepts 2.5 to review the effects of tectonic plates shifting deep underground or under the sea. Then have them predict the effects of a huge tsunami. Tell them that they will read more about this during the Case Study.

Read While students read Geography of a Disaster, ask questions found in **Guide on the Side** to build understanding of Key Ideas and lesson objectives.

ELL Intermediate Post a diagram that shows the relationship between the prefix and root of the word *evacuate* and its meaning: *e-, ex-* ⟶ out, from; *vacuus* ⟶ empty; to withdraw or depart from; to empty out.

myWorld Activity: Tsunami Reactions Pass out *Activity Support: Analyze Viewpoints*. Have partners read the first-hand accounts of an official and a tourist in Thailand during the tsunami of 2004. Students should answer the questions below the excerpts to analyze and summarize the experiences of the people offering the accounts. Then discuss the effects of natural disasters on developing countries such as Thailand. **(Verbal)**

20 min

L2 Extra Support For extra support with summarizing, have students go to **21st Century Skills Online Tutor** *Summarize*.

L4 Challenge Ask partners to create a newscast dramatizing reports on the tsunami of 2004 and offering advice for people to follow should they ever experience a tsunami.

3 Understand

Review Go over students' responses to the questions, focusing on ways to prepare for a tsunami. Have them recall their predictions about the effects of a tsunami. As a class, see if the Case Study supported or contradicted their predictions.

Assess Check students' answers to the Assessment questions for completeness and accuracy. Evaluate students' understanding of the two aspects of preparation for a natural disaster: mitigation and response.

Remediate If students struggle to understand how mitigation differs from response, create a "Before Disaster and After Disaster" chart. In the "Before" section write down steps used to limit damage from a disaster, and add the label "mitigation" to this side. In the "After" column write ways of meeting an emergency caused by a natural disaster, and add the label "response" to this side of the chart.

Name _____ Class _____ Date _____

myWorld Activity Support   **Analyze Viewpoints**

Tsunami Reactions

Directions Read the first hand accounts from people who experienced the tsunami of 2004, and then respond to the questions that follow. While you read, consider how to summarize their experiences. Find a few words to capture each experience.

First Hand Accounts

"Government is almost dysfunctional, administration is almost in a void. . . . Even if there are personnel, they are dispirited. We don't have air transportation to move in replacements. Most people are depressed. People say, 'Where is the army? Where are the police?' They are depressed. They can't be replaced in one or two days."

—Alwi Shihab, Minister for Social Services, Indonesia, January 2, 2005

"The second wave was the largest . . . . I'd say it was about 15 feet (4.5 meters). The water just smashed everything in its path. It came up over the beach, over the road running along the beach front, behind the main part of the hotel, and swept away large four-wheel drive vehicles. . . . Water surged into the hotel lobby of our wing, on the other side of the road, and smashed the windows of shops fronting the street."

—Beverly Howie, tourist in Phuket, Thailand, December 26, 2004

1. Describe the experience of Alwi Shihab shortly after the tsunami of 2004.

   _____

   _____

2. Describe the experience of Beverly Howie during the tsunami.

   _____

   _____

3. Summarize how you think people felt who experienced the tsunami first hand accounts.

   _____

   _____

4. Compare and contrast the viewpoints of the minister of social services and the tourist.

   _____

   _____

T85

CORE CONCEPTS: FORCES INSIDE EARTH

Review Core Concepts 2.5 before discussing the tsunami of December 26, 2004, with your students. This lesson will help them better understand the relationship between tectonic plates and earthquakes that may bring on devastating tsunamis. Have students read and summarize Earthquakes and Volcanoes. Ask them what causes earthquakes. (The plates slide against each other.) Where do earthquakes often occur? (They occur at the seams, or faults, between plates.) Review the Continental Plates map. Ask, What three plates cause earthquakes in Southeast Asia? (the Philippine Plate, the Pacific Plate and the Indo-Australian Plate). In what direction does the Pacific Plate move? (east to north and west) In what direction does the Indo-Australian Plate move? (south to north and east).

GUIDE ON THE SIDE

Geography of a Disaster

Key Ideas
- Undersea earthquakes cause tsunamis in South and Southeast Asia.
- People in the region are finding ways to prepare for natural disasters.

Key Terms • tsunami • plate • evacuate • tsunameter

The Tsunami of 2004

- **Cause and Effect** What were some effects of the tsunami of 2004? (Almost 230,000 people died. Survivors lost homes and livelihoods, as farms and fishing grounds were destroyed.)

- **Make Inferences** Why are tsunamis so destructive? (The giant waves blast into areas where people live and work.)

Causes of the Tsunami

- **Cause and Effect** What geological events led to the tsunami of December 2004? (The Indo-Australian Plate moved under the Philippine Plate. The shifting of plates caused an underground earthquake. The earthquake set off the tsunami.)

Natural disasters strike populations all over the world. Floods and earthquakes in heavily populated areas often lead to much loss of life and destruction of property. One kind of natural disaster is called a **tsunami**, a series of huge waves. Tsunamis can be triggered by underwater earthquakes. When these powerful waves reach land, they may rise to more than 50 feet. The water, weighing millions of tons, can destroy buildings, farms, and forests.

The Tsunami of 2004

The worst tsunami in history struck 14 countries around the Indian Ocean on December 26, 2004. It was set off by a 9.1-magnitude earthquake near Sumatra. Sumatra was hit within minutes of the earthquake. Two hours later, thirty-foot waves reached India and Sri Lanka, 750 miles from the quake. Almost 230,000 people died, around three quarters of them in Indonesia. Survivors lost their homes and livelihoods, as farms and fishing grounds were destroyed.

Reading Check **What set off the Indian Ocean tsunami of 2004?**

Cause of the Tsunami

Earthquakes are caused by the movement of tectonic **plates**, huge blocks of rock that form the outermost layer of the earth. This movement is very slow, but over time, enormous pressure builds up as plates are forced against each other. Eventually one plate will suddenly shift under another. When the Indo-Australian plate slid under the Philippine plate on December 26, 2004, the planet shook. The shifting plates caused an underwater earthquake that set off the tsunami. According to the U.S. Geological Survey, the force of the

◀ U.S. Navy helicopter crew distributes food and water to tsunami victims in Indonesia.

READING CHECK an earthquake

PRIMARY SOURCE

From the Scene of the Disaster Many people shared their experiences during the tsunami of December 26, 2004. Don Howie, a tourist in Phuket, Thailand, gave CNN this description: "The sea suddenly surged out for about 200 meters (656 feet) . . . . There was nothing left but sand. Luckily, I was left standing on the rocks where I had been looking at the fish and coral. Anyone swimming in the middle of the beach must have been dragged well out to sea. My boss, who is not a strong swimmer, was wearing a buoyancy vest, which was just as well."

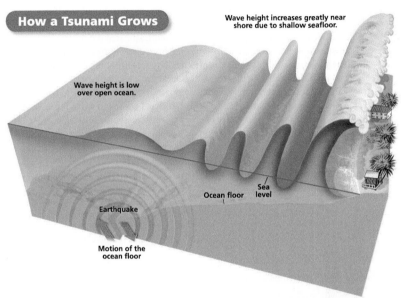

How a Tsunami Grows

Wave height increases greatly near shore due to shallow seafloor.

Wave height is low over open ocean.

Sea level

Ocean floor

Earthquake

Motion of the ocean floor

2004 tsunami was comparable to the power of 23,000 atomic bombs.

For people on the beaches, there was little warning. Many reported seeing animals fleeing for higher ground shortly before the tsunami struck. In some areas, the ocean receded, exposing fish on the sand. Then came the sound of the approaching tsunami like the rush of a jet. In some places the tsunami arrived in waves. In other places, water rose like a flood. Many were killed by the force of the waves. As the sea retreated, it swept thousands of people out with it. Miles of coastline were destroyed and many islands were submerged.

Reading Check **What were some signs of the approaching disaster?**

Preparing for a Disaster
In the tsunami of 2004, many deaths might have been prevented if people had been **evacuated,** or moved to other areas. However, tsunamis rarely occur in the Indian Ocean, and there was no system in place for detecting them or alerting people.

There are two parts to preparing for a natural disaster: mitigation and response. Mitigation includes taking steps to limit the damage a disaster can cause. Buildings, bridges, and other structures must be built in safe locations and with the right materials to withstand damage. Mitigation also includes creating systems for detecting and warning about disasters. Finally, mitigation includes teaching the

- **Draw Conclusions** What do the reports of animals fleeing to higher ground suggest? (They suggest that the animals sensed a tsunami approaching before humans did.)

Preparing for a Disaster

- **Main Idea** What is mitigation? (Mitigation refers to measures that prevent or reduce the destructive effects of natural disasters.)

READING CHECK Animals fled for higher ground. The ocean receded. They could hear the sound of the tsunami approaching.

QUICK FACTS

More on Earthquakes and Tsunamis

Tsunamis are secondary effects of earthquakes. The strongest earthquake on record, with a 9.5 magnitude, occurred in May, 1960, in southern Chile. It set off a huge tsunami that spread across the Pacific Ocean, reaching Japan. Between 2000 and 2007, Southeast Asia experienced seven major earthquakes with magnitudes of 6.0 or greater.

Date	Location	Magnitude	Deaths
June 4, 2000	Sumatra, Indonesia	7.9	103
Feb 4, 2004	Paupua, Indonesia	7.0	37
Dec 26, 2004	Sumatra	9.1	226,328
Mar 28, 2005	Islands off Sumatra	8.6	1,000+
May 27, 2006	Java, Indonesia	6.3	5,749
July 17, 2006	South of Java	7.7	403
Mar 6, 2007	Southern Sumatra	6.4	70

Source: World Almanac 2009

- **Express an Opinion** How important do you think education is in preparing for a natural disaster? (Sample: Educating people to pay attention to warnings and protect themselves is very important.)

- **Draw Conclusions** How does response preparedness save lives? (Rescue workers are ready to respond as soon as a disaster strikes.)

public how to prepare for and respond to an emergency.

One of the best ways to prepare for a disaster is to know how to respond to one. Rehearsals and drills can help people meet the emergency when a disaster strikes. In such a situation, experts would rush to the site to assess damage and decide what needs to be done. Police officers, firefighters, and medical personnel would work together to save lives. Government officials at different levels would communicate with each other and with relief agencies, like the Red Cross.

Supplies and equipment would be brought to the stricken area.

Southeast Asian nations are learning from disaster preparations in other regions. Countries bordering the Pacific Ocean have had long experience with tsunamis. Instruments called **tsunameters** can detect a tsunami when it passes. A tsunameter sits on a floating platform and is anchored by a line to the ocean floor. These devices send a signal to warning centers, which then issue alerts.

Reading Check How have countries on the Pacific Rim prepared for tsunamis?

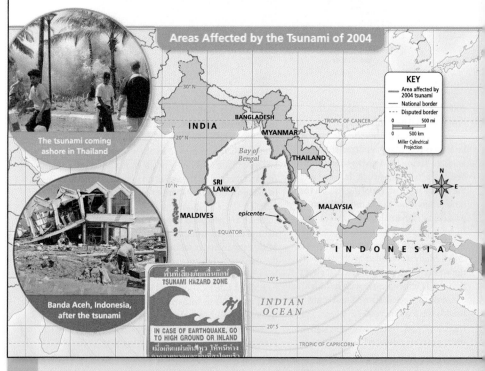

Areas Affected by the Tsunami of 2004

The tsunami coming ashore in Thailand

Banda Aceh, Indonesia, after the tsunami

TSUNAMI HAZARD ZONE
IN CASE OF EARTHQUAKE, GO TO HIGH GROUND OR INLAND

KEY
Area affected by 2004 tsunami
National border
Disputed border
0   500 mi
0   500 km
Miller Cylindrical Projection

BANGLADESH
INDIA
MYANMAR
TROPIC OF CANCER
Bay of Bengal
THAILAND
SRI LANKA
MALAYSIA
MALDIVES epicenter
EQUATOR
INDONESIA
INDIAN OCEAN
TROPIC OF CAPRICORN

READING CHECK They have prepared with early warning systems and education. They have also trained rescue workers and agencies for disaster-relief efforts.

READING CHECK Indonesia has been educating the public about how to respond to a disaster.

GEOGRAPHY

FEMA Tsunami Guidelines The Federal Emergency Management Agency offers four guidelines for what to do if a tsunami is likely in your area:

- **Turn on your radio.** If an earthquake occurs near a coastal area and a tsunami is detected, radio stations will issue a tsunami warning.
- **Move inland to higher ground.** Do this immediately and stay there.
- **Stay away from the beach.** Never go down to the beach to watch a tsunami come in. If you can see the wave you are too close to escape it.
- **CAUTION — If there is noticeable recession in water away from the shoreline, this is nature's tsunami warning and it should be heeded.** You should move away immediately.

Disaster Preparation in Indian Ocean Nations

Since 2006, the Indian Ocean Tsunami Warning System has been set up to monitor the Indian Ocean. Because of this new system, the entire region of the Indian Ocean has a way of tracking tsunamis and issuing warnings. The Indian government also began placing detectors in the Indian Ocean. International groups have helped countries in the area with mitigation and response systems.

Since 2004, countries in the area affected by the tsunami have focused more on disaster preparedness. In Southeast Asia, Indonesia is teaching its people how to respond to a disaster. In South Asia, Sri Lanka and other countries have moved people from the coast to safer areas inland. But many worry about densely populated countries bordering the Bay of Bengal, where millions of people live. Bangladesh, also prone to cyclones, has built a warning system and hundreds of shelters along the coast.

The potential for a future disaster remains, however. Cyclones frequently strike in the Indian Ocean. Some scientists think the region is likely to suffer

▲ Worker in the tsunami early-warning center that has recently opened in India

another major earthquake and tsunami in the next 30 years. There are new concerns about an area along the coast of Myanmar. In 1762, a serious earthquake damaged parts of this coast. A similar quake today could have a disastrous effect on the region. Faced with these concerns, United Nations officials believe the countries of the region are not completing mitigation work rapidly enough.

Reading Check What is Indonesia doing to prepare for possible disasters?

Disaster Preparation in Indian Ocean Nations

- **Cause and Effect** What effect did the 2004 tsunami have on improving preparations for natural disasters in the Indian Ocean region? (It caused Indian Ocean nations to set up a tsunami warning system.)
- **Make Inferences** Which mitigation efforts do you think would be most difficult? Explain. (Sample: Moving people to safer areas inland and finding them new jobs would be difficult and costly. Convincing people to leave their homes would also be hard.)

Assessment

1. What causes a tsunami?
2. What is the difference between mitigation and response?
3. Why are many countries in the Pacific region prepared for natural disasters?
4. Why might the United Nations want the nations around the Indian Ocean to put more stress on mitigation?
5. Why are some scientists concerned about the coast of Myanmar?

ASSESSMENT **1.** When a tectonic plate shifts beneath the ocean, causing an underwater earthquake, the earthquake may trigger a tsunami. **2.** Mitigation includes steps taken before a disaster to prevent damage or death. Response includes steps that would help save lives after a disaster occurs. **3.** They are prepared because of the frequency of past disasters in the region. **4.** Steps taken for prevention can mean smaller loss of life and lower costs of repair, rescue, and relief. **5.** They believe that a serious earthquake is likely there.

1. Farming populations settled in fertile river valleys, coastal plains and deltas; traders and migrants sailed through the gentle seas and settled on different islands.

2. Summer monsoons create heavy rain and river flooding.

3. India and China were early influences. Later Europeans influence spread.

THINK CRITICALLY

9. They have used rich soil for farming, terracing to farm in highlands, gentle seas and resources for trade.

10. The north-south cordilleras isolated early societies and allowed diverse groups to develop; gentle waterways and resources drew traders and immigrants from many lands.

11. Maritime trade allowed the islands contact with Muslim traders from India.

12. The watery lowlands and coastal areas led people to build houses on stilts, encouraged development of rice farming, encouraged fishing, and led to water-related cultural activities and festivals.

4. The Khmer built reservoirs that allowed them to utilize rainwater for irrigation.

5. The spice trade and resources drew Westerners. In turn they introduced new crops and replaced small farms with plantations. These farms attracted migrants and increased ethnic diversity.

6. Insurgents hope to establish an independent state in the Philippines.

7. The Strait of Malacca is a global shipping lane through which one third of the world's trade and one half of its oil pass.

8. Richest countries: Brunei, Singapore, and Malaysia; Poorest countries: Cambodia, Myanmar, East Timor, and Vietnam

Southeast Asia

Chapter Assessment

Key Terms and Ideas

1. **Discuss** How did physical geography determine where people settled in Southeast Asia?

2. **Explain** What kinds of weather conditions do the summer **monsoons** create?

3. **Recall** Which civilizations influenced Southeast Asia?

4. **Explain** How did the ancient Khmer create a food **surplus**?

5. **Summarize** What were the causes and effects of Western colonialism in the region?

6. **Recall** What is the goal of the **insurgency** in the Philippines?

7. **Explain** Why is the Strait of Malacca so important today?

8. **Describe** Which are the richest and the poorest countries in Southeast Asia?

Think Critically

9. **Draw Conclusions** How have the people of Southeast Asia used the environment to meet their needs?

10. **Synthesize** How did geography contribute to the diversity of the region?

11. **Make Inferences** Why did Islam spread through the islands?

12. **Core Concepts: Culture and Geography** How has the environment shaped culture in Southeast Asia?

Places to Know

For each place, write the letter from the map that shows its location.

13. **Mekong River**
14. **Singapore**
15. **Strait of Malacca**
16. **Bangkok**
17. **The Philippines**
18. **South China Sea**
19. **Estimate** Using the scale, estimate the distance between Bangkok and the Philippines.

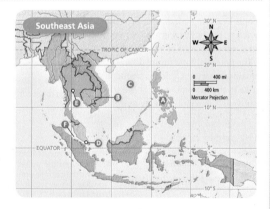

PLACES TO KNOW

13. B
14. D
15. F
16. E
17. A
18. C
19. about 1500 miles

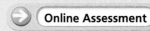

 myWorld Chapter Activity

Gaining Wealth Through History Find Step-by-Step Instructions, Student Instructions and Rubric, and an Activity Support on pp. T61–T63. **(Logical/Verbal)**

21st Century Learning

Develop Cultural Awareness Students' charts should reflect a careful search and thoughtful choice of unique cultural features and ideas about the origins of these features. If students need help with this skill, direct them to the online tutorial.

Online Assessment

Tailor review and assessment to each student's needs with an array of online assessments.
- On Assignment Article or Slideshow
- Self-Test
- Success Tracker

? Essential Question

myWorld Chapter Activity

 Gaining Wealth Through History Follow your teacher's instructions to investigate the geographical factors that have contributed to the economic success of each historical character. Then rank the characters on an economic assessment scale and explain the reasons for your assessment.

21st Century Learning

Develop Cultural Awareness

 Look back over the chapter and make a list of features that make Southeast Asian culture unique. Then consider why each feature might have developed—was it because of geography, climate, or history? Create a table that lists each feature and your theory about its origin.

WRITING TASK TIP

WORKING WITH QUESTIONS Suggest that students turn the writing task into a question: What has been Malacca's significance to world trade over the centuries? Then have them list one or two points based on each document.

Document-Based Questions

Online at myworldgeography.com

Use your knowledge of Southeast Asia and Documents A and B to answer Questions 1–3.

Document A

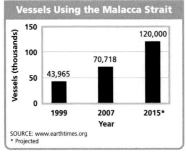

Vessels Using the Malacca Strait

120,000 (2015*)
70,718 (2007)
43,965 (1999)

Vessels (thousands) — 0, 50, 100, 150

Year: 1999, 2007, 2015*

SOURCE: www.earthtimes.org
* Projected

1. What does Document A tell you about shipping in the Strait of Malacca?

A The number of vessels is decreasing every decade.

B The number of vessels peaked in the 1990s and then declined.

C The projected number of vessels will have nearly tripled in a 16-year span.

D The projected number of vessels will decline sharply by 2015.

Document B

" He who is lord of Malacca has his hand on the throat of Venice."

—Duarte Barbosa describing world trade in the 1400s and 1500s

2. Which of the following best describes the meaning of Document B?

A The European trading city of Venice depends on goods traveling through the Malacca Strait.

B The trading city of Venice is being attacked by the lord of Malacca.

C The cities of Venice and Malacca have little contact with each other.

D Venice defeated Malacca after a long war.

3. **Writing Task** Use Documents A and B to write a short paragraph explaining the role of the Malacca Strait in world trade.

DOCUMENT-BASED QUESTIONS

1. C   **2.** A

3. Sample: The Malacca Strait has long been important to world trade. Early merchants sailed the strait in search of valuable spices, while modern merchants ply the strait for oil. Early Europeans recognized that the economic health of their big cities, like Venice, depended on the good will of Malacca's rulers. So too, Western nations today would suffer if access to the strait were cut off, given that so much oil passes through there each year. Based on projections in the table, the importance of the Malacca Strait will only continue to grow in the future.

CORE CONCEPTS: URBANIZATION

Review Core Concept 6.4 with the class before assigning this activity. Ask, What are the reasons why cities grow? What problems occur when cities grow too quickly? Help the class to remember some of the issues connected with urbanization that they have encountered in previous chapters. These include lack of housing, poor sanitation, spread of diseases, pollution, and crime.

Encourage students to think of their assignment as a plan to solve some of those problems. Remind the class that it is difficult to solve many problems all at once. Suggest that as students do research about their cities, they look for information to help them decide which problems are most urgent. Then they can choose to brainstorm solutions for one or two of these problems.

21st Century Learning

Give an Effective Presentation
Ask students to name things that make speeches or classroom presentations interesting. Answers may include such techniques as using humor, including graphs or photographs, and supporting points with interesting stories about people. Have students think, pair, and share at least three techniques that they think will make their presentation more effective. Suggest that students try to use two or three of the techniques suggested in their group presentation.

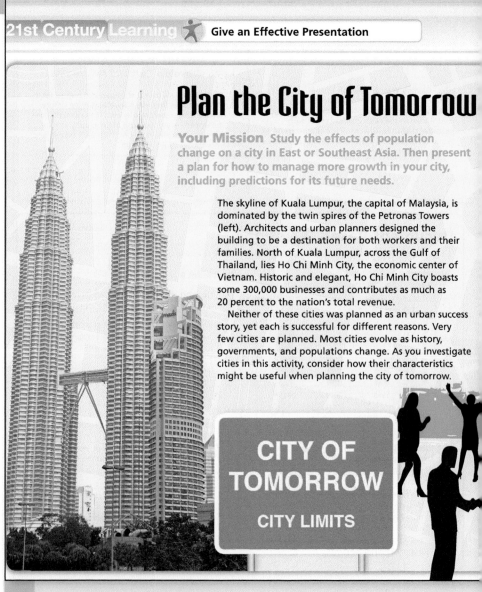

21st Century Learning ★ **Give an Effective Presentation**

Plan the City of Tomorrow

Your Mission Study the effects of population change on a city in East or Southeast Asia. Then present a plan for how to manage more growth in your city, including predictions for its future needs.

The skyline of Kuala Lumpur, the capital of Malaysia, is dominated by the twin spires of the Petronas Towers (left). Architects and urban planners designed the building to be a destination for both workers and their families. North of Kuala Lumpur, across the Gulf of Thailand, lies Ho Chi Minh City, the economic center of Vietnam. Historic and elegant, Ho Chi Minh City boasts some 300,000 businesses and contributes as much as 20 percent to the nation's total revenue.

Neither of these cities was planned as an urban success story, yet each is successful for different reasons. Very few cities are planned. Most cities evolve as history, governments, and populations change. As you investigate cities in this activity, consider how their characteristics might be useful when planning the city of tomorrow.

CITY OF TOMORROW

CITY LIMITS

ANSWERS

PLAN THE CITY OF TOMORROW RUBRIC
3. The plan reflects research of the history of their city's name and the causes and effects of population growth. The plan clearly describes ways in which to improve life for city residents. Their presentation summarizes research and relates the plan to residents' lives. The presentation is highly persuasive.

HISTORY

Famous Urban Planners Large urban planning projects go back at least 2,000 years. Caesar Augustus boasted that he found Rome a city of brick and left it a city of marble. During his reign, he sponsored the construction of public buildings, temples, theaters, and warehouses. During the reign of Emperor Napoleon III of France (1852–1870), Baron Haussmann transformed Paris from a medieval city of tiny winding streets to a modern city with wide avenues that connected major points. He also renovated the sewer system. Inspired by these two models, city planner Daniel H. Burnham helped to rebuild Chicago after fire destroyed it in 1871. During the 1880s and 1890s, his architectural firm devised methods to construct buildings as high as 21 stories. Later, he introduced a plan to develop many large city parks in Chicago.

Go to myWorldGeography.com for help with this activity.

STEP 1

What's in a Name?

The name of the city you are researching may have changed over the years. City names can change, for example, if the country was once a colony that later declared independence. When this happens, large groups of people may move in or out of a region. Investigate the history of your city's name and begin your presentation with this brief overview—it will engage your listeners right from the start.

STEP 2

What's Your Plan?

Your main goal is to improve life for the people of your city. But you need a solid plan. Gather facts and figures about population trends. Identify areas where your city functions well and areas that need improvement. Remember that you are offering a solution for the future and that you can't always predict what will happen. Thus, your plan should offer reasonable expectations for implementing your ideas.

STEP 3

The Big Finale

An effective presentation ends with a summary of what you have already said. If you have any final arguments, make them with confidence. Avoid arrogance. Chances are that your audience will agree with your proposals—after all, they live in this city!—but they may be concerned with the costs associated with your plan. Keep in mind that planning the city of tomorrow begins with understanding cities of today.

2. The plan reflects some research into the history of their city's name and the causes and effects of population growth. It partially describes ways to improve city life. The presentation partially summarizes research or relates the plan to residents' lives. It is somewhat persuasive.

1. The plan reflects little research into their city's name or the causes and effects of population growth. It describes the need for improvement but does not suggest how to achieve it. The presentation summarizes little research, does not link to residents' lives, and is not persuasive.

ANSWERS

GUIDE ON THE SIDE

TakingITGlobal for Educators

Have your students go to myworldgeography.com to find solutions to this 21st Century Learning Activity, *Plan the City of Tomorrow.*

21c Online Tutor

Using the 21st Century Online Tutor, students can get more tips on how to give more effective presentations. Students respond onscreen to learn how to plan successful presentations.

China and Its Neighbors

See rubric on p. T6.

myWorld Chapter Activity: A Changing China: Who Benefits Most?

Answers will vary. Sample answers are for Activity Card 121: Wealth Gap.

Differences Between Chinese Citizens	
The data compares people in China with a high per-capita GDP and people in China with a low per-capita GDP.	
Benefits	**Provide at least one reason.**
people with a high per-capita GDP	They have more income to buy what they need.
Disadvantages	**Provide at least one reason.**
This issue affects people with a low per-capita GDP. They don't have enough money to buy what they need.	There aren't enough high-paying jobs in their region.

Sample Notes: People in eastern China seem to deal with more pollution than people in western China. People in urban areas have more food, clothing, and cultural activities than people in rural areas.

Section 1
China and Its Neighbors

myWorld Activity: Should I Migrate? Make a Decision

1. Sample: The son and daughter will go to the city because they are young and healthy. The mother and father will stay at home to care for the grandmother and grandfather.

2. Sample: The son and daughter will probably earn more money in the city, which they can send home to help the family. Also, the grandmother and grandfather will be taken care of.

3. Sample: If more of the family went to the city, more money would be earned.

Enrichment: Tibet's Conflicts With China

1. The Dalai Lama's followers consider the him the political ruler of Tibet and their supreme spiritual leader.

2. In the 1960s and 1970s, the communists harshly enforced socialism. Then in the 1980s, the Chinese government loosened its restrictions.

3. Timeline dates: 1600s: Dalai Lama starts to rule an independent Tibet; early 1700s: China conquers Tibet; 1911: Tibet gains independence from China; 1949: Communists take control of China; 1950: China takes control of Tibet; late 1950s: Riots take place in Tibet, and the Dalai Lama flees to India; 1960s and 1970s: Communists strictly enforce socialism in Tibet; 1980s: China loosens restrictions in Tibet; Situation between Tibet and China is still unresolved.

Section 1 Quiz

1. a   2. d   3. c   4. b   5. a
6. The west and north of China tend to be very dry. In fact, a huge, uninhabitable desert covers part of this region. The terrain in the west is very rugged, with extremely cold winters. Good farmland in these areas is limited. As a result, the population is sparse. In contrast, the climate in the south and east along the coast is much warmer, with mild winters. These areas get plenty of rainfall. Good farmland is more plentiful, and the population is denser.

Section 2
China and Its Neighbors

myWorld Activity: Command Economy vs. Market Economy

Wrap-up Sample: A market economy would benefit my region more than a command economy. Under the command economy, my region was told to make tanks. But my region has few iron deposits and low-quality iron ore. So we could not make enough good-quality tanks. In a market economy, my region could decide what to produce based on our strengths. As a result, because of our many forests, we produced high-quality furniture.

Enrichment: Silk Making

1. The silkworm forms a cocoon by secreting a fluid that hardens immediately into silk threads.

2. Sample: Yes, being a wealthy woman, Xi Ling-Shi probably had enough free time to notice the worms eating mulberry leaves and making shining cocoons.

3. Sample: Each step will have a corresponding illustration.

   1. Moths called the *Bombyx mori* lay hundreds of eggs.

   2. The eggs hatch into young silkworms.

   3. The silkworms are fed mulberry leaves day and night.

   4. Once fully grown, the silkworm stops eating and spins its cocoon out of silk thread.

   5. Most cocoons are then placed in a hot oven, thereby killing the worm.

   6. The cocoons are soaked in hot water, causing them to unravel into silk filaments.

   7. The raw silk is strengthened through a series of processes that involves twisting the strands together.

   8. A glue-like substance is boiled off the fabric, revealing the natural beauty of the silk.

   9. Brilliant dyes are often applied to the silk thread.

Section 2 Quiz

1. b   2. b   3. b   4. d   5. c   .

6. China began to open up to international trade. It also started to move toward a market economy. Some farmers and businesses were told that they could decide what crops and goods to produce. New businesses opened, competing with each other to make the best, cheapest goods. However, the Chinese Communist Party's hold on the government stayed as strong as ever.

Primary Source: Confucianism and Imperial Law

myWorld Activity: Law and Punishment

2. Sample Laws: 1. Respect your father and mother. 2. Take care of your parents' needs. 3. Do not physically harm your parents. 4. Do not quarrel with your siblings.

   Sample Punishments: 1. Stay at home for one month. 2. Pay a fine to your parents. 3. Receive imprisonment for life. 4. Become your sibling's servant for one month.

3. Starting at age 21, a son or daughter should take care of their parents' basic physical needs, including food, clothing, and shelter. The only exception to this law is if the son or daughter is sick.

4. If a son or daughter who is age 21 or older fails to provide for the basic physical needs of his or her parent, the son or daughter will have to pay a fine of 100 units. For each repeat offense, the fine will double. If the son or daughter is sick, then no fine will be imposed.

Section 3
China and Its Neighbors

myWorld Activity: Take a Stand on the Three Gorges Dam

Defend Your Position Sample answer: The dam is worth what it costs due to the energy it will create. The huge Three Gorges Dam will produce large amounts of hydroelectricity, which will be used to power large sections of China. Also, this energy is renewable, so it will not deplete nonrenewable resources. In addition, the energy produced by the dam will help China's economy. All of these reasons offset the wildlife damage and the displaced persons caused by building the dam.

Enrichment: The Chinese River Dolphin

1. Pollution made it difficult for the Chinese river dolphin to find food. Also, illegal fishing and collisions with cargo ships reduced their population.

2. Sample: People might want to protect endangered species in China because it would help preserve the Chinese heritage, be good for tourism, and help keep the ecosystem in balance. People might not want to protect endangered species in China because doing so would put too many limits on industry and thereby harm the economy.

3. Students should create a map as described.

Section 3 Quiz

1. a   2. a   3. d   4. b   5. a

6.

What has been the impact of economic changes in China on . . .
the standard of living? In general, the standard of living has risen for people living in the east, and most likely has not risen for people living in the west.
where people live? Many more people have moved to cities.
the environment? Growth of industry has caused severe water and air pollution throughout large sections of China.

Case Study: Information Control in China

1. The only source of information was from the Chinese government.

2. The information given out by the government is unreliable.

3. China's government

4. Many people with different ideas and voices caused great confusion on the Internet. To create stability, the government shut down the message boards.

5. Both the journalist and the student claim that the Chinese government controls information in China.

Japan and the Koreas

See rubric on p. T34.

myWorld Chapter Activity: Mission Earth

Sample answers in order of country, change, benefits, drawbacks, adaptation, benefits, and drawbacks:

Japan

Change: Land reclamation; provides more land for industry and businesses; threatens the environment. Adaptation: Underground construction; provides more space for urban growth; people could easily get lost in underground structures.

South Korea

Change: Pollution; more pollution means that industrial development is increasing; harms the environment. Adaptation: Solar energy; renewable energy source that doesn't pollute; is expensive.

North Korea

Change: Constructing dams; provides hydroelectricity; dams are expensive to build and take money away from more pressing needs.
Adaptation: Heating with ondols; cheap, efficient, and environmentally friendly way to heat a building; have become unpopular.

Section 1
Japan and the Koreas

myWorld Activity: Trade-off

1. Sample: Yes, many of the countries didn't want to trade away many raw materials because doing so would put them below five tokens of that resource.

2. Sample: Yes, I needed four more food tokens. Trying to get that number of tokens was difficult because countries did not want to trade away too much food and end up with fewer than five food tokens.

Enrichment: Japan's Temperatures

1. 90° in August in Fukuoda

2. 30° in January in Sapporo

3. There is more of a difference between the temperatures of Tokyo and Sapporo than between Tokyo and Fukuoka. The yearly average high temperature is about 55° in Sapporo and 65° in Tokyo. This is a difference of 10°. The difference in the yearly average high temperature of Tokyo and Fukuoka is about 3°.

4. Sample: I would like to study during July, August, and September in Sapporo because I like hot weather.

Section 1 Quiz

1. b   2. a   3. b   4. d   5. a

6. Japan has many mountainous areas and few flat areas where large numbers of people can live. As a result, Japan has a dense population that is packed into a few flat areas.

Section 2
Japan and the Koreas

myWorld Activity: Best of the Best

Events and Descriptions	Reasons
1. Tokugawa tried to bring peace to Japan by taking control.	1. Tokugawa's takeover of Japan started a period of Tokugawa rule that lasted for over 250 years and had a great effect on the culture of the nation.
2. Korea splits into North and South Korea. The Korean War ended with a treaty that divided Korea into two nations.	2. The division of Korea into North and South created a conflict between the two countries that had a great effect on them and the rest of the world.
3. Japan's economic boom; after World War II, the government of Japan started certain policies that caused strong economic growth.	3. Japan's economic development has had a great effect on technology throughout the world.
4. Meiji Restoration; new leaders pushed out the Tokugawa shogun and brought back Emperor Meiji.	4. The Meiji Restoration spurred industrial and military development in Japan that led to World War II.
5. The kingdom of the Silla conquered Korea; The Silla pushed the Chinese out of Korea and set up a strong government.	5. The Silla rulers strongly influenced Korean culture. For example, they fostered the creation of a new writing system.

1. Sample: No, I think the split of Korea into North and South Korea is the most important event. This event has had a major impact on the world today.

2. Sample: My team also discussed the arrival of Commodore Perry in Japan and the bombing of Pearl Harbor by the Japanese. If Perry did not arrive in Japan, the Japanese probably would still have eventually opened up to the rest of the world. Also, if Japan didn't bomb Pearl Harbor, Japanese aggression probably would have eventually caused the United States to enter World War II.

Enrichment: Making Celadon

1. The Koreans were the first to use inlaid decorations in celadon making.

2. A kiln is an oven used for heating clay for pottery or bricks.

3. Designs will vary but should be based on designs found on Korean pottery.

Section 2 Quiz

1. c   2. b   3. a   4. a   5. b
6.

Five Levels of Medieval Society in Japan
1. Large landowners
2. Samurai
3. Peasants
4. Craftspeople
5. Merchants

Primary Source: Japan's Occupation of Korea

myWorld Activity: A Call to Protest

Protest Song Songs will vary but should use key points from the two primary source documents, use a popular melody, and have stanzas that rhyme.

Protest Poster Posters will vary but should depict ideas found in the two primary source documents, use images that convey strong emotion against Japanese oppression and for Korean independence, and use a slogan that conveys the Korean desire for independence.

Protest Leaflet Leaflets will vary but should use evidence from the two primary source documents, have a list of rights for the Korean people, include a description of Japan's oppression, and use an attention-grabbing headline.

Wrap-up Sample: Common themes were the oppression of the majority of people by a few people in power and a lack of freedom for most people. Yes, many countries today, such as North Korea, have people who are oppressed and lack freedom.

Section 3
Japan and the Koreas

myWorld Activity: Political Manga

1. South Korea is given as an example of a limited government. North Korea is given as an example of an unlimited government. South Korea's government allows more freedom of choice for its citizens. North Korea's government strictly controls North Korean society.

2. Sample: I am featuring the North Korean government. I think this government is cruel and unfair to its citizens.

3. Sample: I want to use a large umbrella to represent the North Korean leader. Also, I want show the North Korean people underneath the umbrella.

4. Sample: I want to use rain falling underneath the umbrella to represent the state of the Korean people and a sunny day above the umbrella to show the position of the government.

5. Sample: To show the dominance of the North Korean leader, I am planning to draw a huge umbrella to represent him.

Enrichment: Kim Jong-il

1. to glorify Kim Jong-il in the eyes of his people

2. Sample: I think he has mixed feelings about Western culture. He likes some aspects of this culture, such as Hollywood movies, but doesn't seem to trust Western nations.

Section 3 Quiz

1. b   **2.** b   **3.** b   **4.** c   **5.** d

6. Sample: No, I do not think North and South Korea will reunify. The governments of North and South Korea are too different; the hard feelings about the Korean War are still strong; and Kim Jong-il has shown distrust of South Korea, since it is an ally of the West.

Case Study: Governments and Citizens in Japan and the Koreas

myWorld Activity: A Guide for Citizens

Sample table for a citizen from South Korea:

Top Five Qualities of a Good Citizen in South Korea
1. Able to make informed decisions
2. Respectful of the rights of individuals
3. Responsible about voting
4. Creative
5. Self-motivated

1. Sample: Both deal with a citizen's relationship with his or her government. The South Korean list deals with freedom of choice, creativity, and self-motivation. The North Korean list deals with obedience, fitting in with others, and respect for authority.

2. Sample: North Koreans value obedience to the government, not criticizing the government and its leader, fitting in with other people, and doing what's best for the whole of society. South Koreans value being creative and self-motivated, making good choices, and doing what is best for the individual.

Southeast Asia

See rubric on p. T62.

myWorld Chapter Activity: Gaining Wealth Through History

Sample:
Character: King Jayavarman VII
Home: Southeast Asia
Work: Rules empire; builds temples, hospitals, highways
Goals: to gain wealth from agriculture
Methods: Grows more rice crops by irrigating fields during dry season
Geography: Warm, rainy climate promotes farming; irrigation channels and reservoirs sustain farming in dry season
Economic benefits: The king benefits by expanding agriculture and increasing food surpluses in the region.

Section 1
Southeast Asia

myWorld Activity: Why Settle in Southeast Asia?

Sample:

This settler is from China, arrived after 1800, traveled by sailing ship, and settled in Singapore.

First Answer: I settled here to look for work because demand for labor was high.

Second Answer: I spread my culture.

Third Question: Sample: What kind of work do you do?

Third Answer: Sample: I unload ships that bring in trade items through the Malacca Strait.

Fourth Question: Sample: What is the climate like in your new home?

Fourth Answer: Sample: It is a tropical-wet climate, so it is warm, and we often have rain.

Enrichment: Krakatoa

1. The information shows that people knew very little about the science of volcanoes in 1883.

2. Sample: Scientists may have been interested in the effects of the landslides, gases, and ashes from the eruptions on surrounding areas. They probably collected data from the remains of Krakatoa and ashes from other lands.

3. Sample: After a summer of strange rumblings and billows of ash coming from Krakatoa, the great mountain exploded yesterday. We watched in terror as a black cloud rose over the strait. The sea was growing wild. We grabbed a few belongings and raced inland toward high ground. Black ash blew all around us. We heard the wild waters of the strait behind us. Would we survive? Would we have a home to return to? My family was lucky. We all lived through the disaster. Our town is covered in wet mud, but our home is standing.

Section 1 Quiz

1. c   2. b   3. a   4. c   5. b

6.

Characteristic	Influence on Southeast Asian Settlement and Culture
Tropical wet and dry climate	Rain forest growth, monsoons, typhoons
North-south cordilleras	Isolated early societies, helped define borders
Deltas with rich sediment	Home to early civilizations
Gentle seas	Allowed trade, especially through Malacca Strait

Section 2
Southeast Asia

myWorld Activity: Historical Cartoon

Sample:

Event Sample: The Mongol invasion of the Khmer empire (1287)

Person 1 Sample: Resident of Burmese empire of Bagan; upset because property was destroyed and culture undermined in Mongol invasion (Cartoon might show attackers destroying houses or temples.)

Person 2 Sample: Mongol invader; complains about heat and rain (Cartoon might show invader getting tossed in air by elephant.)

Enrichment: Angkor, City of Temples

1. He was emphasizing that Angkor is a great achievement.

2. Wooden buildings rot while stone does not.

3. Letters will vary but students should express a clear opinion as to what should happen to the statues and why.

Section 2 Quiz

1. d   2. b   3. c   4. d   5. a

6. Students should complete the web to show Southeast Asian cultural influences. Samples: Traders from India and China brought Hinduism and Buddhism; traders from India brought Islam to islands; Europeans set up plantations, used resources, drew immigrants, and set up nations; Japan invaded during World War II.

Primary Source: Southeast Asia in the 1200s

myWorld Activity: Khmer Justice

1. The men would be sent to a tower in front of the royal palace.

2. They would stay there from one to four days.

3. Family members would watch over the two men.

4. The man who came out with a sickness was considered wrong.

5. Sample: Khmer people settled disputes near the royal palace because it was home to a powerful king, who stood for truth and justice and may have observed the trial.

6. Sample: The excerpt shows that the Khmer believed that illness proved right or wrong. I disagree since I know that the cause of illness has nothing to do with right or wrong.

Section 3
Southeast Asia

myWorld Activity: Facing Challenges

Students' evaluations of degree of difficulty and solutions will vary. Sample: Overpopulation is the most pressing problem because it causes other problems, such as hunger, pollution, and disease. The best solution is for the government to give incentives for citizens to migrate to less populated areas and for citizens to have fewer children.

Enrichment: Southeast Asia's Amazing Fruits

1. The region's hot temperatures and abundant rainfall are good for growing a variety of fruits.

2. Nearly one third of the world's pineapples and more than 15 percent of the world's bananas are grown in the region.

3. Maps should accurately show where major fruits grow. Sample: bananas: Indonesia, Malaysia, Philippines, Thailand, Vietnam; pineapples: Indonesia, Philippines, Thailand, durians: Thailand

Section 3 Quiz

1. b 2. a 3. d 4. c 5. d

6.

Issue	Effects	Countries Affected
Political unrest	Unstable government	Myanmar
	Insurgency	Philippines
	Anti-government protests	Thailand
	Corruption, election fraud	Malaysia, Indonesia
Over-population	Strains water supply and other resources, hurts environment	Indonesia
Under-population	Too few young people to support aging population	Singapore
Pollution	Air pollution from fires	Indonesia, Thailand
Poverty	Citizens' basic needs are not met.	Cambodia, Myanmar, Laos, East Timor, Vietnam, Philippines, Indonesia

Case Study: Preparing for Natural Disasters

myWorld Activity: Tsunami Reactions

1. The minister seems overwhelmed with the government's inability to deal with the enormity of the disaster and the peoples' depression caused by shock.

2. The hotel guest was frightened and amazed by the powerful waves.

3. They probably felt shocked and horrified by the waves' immense size and power.

4. The tourist seems impressed by the waves' destructive force, while the government minister is upset because the devastation is more than the goverment or its workers can deal with.

Acknowledgments

The people who made up the **myWorld Geography** team—representing composition services; core design, digital, and multimedia production services; digital product development; editorial; editorial services; materials management; and production management—are listed below.

Leann Davis Alspaugh, Sarah Aubry, Deanna Babikian, Paul Blankman, Alyssa Boehm, Peter Brooks, Susan Brorein, Megan Burnett, Todd Christy, Neville Cole, Bob Craton, Michael Di Maria, Glenn Diedrich, Frederick Fellows, Jorgensen Fernandez, Thomas Ferreira, Patricia Fromkin, Andrea Golden, Mary Ann Gundersen, Christopher Harris, Susan Hersch, Paul Hughes, Judie Jozokos, John Kingston, Kate Koch, Stephanie Krol, Karen Lepri, Ann-Michelle Levangie, Salena LiBritz, Courtney Markham, Constance J. McCarty, Laurie McKenna, Anne McLaughlin, Rich McMahon, Mark O'Malley, Alison Muff, Jen Paley, Gabriela Perez Fiato, Judith Pinkham, Paul Ramos, Charlene Rimsa, Marcy Rose, Rashid Ross, Alexandra Sherman, Owen Shows, Melissa Shustyk, Jewel Simmons, Ted Smykal, Emily Soltanoff, Frank Tangredi, Simon Tuchman, Elizabeth Tustian, Merle Uuesoo, Alwyn Velasquez, Andrew White, Heather Wright

Maps

XNR Productions, Inc.

Illustration

Kerry Cashman, Marcos Chin, Dave Cockburn, Jeremy Mohler

Note: T page numbers below refer to teacher resource pages. Other page numbers refer to Eastern Hemisphere Student Edition pages.

Photography

TABLE OF CONTENTS: **Pages vi–vii, All,** Pearson Education, Inc.

EAST AND SOUTHEAST ASIA REGIONAL OVERVIEW: **Pages 612–617, Bkgrnd sky,** ImageSource/Getty Images; **Page 613, Bkgrnd,** Michele Falzone/JAI/Corbis; **LT,** Pearson Education, Inc.; **TM,** Pearson Education, Inc.; **RT,** Pearson Education, Inc.; **614, T,** China Tourism Press/Getty Images; **B,** Diehm/Getty Images; **615, T,** Robert Harding Picture Library Ltd/Alamy; **B,** Kazuyoshi Nomachi/Corbis; **616, L,** Ken Straiton/Corbis; **R,** Planetary Visions Limited; **617, All,** Pearson Education, Inc.

CHINA AND ITS NEIGHBORS: **Pages 619–621, All,** Pearson Education, Inc.; **622, Bkgrnd,** PanStock RF/Newscom; **B,** Angelo Cavalli/Getty Images; **624, B,** Panorama Media (Beijing) Ltd./Alamy; **RM,** Nigel Hicks/Alamy; **LM,** Hiroji Kubota/Magnum; **LT,** Robert Harding Picture Library Ltd./Alamy; **RT,** Liu Liqun/Corbis; **M,** Kazuyoshi Nomachi/Corbis; **626, T,** Robin Moyer/Onasia.com; **B,** Tim Graham/Getty Images; **627,** Bruno Morandi/Robert Harding World Imagery/Getty Images; **628, R,** Picture Finders Ltd./eStock Photo; **M,** John Slater/Corbis; **L,** Craig Lovell/Corbis; **629,** Gordon Wiltsie/National Geographic Stock; **630, L,** O. Louis Mazzatenta/National Geographic Stock; **630–631,** Peter Gridley/Getty Images; **632, R,** Alan Hills/The British Museum/Dorling Kindersley; **M,** Danny Lehman/Corbis; **L,** Linda Whitwam/Dorling Kindersley; **633,** Bettmann/Corbis; **634, L,** Hulton Archive/Getty Images; **R,** Mark Leong/Redux Pictures; **636, B,** Tamir Niv/Shutterstock; **637, T,** The Granger Collection, New York; **637, B,** Directphoto.org/Alamy; **T25,** Still Pictures/Peter Arnold; **638, L,** Peter Charlesworth/Onasia.com; **R,** Jeff Widener/AP Photo; **640,** Simon Kwong/Reuters/Corbis; **641, R,** Elizabeth Dalziel/AP Images; **M,** David Hartung/Onasia.com; **L,** Gao feng-Imaginechina/AP Images; **641,** Yin Hai/epa/Corbis; **644, R,** Bob Sacha/Corbis; **L,** Keren Su/Corbis; **645,** Pearson Education, Inc.; **646, R,** Baldwin H. Ward & Kathryn C. Ward/Corbis; **646, L,** Getty Images; **647,** Dorling Kindersley; **648, T,** Photos 12/Alamy; **648, C,** Swim Ink/Corbis; **649, B,** Michael Reynolds/epa/Corbis.

JAPAN AND THE KOREAS: **Pages 653–655, All,** Pearson Education, Inc.; **656, Bkgrnd,** Jon Arnold Images Ltd/Alamy; **B,** Kazuko Kimizuka/Getty Images; **658, M,** Robert Harding Picture Library Ltd/Alamy; **R,** TongRo Image Stock/Alamy; **L,** Radius Images/JupiterImages; **659, L,** Yonhap, Yu Hyung-je/AP Photo; **662, L,** Daisuke Akita/amanaimages/Corbis; **M,** Pearson Education, Inc.; **R,** Chad Ehlers/Alamy; **663,** Stringer/AFP/Getty Images; **664,** dbimages/Alamy; **665, LT,** *Portrait of Izumi Tadahira (d. 1189) With a Poem,* from "Famous Generals of Japan" (about 1858) Yoshitora, Color woodblock print. School of Oriental and African Studies Library, University of London/The Bridgeman Art Library; **RT,** Stapleton Collection/Corbis; **RB,** Geoff Dann/Courtesy of the Wallace Collection, London/Dorling Kindersley; **LB,** The Metropolitan Museum of Art/Art Resource, NY; **666,** Asian Art & Archaeology, Inc./Corbis; **667,** Museum of Flight/Corbis; **668,** Gary Knight/VII/AP Images; **670, T,** Hideo Haga/HAGA/The Image Works; **670, B,** Sergiu Turcanu/Alamy; **671, T,** Library of Congress; **T54,** Noboru Hashimoto/Corbis; **672,** ImageGap/Alamy; **673,** Matt Dunham/AP Photo; **674, L,** Paul Gadd/Corbis; **R,** Paul Souders/Corbis; **675, R,** AFP/AFP/Getty Images; **L,** AP Photo/Korea News Service; **676,** Peter Turnley/Corbis; **677,** Issei Kato/Reuters/Corbis; **678, LB,** Laurence Mouton/PhotoLibrary; **LT,** Yoshikazu Tsuno/AFP/Getty Images; **RB,** Courtesy of Warner Bros/Bureau L.A. Collection/Corbis; **RT,** Photos 12/Alamy; **680,** Koji Sasahara/AP Images; **682, T,** blitzjp/Alamy; **682, L,** Ahn Young-joon/AP Images; **682, R,** Issei Kato/Reuters; **683,** Kyodo/Newscom.

SOUTHEAST ASIA: **Pages 686–689, All,** Pearson Education, Inc.; **690, B,** PCL/Alamy; **Bkgrnd,** Reuters/Corbis; **692, R,** Frans Lanting/Corbis; **L,** Ingo Jezierski/Corbis; **M,** Thierry Falise/OnAsia; **695,** Peter Horree/Alamy; **696,** Mickael David/age Fotostock; **698,** David Halbakken/Alamy; **700, R,** Roger Viollet/Getty Images; **L,** Eightfish/Alamy; **702, T,** North Wind Picture Archives; **B,** Shutterstock; **703, T,** Craig Lovell/Eagle Visions Photography/Alamy; **B,** Yi Lu/Corbis; **704,** International Photobank/Alamy; **705, Bkgrnd,** Jon Arnold Images Ltd/Alamy; **R,** Free Agents Limited/Corbis; **L,** Michael Freeman/Corbis; **706,** Chad Ehlers/Photolibrary; **707, Bkgrnd,** Jonathan Head/AP Photo; Inset, Viviane Moos/Corbis; **708, L,** Paula Bronstein/Getty Images; **R,** Travelpix Ltd./Getty Images; **710,** Jacob J. Kirk/U.S. Navy News Photo/Newscom; **712, T,** David Rydevik; **712, C,** Bullit Marquez/AP Photo; **712, B,** Shutterstock; **713,** Pallava Bagla/Corbis.

EAST AND SOUTHEAST ASIA UNIT CLOSER: **Pages 716–717, All,** Shutterstock.

Text

Grateful acknowledgment is made to the following for copyrighted material:

Page 626 Excerpt from "Migrant Couple Struggles to Earn in New China," from *NPR, May 20, 2008.* Copyright © National Public Radio.

Page 651 Excerpt from "Voices from Modern China: Fu Ansi, Migrant Worker," from *bbc.com.* Copyright © BBC.

Page 677
"Crimes by Elderly Hit High in Japan" from *AFP, November 7, 2008.* Used with permission of Agence France-Presse; permission conveyed through Copyright Clearance Center, Inc.

Note: Every effort has been made to locate the copyright owner of material reproduced in this publication. Omissions brought to our attention will be corrected in subsequent editions.